LANGUAGE IN THE CONFESSIONS
OF AUGUSTINE

Language in the *Confessions* of Augustine

PHILIP BURTON

OXFORD
UNIVERSITY PRESS

OXFORD
UNIVERSITY PRESS

Great Clarendon Street, Oxford OX2 6DP

Oxford University Press is a department of the University of Oxford.
It furthers the University's objective of excellence in research, scholarship,
and education by publishing worldwide in

Oxford New York

Auckland Cape Town Dar es Salaam Hong Kong Karachi
Kuala Lumpur Madrid Melbourne Mexico City Nairobi
New Delhi Shanghai Taipei Toronto

With offices in

Argentina Austria Brazil Chile Czech Republic France Greece
Guatemala Hungary Italy Japan Poland Portugal Singapore
South Korea Switzerland Thailand Turkey Ukraine Vietnam

Oxford is a registered trade mark of Oxford University Press
in the UK and in certain other countries

Published in the United States
by Oxford University Press Inc., New York

© Philip Burton 2007

The moral rights of the author have been asserted
Database right Oxford University Press (maker)

First published 2007
First published in paperback 2009

All rights reserved. No part of this publication may be reproduced,
stored in a retrieval system, or transmitted, in any form or by any means,
without the prior permission in writing of Oxford University Press,
or as expressly permitted by law, or under terms agreed with the appropriate
reprographics rights organization. Enquiries concerning reproduction
outside the scope of the above should be sent to the Rights Department,
Oxford University Press, at the address above

You must not circulate this book in any other binding or cover
and you must impose the same condition on any acquirer

British Library Cataloguing in Publication Data
Data available

Library of Congress Cataloging in Publication Data
Data available

Typeset by SPI Publisher Services, Pondicherry, India
Printed in Great Britain
by
Biddles Ltd., King's Lynn, Norfolk

ISBN 978-0-19-926622-7 (Hbk.)
       978-0-19-955445-4 (Pbk.)

1 3 5 7 9 10 8 6 4 2

MATRI

Preface

Readers of this book will probably be staff or students in departments of classics or theology. Such people will be familiar with problems involving language. Can the ancient world be properly understood in translation, or should all students be obliged to learn some Greek or Latin? Are inclusive versions essential if the Scriptures are to retain their pastoral value in the modern world, or is inclusive translation essentially a strategy to conceal the social values encoded in the original? Should students be allowed to get away with split infinitives and comma-splice sentences, or will that ultimately cheapen our degrees and lead to protests from employers' organizations that our graduates lack basic literacy? Are the norms of email and text-messaging corrupting good English usage, or are they helping to strip away some traditional encrustations? *Y-a-t-il d'hors-texte*, and why pose the question in French? Then there are bigger questions with implications far beyond the bounds of academia: for instance, is *God* more, less, or other than a translation of *Allah*, and vice versa? And who decides?

This book seeks to address some related themes as they occur in the *Confessions* of Augustine. It is informed less by a single thesis than by a series of recurrent issues. There is the inadequacy of language, arbitrary and temporal as it is, to describe or invoke an absolute and timeless God; there is the fact—for Augustine—that God not only permits humans to invoke him, but even engages in dialogue with them; even chats with them. There is the primal status of language as the means of God's imposition of order on the formless matter of the universe, constantly replicated in humans' imposition of order on the formless breath. There is the fact that languages exist only by the consent of a community, but also that languages set communities apart from each other; and that even within a community, variations in language use can easily become points for contention and ill-founded pride. And there is the ambiguous status of the paralinguistic—singing, laughing, weeping, groaning—vis-à-vis language itself: do they transcend the limitations of language, or do they fall beneath it? These issues are explored with reference to Augustine's own linguistic practice; for while it is always true to some extent that the content of a work of literature cannot be separated from its language, the *Confessions* is a work of which this is especially true, as any translator will discover.

I have, I hope, resisted the temptation to make any kind of apology for my published translation of the work. Citations from the *Confessions* are given here in ad hoc renderings, intended to emphasize the particular point at issue. As a result, they may lack the smoothness to which most translators aspire. It would indeed be interesting to see a translation of the work as a whole which did not suppress the odd and paradoxical elements in Augustine's language.

This book was commissioned by Hilary O'Shea of Oxford University Press, so might never have been begun without her; and without Lucy Qureshi's constant encouragement (and occasional threat) it might never have been finished. My warmest thanks go to both. I would like to thank also Dorothy McCarthy, Jack Sinden, and Rachel Woodforde for their work in seeing it through the press. The Press's two anonymous readers were full of valuable suggestions and criticisms, and tactfully put me right on numerous points. Gillian Clark's contribution, both practical and moral, was outstanding. Mistakes and shortcomings are my own.

Some debts of gratitude are more general. I am conscious that the influence of several scholars—in particular Peter Brown, Robert Markus, J. J. O'Donnell, and Oliver Lyne—greatly outweighs the frequency with which they are cited in this book. Lyne, indeed, is not cited at all, but for me at least *Words and the Poet* was a book which remains unexampled in the way traditional skills of close reading are integrated with what was cutting-edge technology (and an unobtrusive awareness of other critical approaches). As for O'Donnell's edition of the *Confessions*, I assume that any reader of this will have it available and will use it throughout. Often in preparing this book I have found a happy notion of mine explored *ad loc.* by O'Donnell, copiously documented, and then politely shown to be erroneous if not simply beside the point; and no doubt many such cases have escaped me. I should also note the use I have made of the Perseus Digital Library in the research for this book. The academic community has yet to decide what sort of *auctoritas* online resources as a whole they should enjoy, but I have found immensely stimulating the possibilities the Perseus site offers, not least in demonstrating the continuing potential of empirical, linguistic approaches to classical literature.

Various audiences have heard and commented on material from this book; I am grateful for the comments and suggestions I have received. Versions of Chapter 3 have appeared in Pollmann and Vessey (eds), *Augustine and the Disciplines: From Cassiciacum to Confessions* (Oxford: Oxford University Press, 2005) and in López Férez (ed.), *La lengua científica griega. Orígenes, desarollo e influencia en las lenguas modernes europeas.* (Madrid: Ediciones clásicas, 2004); material in Chapters 6 and 7 overlaps with a essay in Arias Abellán (ed), *Latin vulgaire-latin tardif. Actes du VIIème colloque sur le latin vulgaire et tardif* (Seville: Universidad de Sevilla, 2006).

Finally, I must thank the friends and colleagues not so far mentioned whose support has kept me going at critical stages. In particular I should name Jon Balserak, Paul Bibire, Allen Brent, Catherine Conybeare, Tom Harrison, Thirza Hope, Hugh Houghton, John and Milly Hurst, David Parker, Eleanor Payton, Mirjam Plantinga, and Amy Wright. Last of all, I would like to thank my family for their patience and help, especially in the matter of the paralinguistic and of language acquisition.

PHB
Birmingham, February 2006

Contents

1. *Sermo* — 1
2. Alternative Comedy: The Language of the Theatre — 35
3. The Vocabulary of the Liberal Arts — 63
4. Talking Books — 88
5. Biblical Idioms in the *Confessions* — 112
6. The Paralinguistic — 133
7. Epilogue — 173

Appendix. Greek Words in the Confessions — 178
Bibliography — 179
Index locorum — 189
Index rerum — 195
Index verborum graecorum — 196
Index verborum latinorum — 197

1

Sermo

INTRODUCTION

Virgil

In his sixth *Eclogue*, Virgil puts into the mouth of the satyr Silenus a vivid and allusive creation myth. Atoms of the four elements of earth, air, sea, and fire shoot through the void; coalescing, they come to form the young world. The land hardens and becomes separate from the sea. The sun appears for the first time, and gathers up clouds of water; the first rains fall. Woods appear, and through the mountains the first few beasts roam. Pyrrha—sole survivor with her husband Deucalion of the great deluge of Greek mythology—throws the stones which become the race of men. The Golden Age begins. Then Prometheus steals fire; technology, agriculture, and weaponry become possible.[1] Men get restless; the Quest of the Golden Fleece is begun, in which (as Virgil's readers would recall) the primal separation of the elements is reversed, as mountain pines form the timbers that will furrow the sea.[2] Only one story is told of that great adventure; how the Argonauts wandered along the beach calling for

---

[1] The implications of Prometheus' theft are not spelt out in the *Eclogues*, but would be familiar to readers who remembered Hesiod's account of the Golden Age of Cronus and how it was succeeded by the Ages of Bronze and Iron; see Coleman (1977: 187–8) on this and the interpretation of this passage generally.

[2] Virgil's account is highly compressed, but any educated readers of his day would recall Catullus' account of how 'the pine-trees born on Mount Pelion are said to have floated through Neptune's bright waves' (Poem 64. 1–2). Arguably the confusion of the elements begins with Prometheus' theft of fire, bringing one of the higher elements into contact with one of the lower (earth).

the young sailor Hylas, who—as we are to know—has been seduced by water-nymphs and dragged into their pool: 'Moreover, Silenus sang how the sailors called for Hylas, whom they had left at the fountain, and how the whole shore re-echoed the cry, "Hylas, Hylas!"'

> his adiungit Hylan quo fonte nautae relictum
> clamassent, ut litus Hyla Hyla omne sonaret.

We might expect this, the first moment in Silenus' account when humans are heard to speak, to be the occasion for reflection on the special capacity humans have for language, and on their distinction from the inarticulate beasts. Virgil makes every effort to ensure we do not read it this way. Taken completely out of context, the cry *Hyla Hyla* has an ululating quality to it; in context, Virgil exploits a Greek metrical licence very rare in Latin in order to fit the hexameter scheme of the verse.[3] His educated reader would notice the Greek vocative form, but would presumably be educated enough to notice a homonym within Greek: *Hyla* ("Υλα) represents not only the vocative of the name Hylas ("Υλα) but also the imperative of the poetic verb 'to bark' (ὑλάω).[4] The sailors' cry, then, is both 'Hylas!' and 'Howl!' It is not even clear who produces this cry, as Virgil shifts the subject from the sailors (*nautae*) to the shore (*litus*), and exploits the ambiguity of the verb *sonare*—both 'to sound' and 'to resound'. Man's first recorded utterance, then, is an animal howl of loss, taken up by inanimate nature. It is an inauspicious first attestation of language.

Ignatius

At some point around eighty years after the crucifixion of Jesus of Nazareth, Bishop Ignatius of Antioch-in-Syria was arrested and taken

---

[3] The final vowel of the first *Hyla* is not elided before the following vowel (the /h/ being effectively silent); the final vowel of the second *Hyla* is not elided, but is shortened in hiatus with the following *omne*. Neither effect is usual in Latin; the effect (as often in the *Eclogues*) is that of a language somewhere between Greek and Latin.

[4] Compare a similar play on words in Sophocles' *Ajax* 430–3. For recent studies on name-games in Virgil, see Paschalis (1996) and O'Hara (1996). Neither, however, discusses this passage.

off to Rome to face martyrdom. In the course of his last journey he wrote a series of letters to various Christian communities in western Asia Minor—at Ephesus, Magnesia, Tralles, Philadelphia, and Smyrna, plus one to Bishop Polycarp of Smyrna—and to the church at Rome. One of the recurrent motifs of Ignatius' writing is his emphasis on speech and silence, in both literal and metaphorical senses. To the church at Ephesus he writes:

It is better to be silent and to be than to speak and not to be. Teaching is a fine thing, provided that he who speaks also does; there is 'one Teacher' who 'spoke and it was done', and what he has done in silence is worthy of the Father. He who possesses the word of Jesus can in truth also hear his silence, so as to be perfect, and so that through what he speaks, he may act, and through what he keeps silence, he may be judged.

ἄμεινόν ἐστι σιωπᾶν καὶ εἶναι ἢ λαλοῦντα μὴ εἶναι. καλὸν τὸ διδάσκειν, ἐὰν ὁ λέγων ποιῇ:. εἷς οὖν διδάσκαλός ὃς εἶπεν καὶ ἐγένετο. καὶ ἃ σιγῶν δὲ πεποίηκεν ἄξια τοῦ πατρός ἐστιν. ὁ λόγον Ἰησοῦ κεκτημένος ἀληθῶς δύναται καὶ τῇ ἡσυχίᾳ αὐτοῦ: ἀκούειν ἵνα τέλειος ᾖ, ἵνα δι᾽ ὧν λαλεῖ πράσσῃ καὶ δι᾽ ὧν σιγᾷ γινώσκηται. (ad Ephesios 4. 1–2).

Jesus is the 'one Teacher' (compare Matthew 23:8), who 'spoke and it was done' (Psalm 32:9, 148:5). The Word, to be identified with the Son of God, was the one through whom all things were brought into being, even though—as there was yet no physical world—the initial speech-act of creation took place in silence. This being so, silence can be more a mark of existence than physical speech. But theological statements have historical contexts; and the immediate context of this appears to be the 'silence' or inaction of the anonymous Bishop of Ephesus.[5] Ignatius, the great exponent of episcopacy, is comparing the Ephesians' silent bishop to the silent Christ. 'It is he who does not speak without backing up what he says with deeds. The clear implication is that precisely such empty talk characterizes the false teachers'.[6]

However, the bishop's silence may have wider theological repercussions. As Chadwick argued, Ignatius stresses the bishop's role as the 'type of God': 'God is silence; therefore when men see their

---

[5] Compare ad Ephesios 4. 1, 'The more you see the Bishop keeping silence (σιγῶντα) the more you should fear him.' For a discussion and bibliography, see Trevett (1983: 9–10).
[6] Schoedel (1985: 77), a very useful discussion.

bishop silent... it is then that he is most like God. And if he should preach, that sermon might perhaps be considered as a "Logos proceeding from silence"' (Chadwick 1950: 171–2). A recent study (Maier 2004) has persuasively located the bishop's silence falls within ancient rhetorical theories on well-timed and temperate speech. This does not, however, preclude us from interpreting Ignatius' 'it is better to be' in a more general, existential sense. Although the phrase is generally understood elliptically ('to be [bishop]'), and although this interpretation is persuasive, it is not inevitable. And indeed Ignatius' interest in the matter goes beyond the immediate imperative for subjection to the Bishop as to God. The linguistic theme is developed again in his letter to the Magnesians:

It is inconsistent to speak Jesus Christ and to talk Jewish. For it was not Christianity that believed in Judaism but Judaism in Christianity, so that 'every tongue' that has believed in God should 'be gathered together'.

ἄτοπόν ἐστιν Ἰησοῦν Χριστὸν λαλεῖν καὶ ἰουδαίζειν. ὁ γὰρ Χριστιανισμός οὐκ εἰς Ἰουδαισμὸν ἐπίστευσεν ἀλλὰ Ἰουδαισμός εἰς Χριστιανισμόν, ἵνα πᾶσα γλῶσσα πιστεύσασα εἰς θεὸν συνήχθη. (ad Magnesios 10. 3)

The translation given here may appear tendentious. The phrase 'to speak Jesus Christ' may mean no more than 'to speak of Jesus', 'to bespeak Jesus'.[7] Likewise the verb ἰουδαίζειν normally signifies 'to follow Jewish practices' (as it does at Galatians 2:14). But its form recalls such familiar Greek verbs as ἀττικίζειν 'to speak Attic Greek' or αἰολίζειν 'to speak Aeolic'; and, given Ignatius' references to 'speaking' and 'tongues', it is at least plausible if not positively required to take them in a linguistic sense.[8] Christianity, then, may be seen as a language, a form of discourse in its own right, destined to subsume all other forms of language.

Ignatius' attitude to language we may term a form of mysticism. It is mystical in the sense that he repeatedly uses what appears to be a system of metaphors to describe his experience, yet these metaphors are never cashed in to give his readers what they regard as a literal or

---

[7] See Liddell, Scott, and Jones under λαλέω sense 2.
[8] The reference to 'every tongue' being 'gathered together' itself recalls Isaiah 66:18 ('I am coming to gather together all nations and tongues') and Philippians 2:11 ('every tongue shall confess that Jesus Christ is Lord', itself echoing Isaiah 45:23; see Schoedel above note 6.

plain account of what he means; they remain μυστήρια, in Latin *mysteria* or *sacramenta*, sacred symbols referring to truths which are beyond full comprehension, and so beyond full expression even by the most articulate.[9] His preoccupation with Christianity-as-language leads him to speculate also on the relationship between spoken and written words. To the church in Philadelphia he writes:

If someone should translate Judaism for you, do not listen to them. It is better to hear Christianity from a man who has been circumcised than to hear Judaism from the uncircumcised. But if neither speak about Jesus Christ, they are to me mere gravestones and monuments to the dead, on which are written only the names of mortals.

ἐὰν δέ τις ἰουδαϊσμὸν ἑρμηνεύῃ ὑμῖν μὴ ἀκούετε αὐτοῦ. ἄμεινον γάρ ἐστι παρὰ ἀνδρὸς περιτομὴν ἔχοντος χριστιανισμὸν ἀκούειν ἢ παρὰ ἀκροβύστου ἰουδαϊσμόν. ἐὰν δὲ ἀμφότεροι περὶ Ἰησοῦ Χριστοῦ μὴ λαλῶσιν οὗτοι, ἐμοὶ στῆλαί εἰσιν καὶ τάφοι νεκρῶν ἐφ᾽ οἷς γέγραπται μόνον ὀνόματα ἀνθρώπων. (*ad Philadelphios* 6. 1)

Again, Christianity and Judaism are presented as separate languages, requiring 'translation' between them; the novelty here is that *viva voce* speech[10] (identified with discourse about Jesus) is contrasted with the deadness of merely written language.[11] The tension between written and spoken word has a rich prehistory in classical thought, and will be discussed further below (Chapter 4).[12]

[9] The definition of mysticism given here is necessarily a partial one, as the term may be used in both highly specialized senses and in very general ones. I follow here the commonplace distinction of mystical theology from natural theology (the apprehension of God from the created world) on the one hand, and revealed religion on the other, my emphasis being not so much on the religious person's alleged experience as on his or her account of it.

[10] The verb λαλέω in classical Greek has the sense 'to chat, talk idly'. From an early date, however, it is also used in the more neutral sense 'to speak, talk', but with the notion of conversational rather than formal or written use of language subsisting. On the similar development of Latin *loquor*, see below in this chapter.

[11] See again the comments of Schoedel: 'Thus old age was said to render a man like a grave with nothing but a name left on it (Macrobius *Sat*. 2. 7). Or a person ignored by others was compared to an old tombstone passed by and unread (Lucian *Tim*. 5). Also interesting are the references to the Pythagorean practice of building cenotaphs to those who abandoned the sect (Clement Alex. *Strom*. 5. 9, 57. 2–3; Origen *Cels*. 2. 12; 3. 51).'

[12] What has been identified here as Ignatius' linguistic mysticism does not appear to have attracted any great notice previously. In addition to the passages discussed above, the following seem particularly relevant: *ad Ephesios* 15. 2, 19. 1; *ad Trallenses* 9. 1; *ad Romanos* 2. 1, 8. 2; *ad Smyrnaeos* 10. 1; *ad Magnesios* 8. 2; *ad Philadelphos* 1. 1.

Jerome and Rufinus

In AD 384 Jerome wrote a letter from Palestine to his friend Eustochium at Rome. Eustochium was a young woman of noble family, who had recently vowed herself to virginity. Jerome—whose familiarity with such noble virgins was to attract some comment among his contemporaries—wrote to encourage her in her vow, reminding her of the restless drudgery of domestic life and painting her a vivid, if impressionistic, picture of the life of the monastery. The brothers of the common life, he said, meet every afternoon to hear a discourse from the abbot:

While he is speaking, there is such an intense silence that no-one dares look at another or even to clear his throat. The speaker's glory is the tears of his audience; but the tears roll down their cheeks in silence, and their grief does not even burst into a sob.

quo loquente tantum silentium fit ut nemo ad alium respicere, nemo audeat excreare. dicentis laus in fletu audientium est; tacite volvuntur per ora lacrimae et ne in singultus quidem erumpit dolor.

After a communal dinner—again held in silence—they rise, sing a hymn, and then go back to their cells. At this time they do have their few words of daily conversation:

'Have you seen so-and-so? Have you noticed what grace there is in him, what silence, and how modestly he bears himself?' (Jerome *Epistle* 22. 35)

vidistis illum et illum? quanta in ipso sit gratia, quantum silentium, quam moderatus incessus?

This emphasis on silence is something we easily miss, either because it is something we expect of monks anyway, or because modern concerns leave us less attuned to this particular form of the care of the self than (say) to matters of sexuality or food. We find a rationale for this silence in the *Historia Monachorum* of Rufinus of Aquileia. Of the Egyptian Abbot Benus he wrote that he was believed never to have sworn an oath, never to have lied, never to have got angry with anyone, and never to have uttered a superfluous or idle word (*neque... sermonem superfluum otiosumque proferre*); rather, he 'lived a life of the greatest silence' (*summo silentio*) (*Historia Monachorum* 4). Apart from the value of Benus' silence in avoiding these negative uses of language, there is a potentially positive aspect to it. The related *Historia Lausiaca* of Palladius likewise describes Benus as 'very silent' (λίαν ἡσύχιος; *Historica Lausiaca* 49). The Greek ἡσυχία suggests quiet, peace, repose, and freedom from distraction, a concept highly valued in particular by the Pythagoreans: Lucian's Pythagoras, who begins his educational curriculum with 'great quiet, absence of speech, and five whole years without saying a word' (ἡσυχίη μακρὴ καὶ ἀφωνίη καὶ πέντε ὅλων ἐτέων λαλέειν μηδέν; *Vitarum Auctio* 3), represents no more than a mild parody of the Neoplatonist shaman depicted in Iamblichus' *Vitae Pythagorae*.[13] This sense is sometimes associated with *silentium* in classical Latin, though less frequently than is the case in Greek; Rufinus on occasion links *silentium* and *quies* ('silence and rest') as equivalents to ἡσυχία, making it clear that literal silence is not the final goal of the contemplative life.[14] Sometimes, indeed, it is good to talk; the monks of Cellia, for instance, avoid contact with each other, maintaining a 'great silence and immense repose' (*silentium ingens et quies magna*), but will speak to each other if they can offer some instruction, 'as if anointing an athlete in a contest with a strengthening word' (*velut athletas in agone positos sermonis consolatione perungere*; *Historia Monachorum* 22, PL 21. 444–5).

Augustine

Virgil and Ignatius are perhaps not often found in the same company as Jerome and Rufinus. Nor are they equidistant from Augustine, who will be the focus of this book. Virgil's poetry he knew and loved,

[13] See Iamblichus, *de Vita Pythagorica* 68, 72. In a Christian context, we can trace the phrase ἡσυχία θεοῦ: back (again) to Ignatius, *ad Ephesios* 19. 1. The spiritual value of this form of 'silence' is specially emphasized within the Orthodox practice of hesychasm, the origins of which appear to date from the second half of the fourth century; see Murphy (2003).

[14] Most notably at *Historia Monachorum* 1 (*Patrologia Latina* 21. 404), where *quietem silentiumque* correspond to Palladius' ἡσυχίαν; apparently also *Historia Monachorum* 22 (PL 21. 444), where however the Greek text of *Patrologia Graeca* appears to lack the main clause of the sentence (the Latin rendering is *multa quiete*). The literary relations between Rufinus' *Historia Monachorum*, its Greek source, and Palladius' work are complex, but it is notable that Rufinus refers to *silentium* at various passages where it is not found in the parallel passage of Palladius: e.g. *Historia Monachorum* 15 (PL 21. 433), 17 (PL 21. 440), 22 (PL 21. 444).

with Jerome and Rufinus he corresponded; there is no reason to think he was aware of Ignatius' existence at all. The passages we have considered, however, have all in some sense helped shape the religious and intellectual tradition to which he belonged. And each shows a complex attitude towards language, in part spelt out explicitly, but to a greater extent implicit; none of these writers is known primarily as a linguistic theorist. Among the Christian writers it is notable how their attitudes compare with those found in classical authors more generally. The views of Iamblichus' (or Lucian's) Pythagoras on the value of silence would not sound out of place in the *Historia Monachorum*, but even Neoplatonic Pythagoreanism is not mainstream. And while Rufinus' rationale for the avoidance of speech contains much that is classical (avoidance of lying, of expressions of anger, and of casual chat), the prominence given to avoidance of oath-taking is distinctly Christian; and not all classical thinkers would put idle conversation on the same moral level as lying. Moreover, each of the Christian writers cited is in some way inconsistent, or at best ambivalent, about the power of language. Even Jerome, typically forthright in his attack on the 'racket' (*strepitus*) caused by language, allows his monks to speak in praise of silence. These educated Christian authors, then, inherit and develop a classical tradition of thought about the nature and correct use of language. This tradition is modified by their familiarity with various biblical passages in which language plays a key part. The mission of the Christian Church begins with the bestowal of the gift of speaking (or being understood to speak) in foreign languages (Acts 2:1–13), thereby undoing the division of tongues in the story of the Tower of Babel (Genesis 11:1–9). But there are many other such passages: for instance, the invention of the shibboleth and its murderous consequences (Judges 12:1–6), the cultural politics of Daniel's mastery of Chaldean language and literature (Daniel 1:4, 17), and the curious phenomenon of 'speaking in glosses' which caused such division at Corinth (1 Corinthians 12–14). These passages do not all point in one direction, but rather afford material for reflection and elaboration by Christian intellectuals. Most familiar of all will be the references to the 'Word', identified with Jesus of Nazareth, in the Prologue to the *Gospel according to John* (John 1:1–18); the Prologue in fact stands apart from the rest of *John*, though—as we will see—language is a key theme in the Gospel, and one which is exploited by Augustine.

Augustine himself is both an important witness to ancient thought on language and the single most important exponent of Christian language theory in the West. His early works include a dialogue on the nature of language and signs, the *de Magistro* of 389; he also composed a treatise on grammar, probably to be identified with the work preserved as the *Ars Augustini pro Fratrum Mediocritate Breviata*,[15] and a summary of Stoic logic, the *Principia Dialecticae*. Between 395 and 426 he composed a major work on Christian education, the *de Doctrina Christiana*, which is itself largely concerned with the interpretation of the Scriptures and so with the linguistic and philosophical questions of intention, hermeneutics, and signification. In the work which principally concerns us here, the *Confessions* (397–9), he is similarly preoccupied with the importance of language both in human life generally, and in particular in relation to God. It is possible to see Augustine's own encounters with language as a key structural feature of the work. In Book 1 of the work, he moves from being a baby, an *in-fans* lacking any knowledge of language, to being a schoolboy orator. From here he becomes first a student, then a teacher of rhetoric; he also falls in with the Manichees, a group characterized—in his mind—by their incessant talking. His rhetorical career reaches its acme with his appointment as Court Orator in Milan; but his move to Milan allows him to hear the sermons of Bishop Ambrose, as a result of which he rethinks his Manichee views on the interpretation of Scripture. His consequent spiritual crisis leads him to abandon the profession of rhetoric, as being incompatible with his profession of Christianity. In the last three books of the work we encounter Augustine as a different sort of language professional, a Christian commentator revealing the hidden meaning of the biblical Creation narrative.[16]

---

[15] On the identification, see Law (1984). The *Ars Breviata* remains difficult of access. Further bibliography on Augustine the grammarian is currently available at <http://htl.linguist.jussieu.fr/site%20bgl/grammairiens/augustinus.htm>.

[16] On Augustine's scheme of the Six Ages of Man, see Mayer (1969. i: 51–93), with O'Donnell (1992. ii. 52–6).

This is, of course, a schematized account, but not an unrecognizable one. Our concern in this book is to examine Augustine's attitude towards language as displayed in the *Confessions*. At this point our enquiry might go in one of several directions. Traditional studies tend to treat the higher philosophical questions of the relation of language to theology in relative isolation to questions on the history of grammar and the theorization of language—which are in turn treated separately from the more strictly philological approach, with its interest in the individual words and constructions used by the author.[17] This philological approach itself often appears to start from the assumption that what is interesting about the language of this or that text is the extent to which the *Confessions* is a document illustrative of the history of the Latin language. The extent to which Augustine is an individual author, with linguistic preferences of his own, is seen as a matter for the literary critic, or at best the stylistician. The approach adopted here will be to examine both aspects of Augustine's use of language and his attitude towards it, and the relationship between the two. In the course of this enquiry we will make two claims. First, that the *Confessions* is a work in which language is especially important. This is true not just in the sense that all literary works are first and foremost pieces of language, nor in the sense used by those critics according to whom all texts are ultimately recursive and self-referential. It is true in a stronger and more specific sense. Secondly, that much of the interest in the *Confessions* lies in the ways in which Augustine stretches at language, through metaphor, paradox, and the delicate tension between classical and Christian uses. This approach may be illustrated by a consideration of a single short phrase:

---

[17] There are excellent surveys of Augustine's 'philosophy of language' in Kirwan (1994 and 2001) and in Markus (1996), as well as the monumental work of Mayer (1969) on his sign theory. Ancient linguistic theory in general is now excellently covered in a single accessible volume by Law (2003); the work of Vecchio (1994) on Augustine, whom she recommends, *non vidi*. For a fascinating account of the different attitudes among the Church Fathers to the knowability and effability of God, see Young (1979). There is a useful summary of Augustine's style in Solignac (1962: 207–65), with a bibliography of older work on pages 264–5. Pizzolato (1972) is of interest as a study of aspects of Augustine's imagery. Verheijen's (1949) study remains useful, especially on the semantics of *confiteor* and related terms.

'MAKING THE TRUTH'

Modern study of Augustine's *Confessions* reached a landmark in 1992, with the publication of James O'Donnell's three-volume edition and commentary on the work; arguably the most important edition of it since Augustine's own day. O'Donnell begins his introduction with the following words:

> 'He who makes the truth comes to the light.' The truth that Augustine made in the *Confessions* had eluded him for years. It appears before us as a trophy torn from the grip of the unsayable after a prolonged struggle on the frontier between speech and silence. What was at stake was more than words. The 'truth' of which Augustine spoke was not merely a quality of a verbal formula, but veracity itself, a quality of a living human person. Augustine 'made the truth'—in this sense, became himself truthful—when he found a pattern of words to say the true thing well.

Having noted the biblical allusion (John 3:21, cited at *Confessions* 10. 1. 1), O'Donnell states:

> The translation may seem deliberately tendentious: for the Greek ὁ δὲ ποιῶν τὴν ἀλήθειαν and the Latin 'qui autem facit veritatem', English translations prefer 'he who *does* the truth' (and Luther: 'Wer aber die Wahrheit tut'). What 'doing the truth' might mean is anybody's guess, and the phrase is probably preferred out of fear of the implication in 'making truth' that the truth does not exist until it is made.

O'Donnell's proem here is in several ways reminiscent of Augustine's own proems to various books of the *Confessions*. We have the biblical citation taken as the *Leitmotif*, we have some striking if rather impressionistic metaphors (trophies and frontiers), and we have an analysis of the text in question far more challenging than is familiar or comfortable. We may respond to his challenge in various ways. O'Donnell may well be right to suggest that previous commentators have been reluctant to consider the interpretation of *veritatem facere* as 'making the truth'. His own suggestion, however, comes close to placing Augustine in the twentieth-century, 'de-Hellenized' school of 'process theology', according to which God is '[not] absolute and immutable, [but] supremely relative, sensitively responding to every change in the world' (Ford 2003: 731). It is hard to make a convincing case for this—Augustine is, after all, the theologian *par excellence* through whom the Hellenistic concept of the absolute, immutable deity was canonized in Western Christianity—though Augustine himself is supremely aware of the tension caused by the relation between an eternal God and a temporal creation.

Alternatively, we may argue that while O'Donnell's suggested interpretation, for all its theological ramifications, arises from a strictly linguistic point of interpretation: should *facere* be translated as 'to do' or 'to make'? Put in these terms, the question is potentially answerable through traditional linguistic means. We might, for instance, go back to the underlying Greek text (ὁ δὲ ποιῶν τὴν ἀλήθειαν ἔρχεται πρὸς τὸ φῶς), and consider whether the Greek phrase 'to do/make the truth' (ποιεῖν τὴν ἀλήθειαν) has an obvious interpretation. This is most obviously done by comparing similar usages by the same author. It is certainly true that the verb 'to do/ make' has special importance for the author of the *Gospel according to John*.[18] He uses it more frequently than do the authors of the (longer) *Matthew* and *Luke*, and moreover uses it in some very elevated contexts (e.g. John 5:19, 'Amen amen I tell you, the Son can *do* nothing by himself, unless he sees the Father *doing* something; whatever he *does*, the Son likewise *does* the same'). There are two formal parallels for the use of the verb plus an abstract noun (like ποιεῖν τὴν ἀλήθειαν). Most common is the repeated phrase 'to do the will (ποιεῖν τὸ θέλημα) of my Father' (John 4:34, 6:38, 7:17, 9:31), where the verb should surely be interpreted as 'to act in accordance with, to work out', rather than 'to make'. Also notable is the phrase 'to make a beginning' (ποιεῖν τὴν ἀρχήν) at John 2:11: 'Jesus *made this beginning* (ταύτην ἐποίησε ἀρχήν) of his signs in Cana of Galilee', with the periphrasis serving in place of a simple verb ('began', ἤρξατο).[19] On this basis, it is tempting to see the expression 'to do/

---

[18] Copenhaver (1992: 105) notes that in the Septuagint ποιεῖν is particularly associated with the activity of God as creator, with κτίζειν occurring sometimes and δημιουργεῖν never, and that the same preferences are observed (but more so) in the *Corpus Hermeticum*. This appears, then, to be a point of contact between John and the Hermetic corpus.

[19] The use of periphrases involving an all-purpose verb plus objects may be simply a stylistic tic on the part of the author of *John*. Compare the various periphrases involving the verb 'to have' (ἔχειν): 'to have life', e.g. John 3:36, 5:24–6, 10:10; 'to have sin', John 9:41; 'to have maturity', John 9:21–3. Most notable perhaps is 'not to

make the truth' as being simply a Johannine expression meaning 'to be true/genuine' (perhaps ἀληθινὸς εἶναι). Perhaps the closest parallel is Jesus' statement (John 7:19) that 'Moses gave you the Law and none of you makes the Law' (*nemo ex vobis facit legem*). Here the obvious interpretation of *facere* is 'act in accordance with, put into practice'. Examination of parallels in *John* is not the only linguistic approach to the phrase 'to do/make the truth'. We might look at other Greek writings—the Septuagint being the prime candidate—for similar constructions. We might ask whether one can distinguish in Greek (or Latin) between 'doing' and 'making' truth; and if not, whether the context alone would provide sufficient grounds for discovering which sense was meant.[20] These approaches, however, only cast so much light on the question of what Augustine meant by 'doing/making the truth' (*veritatem facere*). His own view on the question of working out an author's meaning is clearly set out in Book 12. There, commenting on the biblical words 'In the beginning God created heaven and earth', he notes that any interpretation is acceptable so long as it is in line with the truth. Although this argument is developed specifically with reference to the interpretation of the Scriptures, it is at least possible that he would have accepted it as a sound principle of interpretation of his own writings.[21] But the linguistic

have honour' (John 4:44) for 'not to be honoured'; John appears to have altered the expression 'to be dishonourable' (ἄτιμός εἶναι) found in Matthew 13:57 and Mark 6:4.

[20] Tentatively, we may say that the distinction can be made in either language, using *facere* and ποιέω in the sense 'to make', and *agere* and πράσσω in the sense 'to do'. Alternatively, we may ask whether the verb should be understood in the sense of the English 'to do one's homework' (where 'to do' means both 'to perform an activity' and 'to create something which was not there previously').

[21] The main problem with this theory of Scriptural hermeneutics is that in principle it means that Scripture cannot add to our stock of knowledge; since it is not merely by reading that we learn, but also through establishing which truth the author intended us to learn; and that we cannot establish this unless we first know the truth in question. This problem is posed here in its stronger form, and Augustine might have modified his position to state that we should accept only those interpretations which are in line with other known truths. But in fact his theory of language, as outlined in the *de Magistro*, takes a different route. The biggest objection to applying this theory to non-Scriptural use of language is that humans may not be speaking the truth, in which case they may not have intended us to learn a truth in the first place. But though Augustine admits that only God never lies, and that humans may lack the self-knowledge to know that they are lying, he still expects his readers to make the charitable assumption that he is telling the truth (10. 3. 3).

approach has its value. At least implicit in Augustine's theory is the notion that there is a limit to the extent to which different meanings may be inferred from a single passage.

O'Donnell's proposed interpretation of *veritatem facere* as 'making the truth' cannot, then, be guaranteed by a linguistic approach to the passage. But his questioning of the traditional interpretation rests on a sound linguistic observation. In formal terms, the verb *facere* tends not to have *veritas* (or other nouns formed from adjectives) as its object.[22] There is no doubt that Augustine would be likewise aware of possibilities of interpretation that this unusual phrase opened up. Although the phrase was one he had taken over from biblical Latin, he was in principle free to paraphrase, smooth it down, or omit it altogether. Instead, he chose not to. What follows is an examination of some of the linguistic choices he makes in the *Confessions*, and a consideration of the place of language within the wider scheme of the work. This must begin, however, with some consideration of how Augustine deploys some of the most basic Latin linguistic vocabulary: the verb 'to speak', *loquor*, and the noun 'language', *sermo*.

DEUS LOQUENS

'I see it absolutely, but I do not know how I should express it, except that everything which begins or ceases to be, does so at that moment when it is deemed that it should have begun or ceased—deemed so in the eternal Reason in which nothing either begins or ends. And that is your Word, and also "the Beginning, since he also speaks to us"' (*utcumque video, sed quomodo id eloquar nescio, nisi quia omne quod esse incipit et esse desinit tunc esse quando debuisse incipere aliquid vel desinere in aeterna ratione cognoscitur, ubi nec incipit aliquid nec desinit. ipsum est verbum tuum, quod et principium est quia et loquitur nobis*; *Confessions* 11. 8. 10). Much of Book 11 of the *Confessions* is taken up with a meditation on the relationship between God and the

---

[22] In this respect, the formal parallel between *veritatem facere* and *voluntatem patris facere* breaks down, in that *voluntas* is not transparently deadjectival. There is, however, another parallel in the biblical phrase *facere misericordiam*, 'to mercy, be merciful', where the noun is derived from an adjective.

created universe. This takes the form of an extended commentary on the opening words of the Book of Genesis: 'In the beginning God created heaven and earth'. The nature of this 'beginning' is problematic. If all that existed before the material world was an absolute and eternal God, what 'beginning' could there be, seeing as the word is normally used within the context of a world where time and sequence is the norm?

Part of Augustine's answer lies in his citation of John 8:35: 'So they said to him, "Who are you?" Jesus said to them, "The Beginning, since I also speak to you."' (*dicebant ergo ei, tu quis es? dixit eis Iesus, principium quia et loquor vobis*). More so even than 'making the truth', Jesus' self-description here illustrates the way the author of *John* can use a limited vocabulary to create a dense style, rich in intratextual cross-references. The obscurity of the original is reflected in both the Latin and English translations. The words require some exegesis if any sense is to be made of them at all. By taking Jesus' statement that he is 'the Beginning' and linking it to the 'beginning' of the Book of Genesis, Augustine is able to give one answer to the problem of how such a 'beginning' could take place within eternity. The phrase 'in the beginning' is taken to mean 'through [the one who is] the Beginning,' the pre-existent Second Person of the Trinity, incarnated as Jesus of Nazareth. In so doing, Augustine is exploiting the possibilities offered by what he called 'the custom of the Scriptures', and what we would call 'biblical Latin'.[23] Although *in principio* would not normally be taken to mean 'through the beginning', the preposition *in* + ablative is often used in this sense in biblical Latin to indicate the instrument or agent of an action, and can be translated as 'by' or 'through'. Tying in further biblical citations, Augustine proceeds: 'In/by/through this beginning, O God, you made heaven and earth; in your Word, in your Son, in your strength, in your wisdom, in your truth...' (*in verbo tuo, in filio tuo, in virtute tua, in sapientia tua, in veritate tua*).[24]

---

[23] *Consuetudo scripturarum*; on this subject, see Chapter 5.
[24] Biblical citations: the universe made through the Word, John 1:10, *mundus per ipsum factus est* (note *per* not *in*, but Augustine clearly regards the two as equivalent). God has 'made everything through Wisdom' at Psalm 103:24. The 'strength of God' is not so obviously described as an agent of creation, but compare Psalm 65:7 (God 'rules in his strength for ever'), Psalm 73:13 (he has 'made fast the sea with his strength').

But this beginning 'also speaks to us' (*et loquitur nobis*). It is not surprising to find the basic verb of speaking occurring repeatedly in a biographical memoir such as the *Gospel according to John*. But there is good reason to think that it is specially important in *John*, and that particular tradition of Christian linguistic mysticism was particularly important for Augustine. The Greek verb λαλέω occurs 39 times in *John*, as opposed to 26 and 31 times respectively in the longer *Matthew* and *Luke*. A few examples will give the flavour: 'I am he who speaks to you' (John 4:26); 'The words which I have spoken to you are spirit and life' (John 6:63); 'As for me, I speak what I have seen at my father's' (John 8:38); 'I speak to you and you do not believe' (John 10:25); 'The words which I speak to you I speak not of myself, but it is my father himself who abides in me that does these works' (John 14:10); 'I have spoken openly to the world... and in secret I have spoken nothing' (John 18:20). As with the verb 'to do' (ποιέω), the subject is usually Jesus, and the activity of speaking is very intimately linked to Jesus' relationship to the Father and to his mission to bring salvation.

Something similar is true also of the *Confessions*. Again, it is only to be expected that the basic verb of speech (*loquor*) will occur many times in a biographical work. But a number of them do command special consideration, in particular the biblical citations. Predictably, the *Gospel according to John* is the major single source of these. It is notable that when Augustine quotes John 8:35 (repeatedly in this passage, and recapitulated at 12. 28. 39) he includes the second half of the verse ('since I also speak to you'). The logic of the verse is unclear even in the Greek (what is the connection between being the Beginning and speaking?). But Augustine immediately spells out his interpretation of it in language reminiscent of his 389 work *The Teacher (de Magistro)*. In *The Teacher* he presents a dialogue between himself and his son Adeodatus about the nature of language (*locutio*). Beginning from a working definition of language as being a means of 'teaching' others (*docere*),[25] Augustine leads Adeodatus to the conclusion that language cannot be used to pass on information

---

[25] The Latin verb has a wider range of meaning than any one English equivalent. It suggests any sort of communication of information, or supposed information. 'Telling' or 'informing' or 'explaining' are alternative translations.

at all: a word tells us nothing unless we know what it means, and it is virtually impossible to explain that except in terms of other words.[26] This, of course, merely displaces the problem. But in fact we do communicate. How? Solely because of the inner presence of 'the one Teacher, who is Christ'[27]—a phrase echoed here in the *Confessions*, where the words spoken outwardly during the Incarnation are meant to prompt people 'to seek and find in the eternal truth, in which the one Good Teacher teaches all his pupils' (*ut... intus quaereretur et inveniretur in aeterna veritate, ubi omnes discipulos bonus et solus magister docet*; *Confessions* 11. 8. 10).

CREATURA LOQUENS

Speech, then, is the characteristic activity of the Son of God, the Word who is intimately linked with the whole process of creation. But God also communicates through the physical world. This idea is not unique to Augustine, or even to Christian writers in general.[28] But it is specially important to Augustine. There is good reason for thinking that he wrote the *Confessions* partly to answer those who criticized his appointment as bishop of Hippo on the grounds that he had been a prominent Manichee before his conversion.[29] Certainly he is at pains to repudiate Manichaeism in general, and in particular the doctrine that the physical world is evil. As part of this, he not only emphasizes his belief in the world as God's creation—many of his Christian contemporaries could do as much while retaining an

---

[26] Similar questions of philosophy of language remain current. Trask (1999: 174–5) puts it in typically crisp terms: 'It seems to be impossible in principle to learn anything about a language without knowing something else about it first.'

[27] See Augustine's own summary at *Retractationes* 1. 11,... *invenitur magistrum non esse qui docet hominem scientiam nisi deum, secundum illud etiam quod in evangelio scriptum est, unus est magister vester* (Matthew 23:8), *Christus*; compare *de Magistro* 11. 38, *ille autem qui consulitur, docet, qui in interiore homine habitare dictus est, Christus*....

[28] In the Christian scriptures, the two key texts are Psalm 18:2, 'The heavens declare the glory of God, and the firmament announces the work of his hands', and Paul's essay in natural theology at Romans 1:21.

[29] On the probable impetus for the writing of the *Confessions*, see Chadwick (1991: xi–xii), Clark (2005: 1–33).

unhealthy scepticism about all things physical—but does so in specifically *linguistic* terms. Again, he does this partly through the careful marshalling of biblical allusions. Consider the account he gives in Book 10 of his search for God in the elements of the physical world:

You have smitten my heart with your word, and I love you. But even heaven and earth and everything in them tell me from every direction that I should love you, nor do they cease from telling everyone ... but you will have mercy on him on whom you have had mercy; for if not, heaven and earth would speak your praises to the unhearing.

percussisti cor meum verbo tuo et amavi te. sed et caelum et terra et omnia quae in eis sunt ecce undique mihi **dicunt** *ut te amem nec cessant* **dicere** *omnibus... misericordiam praestabis cui misericors fueris, alioquin caelum et terra surdis* **loquuntur** *laudes tuas.* (10. 6. 8, quoting in particular Psalm 68:35).

I asked the earth, and it said, 'I am not'; and all that therein is made the same confession. I asked the sea and the deeps and the living creatures that crawl, and they replied, 'We are not your God; look above us.' I asked the winds that blow, and the whole air with all its inhabitants said, 'Anaximenes is mistaken; I am not God.' I asked the heaven, sun, moon, stars. 'Nor are we the God you seek,' they said ... Surely this beauty is apparent to whose senses are intact? Why do they not speak the same to all?

interrogavi *terram, et dixit, non sum; et quaecumque in eadem sunt idem confessa sunt.* **interrogavi** *mare et abyssos et reptilia animarum vivarum, et* **responderunt,** *non sumus nos deus tuus; quaere super nos.* **interrogavi** *auras flabiles, et* **inquit** *universus aer cum incolis suis, fallitur Anaximenes; non sum deus.* **interrogavi** *caelum solem lunam stellas; neque nos sumus deus quem quaeris,* **inquiunt**... *nonne omnibus quibus integer est sensus apparet haec species? cur non omnibus eadem* **loquitur**? (*Confessions* 10. 6. 9–10)[30]

To speak of nature 'speaking' of God might have been little more than a throwaway metaphor. But something more seems to be intended.[31] In the first place, there is the sheer range and volume of linguistic vocabulary: *interrogo, confiteor, respondeo, inquam, loquor.* Then it is notable how Augustine has adapted his biblical text to make

---

[30] For the numerous biblical references, see O'Donnell, above note 16. Note in particular the Johannine repetition of 'I am not' in direct speech; compare e.g. John 1:20–1 (John the Baptist), 18:17, 25 (Peter).

[31] A point emphasized also by Markus (1996: 26–9) in his admirable reading of this passage.

it more openly 'linguistic': his reading of Psalm 68:35 as *loquuntur laudes tuas* contrasts with the more familiar form of the text as simply *laudent*.[32] Finally, we may ask whether this is a metaphor at all. The term is not precise, since different speakers may have different perceptions of when a word is being used in a transferred sense; the question was a familiar one in the ancient grammatical tradition.[33] It is certainly likely that Augustine's imagery of creation 'talking' would indeed be taken as imagery by most of his contemporaries. It is quite possible, however, that he was more or less consciously using linguistic vocabulary (*loquor, dico,* and so on) with a view to extending his readers' view of what constitutes language.

HOMO LOQUENS

However, it is also a human activity. Ancient systems of thought speculated widely on the fact that humans were the one living species with the ability to use language.[34] Eustathius, the twelfth-century

---

[32] The use of *loquor* itself is somewhat surprising, as *laudes dicere* is the more usual Latin idiom. It seems likely that Augustine deliberately avoids the more familiar phrase as being rather trite.

[33] Some typology of metaphor may be useful here. The two commonest types of metaphor are probably extended senses (for example, 'to call someone on the phone') and transferred senses proper (for example, 'to dial a number' on a push-button phone). In the former example, the sense of 'call' is extended to cover any long-distance communication, even if it does not involve raising the voice. In the latter, the sense of 'dial' is transferred to cover something which involves no dialling at all. Metaphor by transference may lose its metaphorical status either if speakers cease to perceive the link with the basic sense (thus creating two homophonous words) or if the transferred sense effectively displaces the basic one. Metaphor by extension may lose its metaphorical status for either of the same two reasons, or because the extended sense simply comes to be perceived as part of the basic sense of the word. The result in any of these cases is the familiar 'dead metaphor' (itself a dead metaphor?). For an example from the Latin tradition, compare Cicero's discussion of *laetus* 'happy, flourishing' as familiarly applied to crops; is it a metaphor or not? (*de Oratore* 3. 155). A third type of metaphor, metaphor by restriction, may occur when a word with an originally wider sense comes to be used in a more restricted sense, with the older, wider sense retained in specific contexts (e.g. formulas, dialect, poetry) where it appears metaphoric in a way it once did not. For example, 'to starve' in older English is 'to die through deprivation'; hence one may in dialect 'starve of cold', i.e. deprivation of heat.

[34] For more recent perspectives, see Aitchison (1996), Dunbar (1996).

commentator on Homer, probably reflects much earlier sources when he glosses the obscure adjective μέροπες (traditionally 'face- or mouth-dividing') of humans because 'they have a mouth divided by nature into words and syllables and letters' (μέροπες δὲ οἱ ἄνθρωποι παρὰ τὸ φύσει μεμερισμένην ἔχειν τὴν ὄπα εἴς τε λέξεις καὶ εἰς συλλάβας καὶ εἰς στοιχεῖα). Various gods and heroes were advanced among the early Greeks as the bestowers of this gift of language (Gera 2003: 112–80). By the classical period, it is simply taken as given, without reference to specific inventors or bestowers.

Augustine himself had advanced a familiar hypothesis. Writing the *de Ordine* shortly after his conversion in 386, he had stated: 'Since one human could not form a stable social relationship with another unless we talked to each other, the rational element in us saw that we should give names to things' (... *illud quod in nobis est rationabile... quia... nec homini homo firmissime sociari posset, nisi colloquerentur... vidit esse imponenda rebus vocabula*; de Ordine 2. 35).[35] In the *Confessions*, his emphasis is changed. Humans use language through the gift of God. This is not only because God is the creator but also because he is the ultimate truth; and so, if the goal of language is to express truth, then the existence of God is the precondition of its existence also. Belief in God is the supreme reason for language; twice in the *Confessions* Augustine quotes Paul's dictum, 'I believe, and therefore I speak' (*credo, propter quod et loquor*; 2 Corinthians 4:13/Psalm 115:10, quoted at 1. 5. 6 and 11. 22. 28). This belief in itself is the result of the 'proclamation' of God: 'May I invoke you, believing in you; for you have been proclaimed to us' (*invocem te credens in te; praedicatus enim es nobis*; 1. 1. 1).[36] This position is not incompatible with his formulation in the *de Ordine*, and is arguably implicit in it. The rational faculty, after all, comes ultimately

---

[35] For an excellent discussion of the background to this, see Duchrow (1965: 94–15).

[36] The 'proclaimer' has been variously identified as Paul, Ambrose, or Christ; see O'Donnell's note. *Praedicare* is used of Paul at 10. 23. 34 (also the *praedicator* at 1 Timothy 2:7 and 2 Timothy 1:11), and at 6. 2. 2 it refers to Ambrose. However, since all knowledge of God rests on God's self-revelation, the ultimate Proclaimer is always the Son, who has 'narrated God' (*deum... enarravit*; John 1:18) or 'spoken the Father' (*patrem dicebat*; John 8:28). Note the typically Johannine emphasis on language, and his typically strained use of it; the Paris Codex Gatianus has smoothed the reading to *patrem esse deum dicebat*. See also Burton (2000: 127).

from God, the source of all reason. But the change of emphasis is clear. Indeed, this is an early sign of a tendency in Augustine's thought which was to become increasingly prominent over the next two decades; a growing stress on God as the source of all that is good in human life, prompting and reinforced by his long-running controversy with Pelagius. But if in the *de Ordine* speech is a human invention, in the *Confessions* it is clearly a gift of God to humans with no prior claim to it. 'Have mercy on me, that I may speak' (*miserere ut loquar*; *Confessions* 1. 5. 5) is Augustine's prayer at the first occurrence of the verb, and this is quickly followed up with another biblical reminiscence: 'Allow me to speak, since it is to your mercy that I speak' (*sine me loqui...quoniam ecce misericordia tua est...cui loquor*; *Confessions* 1. 6. 7, recalling Mark 1:34; also quoted at 9. 2. 22).

Being a gift of God, language is intrinsically good and pleasurable. It is a sign of life. The first thing the son of the widow of Nain does after being raised from the dead by Jesus is to 'begin talking' (Luke 7:22)—a detail noted by Augustine and applied to his mother Monica's prayer for his own 'resurrection' from Manichaeism. As with his citation of John 8:35 ('The Beginning, since I also speak to you') the reference to speaking might reasonably have been omitted; but it is not. Although Augustine does not pursue the point (surely he was 'speaking' already?), we may supply an interpretation: his 'resurrection' as a Catholic Christian would be marked by a return to logical, human discourse. Conversely, the deprivation of speech is associated with pain and divine punishment. The spiritual crisis which resulted in his resignation as Court Orator and professor of rhetoric was immediately preceded by a toothache so painful that he could not speak (*dolore dentum tunc excruciabas me...ut non valerem loqui*; *Confessions* 9. 4. 12)—an incident which recalls Zechariah's punishment for having refused to believe Gabriel's prediction of the birth of John the Baptist (Luke 1:20–2).[37] Language can confer intellectual and moral instruction,[38] which itself is marked by pleasure. Consider, for example, the account of the pleasures of friendship through which he slowly found consolation for the death of his unnamed

---

[37] *Et ecce eris tacens et non poteris loqui...egressus autem non poterat loqui*. Note that Augustine, like Zechariah, is not healed of his speechlessness until he has passed on a message to his friends with a wax tablet.

[38] See in particular Chapter 3, on *colloqui* in the sense 'to engage in dialectic'.

friend in Book 4: 'speaking together, laughing together, reading sweet-speaking books together—by these and other such signs which come from hearts that love and love again, through the face, the tongue, the eyes...' (*colloqui et corridere... simul legere libros dulciloquos... his et huiuscemodi signis a corde procedentibus per os per linguam per oculos*; Confessions 4. 8. 13).

Most importantly, language may be a means to contemplation of the divine. In Book 9 of the *Confessions*, Augustine recounts how he and his mother shared an ecstatic spiritual experience at Ostia-on-Tibur, shortly before her death: 'So we spoke alone together (*colloquebamur*), very sweetly... and we began to ascend inwardly still further, meditating and speaking and marvelling (*adhuc ascendebamus interius cogitando et loquendo et meditando*) at your works, and we came to our own minds and transcended them, to attain the land of unfailing richness... and while we spoke (*loquimur*) and longed for that country, we attained it, in our degree, for a whole heartbeat...' (*Confessions* 9. 10. 23–4). Again, the emphasis on language is striking—one might easily expect accounts of such a beatific vision to focus on inner silence and peace instead—and its ramifications are left to the reader to explore. There is a case for taking the adverb 'inwardly' (*interius*) with both the verb 'to ascend' and with the three verbs that follow ('meditating and speaking and marvelling'). Within both Monica and Augustine an inner dialectic occurs with 'the one true Teacher'; through their outward conversation they share the truths they have each learnt from that source. Human language, like the language of the physical world, may point to God.

HOMO LOQUAX

The joy of speech does not, however, arise from the simple fact of speaking. Language should be used with pleasure as a means to God, but not enjoyed as an end in itself.[39] Augustine's great opening invocation of God closes with a warning about the abuse of language:

---

[39] For the classic Augustinian formulation on the distinction between the 'use' (*usus*) of the created world as a means to the 'enjoyment' (*fruitio*) of the Creator, and the perils of 'enjoying' creation rather than 'using' it, see *City of God*, especially Books

vae tacentibus de te quoniam loquaces muti sunt. Here O'Donnell translates, 'For though they say much [about other things] they are mute [in all that matters],' while noting that 'The oxymoron [*loquax/ mutus*] ... has puzzled'.[40] For Augustine, the 'great talkers' (*loquaces*) *par excellence* are the Manichees, fluent dialecticians with a generous store of mythology (*fabulae*, literally 'speakings').[41] The semantics of this word deserve attention. As we have noted, the distinctive feature of the human being in Greek thought is the possession of speech and reason. (Some thinkers allow animals a degree of rationality, which is not, however, outwardly expressed in speech).[42] These faculties may both be expressed in Greek by the single word *logos* or *to logikon* (λόγος τὸ λογικόν). In purely formal terms, the closest Latin translation of *to logikon* ('the rational/linguistic [faculty]') is *loquax*; but in practice this refers only to the faculty for speech; the sense 'rational' is conveyed by *rationalis*. On top of that, Latin adjectives ending in -*ax* are often pejorative: compare *audax* 'over-bold', *edax* 'greedy', *fugax* 'cowardly', *rapax* 'grasping'. *Loquax*, then, is at best a loaded translation of λογικός even in the sense 'linguistic, language-using'.[43]

The second half of the oxymoron *loquax/mutus* also deserves attention. The adjective *mutus* is well attested in Latin from the Republican period as a translation of the Greek ἄλογος, 'foolish' or 'irrational'. The phrase *loquaces muti sunt*, then, can be glossed as 'those who have the linguistic faculty and indeed use it to an excessive degree, but do not have, or do not exercise, the concomitant faculty of reason'. This (admittedly verbose) gloss is borne out by Augustine's repeated use of the verb *garrire* 'to chatter away' and its

---

8, 11, 14, 19, 21. The vocabulary of use and enjoyment is not prominent in the *Confessions*, but the theory is already implicit.

[40] See the lengthy discussion at O'Donnell (1992. ii. 26–8), who cites (rather cautiously) the alternative interpretation, 'since mute are even the most eloquent'.

[41] Also *loquaces* at *Confessions* 5. 7. 12. Faustus the Manichee bishop is in fact semi-exempted from the charge of *loquacitas*, though Augustine is less than impressed by his skill as a dialectician. On the Manichees' public disputations more generally, see Lim (1995). Manichee *fabulae* are dismissed at e.g. *Confessiones* 4. 8. 13, 5. 3. 3, 5. 7. 12, 5. 10. 19, 6. 5. 7.

[42] On the equation of speech, or at least co-occurrence, of speech and rationality, see Gera (2003, especially 182–212). For rational animals, see Porphyry, *de Abstinentia* 3. 3, with the discussion in Kelber (1958: 86) and the notes in Clark (2000: 163–6).

[43] On other loaded translations in Augustine (e.g. *fabulosus* for μυθικος, *contentiosus* for ἀγωνιστικός see Chapter 3.

cognates of himself and other Manichees: 'I used to say to them, garrulously and ineptly (*garrulus et ineptus*), "Why does a soul made by God get things wrong...?"' (*Confessions* 4. 15. 26).[44] The verb may be used of gossip and idle talk in general, but is particularly applied to talking birds: creatures with the outward appearance of language, but lacking its rational substance.

As with the positive aspects of language, Augustine is able to marshal biblical citations to condemn the misuse of language through empty and meaningless talk. Most important of this is Psalm 143:8, 11: the enemies of the righteous are those 'whose mouth has spoken vanity' (*quorum os locutum est vanitatem*). This is cited twice: at *Confessions* 10. 4. 5 of those uncharitable brothers who take pleasure in Augustine's pre-conversion past, and 11. 30. 40 of those (presumably Manichees) who object to the doctrine of Creation by a supreme God. Also important is Paul's attack on Christian fringe groups as 'empty talkers and misleaders' (*vaniloqui et seductores*) at Titus 1:10,[45] a phrase applied at *Confessions* 8. 10. 22 to dualists (presumably Manichees again) who see the human mind as the locus for conflict between 'good' and 'bad' minds.

Augustine's other key biblical criticism of the misuse of language comes, as we might expect, from the *Gospel according to John*. As with many of the other Johannine references to language, it is hieratic and obscure: 'He who speaks falsehood, speaks of his own' (*qui loquitur mendacium de suo loquitur*; John 8:44). This is cited at *Confessions* 11. 25. 34, 11. 25. 38 as part of Augustine's argument for a pluralist, non-authoritarian exegesis of the Scriptures, against those who wish to claim ownership of them through their possession of a single right interpretation. It is notable that Augustine links 'speaking falsehood' and 'speaking vanity' through his citation of Psalm 4:3, 'Why do you love vanity and seek falsehood' (*ut quid diligitis vanitatem et quaeritis mendacium*; cited at *Confessions* 4. 2. 2 and repeatedly at 9. 4. 9–10). The bridging of Psalm 143:8, 11 and John 8:44 through this verse is unlikely to be coincidental, and invites us to consider—as we

[44] Also at 5. 6. 10 (of Faustus) and 6. 4. 5 (of Augustine again); of over-enthusiastic Christian biblical commentators at 12. 28. 38. Also once, in a positive sense, at 9. 1. 1, of the newly converted Augustine's new-found (and perhaps over-indulged) freedom to talk to God (*garriebam tibi*).

[45] Compare the condemnation of *vaniloquium* by similar groups at 1 Timothy 1:6.

have—Augustine's references to speech collectively and not in isolation from each other.

LOCUTIO: SUMMARY

What we have considered so far are only some of Augustine's uses of *loquor* in the *Confessions*. Some important uses will be considered later on—notably in connection with books and in connection with rhetoric and dialectic.[46] As the verb is a common one in all Latin literature, it should be stressed that its mere occurrence in the work is no proof of its importance. That it is important, however, is guaranteed by its sheer frequency—11.64 instances per 10,000 words, as opposed to around 9.72 per 10,000 words in classical prose generally[47]—and due to its prominent location in biblical citations and in the first paragraphs of three Books (6, 10, and 12). A full examination of all instances is beyond our present scope, but two further points may be made before we proceed. First, the *Confessions* provides an unusually high number of examples of *loquor* governing a direct object. This usage is common, especially in poetry, with adverbial neuter subjects: compare such phrases as *vera loquor*, *falsa loquor*, *haud ignota loquor*. The use with the abstract noun as an object ('to speak vanity', 'to speak falsehood') is rarely if ever found in classical Latin, but quite common in biblical Latin. The phrase *veritatem loqui*, for instance, occurs some 7 times in biblical Latin, the most familiar instance being perhaps Jesus' self-description in the *Gospel according to John* as 'a man who has spoken the truth to you' (*hominem qui veritatem vobis locutus sum*; John 8:40).[48] These may be taken as equivalents to the familiar adverbial neuter accusatives of

---

[46] See discussion in Chapter 3.

[47] The figure for Latin prose as a whole is taken from the Perseus Project website (<http://www.perseus.tufts.edu/>), as of August 2004. We may suggest also that the more frequently a word occurs over a corpus of text, the less variation there is likely be between the frequency levels in individual authors and works. As *loquor* is a relatively high-frequency word overall, its special frequency in the *Confessions* is all the more notable.

[48] Other examples in Psalm 14:3, Isaiah 33:15, Jeremiah 9:5, Zechariah 8:16, Ephesians 4:25.

the adjective (*veritatem loquor* = *vera loquor*), but need not be.[49] Latin (and Greek), like English, have a simple word for 'true' in the sense 'real, genuine' (as in 'the True Cross'); *verus, ἀληθής*. Alongside this there is a more complex word meaning 'truthful, consistent with reality' (as in 'a true copy', 'a true likeness'); *verax, ἀληθινός*. But in all three languages the more basic word tends to encroach on the sense of the more complex. According to this second sense, truth cannot exist without a representation—typically, the representation given in language. In this sense, then, 'speaking truth' is a literally accurate expression; language does not merely reflect truth, but generates it.

One further example of *loquor* with a non-adverbial accusative should be noted: Monica eventually converts her husband Patricius to Christianity after years 'speaking [God] to him through her moral character' (*loquens te illi moribus suis*; Confessions 9. 9. 19). Though this use of *loquor* in the sense 'to bespeak, to intimate' can be paralleled in classical Latin, it remains a striking phrase.[50] As with Augustine's abundant references to the created world 'speaking', we may see this as less a metaphorical use and more an attempt on Augustine's part to broaden the range of what is understood as 'language'.

Finally, we note that *loqui*, though translated here as 'to speak' and the closest thing to a neutral Latin verb meaning 'to use language', is characteristically used of *viva voce* conversation, rather than of harangues, monologues, or written representations of speech.[51]

SERMO

Much the same is true of our other key term, *sermo*. Just as *loqui* is the closest approximation to a neutral verb 'to speak', so *sermo* is the most neutral word for 'language'. It differs from *oratio*, its closest

---

[49] Even in Greek 'to speak the truth' (λαλεῖν τὴν ἀλήθειαν) is not an obvious alternative for the more usual adverbial neuter ἀληθῆ λαλεῖν or λέγειν.

[50] Compare, for instance, Jerome's account of the hermit Paul's words on his encounter with the goat-man in the desert: 'The very beasts bespeak Christ' (*bestiae Christum loquuntur*; Vita Pauli 8, with Cox Miller (1996) and Wisnieski (2000).

[51] On semantics and historical development relative to other Latin verbs of speech, see Ernout and Meillet (1939) under *loquor*.

rival for this title, in that *sermo* tends to refer to conversation and plurivocal speech in a way that *oratio* does not.[52] Alongside this meaning, it gains a range of extended and specialized senses as a recognized technical translation of various Greek words.[53] Translating ἡ διαλεκτή, it may mean either 'accent' or 'dialect' in the modern sense, or 'variety of language, style'; it may also mean 'plain, everyday speech'. Translating ὁ διάλογος, it may mean 'philosophical dialogue' (either oral or written), sometimes broadened to cover literary and scientific topics; the verb *sermocinari* gains the related sense 'to engage in dialectic'. Translating ὁ λόγος, it may mean 'group of words, phrase, sentence'.

In Christian usage, it acquires still more senses. Given the importance of biblical Latin in forming the idiom of Christian writers, it follows that these senses too are derived from the translation of Greek words. In the Latin Bible, *sermo* is found some 590 times (the precise count depending on the form of text).[54] The current Perseus Project text archive cites a total of 1,655 examples, with a frequency of 5.55 per 10,000 words of Latin prose. This, however, *includes* the examples in the Vulgate, which thus make up over one third of the total. The term is thus particularly associated with biblical Latin, and we would expect it to occur more frequently in Christian writers generally. One particularly common use, it should be said, has little impact on the development of a wider Christian usage: *sermo* as a translation of Greek τὸ ῥῆμα, 'thing', itself a Hebrew idiom. Other uses are more important. Particularly notable is the use of *sermo* to translate ὁ λόγος to refer to 'the word of the Lord': for instance, 1 Regnorum 3:1, *sermo domini erat pretiosus in diebus illis*, 'the word of the Lord was rare in

---

[52] On the semantics, see Ernout and Meillet (1939: 713–14), who take the basic sense of *orare* as 'to pray, utter a ritual formula', politely rejecting the Roman popular etymology from *os oris* 'mouth'. However, it remains possible that this was the older sense. The deverbative noun *locutio* is largely confined to learned registers, though compounds such as *colloquium, alloquium* are frequent.

[53] The list given here depends in part on the headings in the *Oxford Latin Dictionary*, which does not, however, consider the potential importance of Greek as a model. Greek influence is admittedly hard to diagnose with certainty where a sense is attested from an earlier date without reference to any Greek term.

[54] This figure is based on the text of the Weber edition available online at <http://www.biblegateway.com/versions/>.

28   Language in the Confessions *of Augustine*

those days.' The phrase is especially common in the formula describing the calling or inspiration of the Old Testament prophets, *factus est sermo domini ad me*, 'the word of the Lord came to me', variously used of Elijah, Jeremiah, and Ezechiel, among others.[55] In this sense it may also translate τὰ λόγια τοῦ θεοῦ, 'the word of God'. It is notably common in the so-called 'Wisdom Literature' of the Old Testament, where the wise speaker invites his youthful hearer to 'take up' or 'keep' his *sermones*.[56]

Particularly important are the uses of *sermo* in the *Gospel according to John*. The same linguistic mysticism in *John* which we have noted in connection with the verb 'to speak' (λαλεῖν) extends also to the use of the noun 'word' (λόγος). This is most famously true in the prologue to the Gospel, where it refers to the divine Word of God, the Second Person of the Trinity. Here *verbum* is the more usual translation, though *sermo* also is attested. But although it is only in the prologue that 'the Word' is explicitly given divine status, there are other instances where something close is more subtly implied: 'This is a hard word; who can hear him/it?' (John 6:61);[57] 'Your word is truth' (John 17:17; compare John 14:6, 'I am the way, the truth, and the life'). Among the other uses of λόγος *sermo* in *John*, it is notably applied to specific Old Testament texts where the other evangelists will typically use the word 'Scripture' (ἡ γραφή): 'So that the word of the Prophet Isaiah which he spoke might be fulfilled' (John 12:38); 'So that the word might be fulfilled which is written in their Law' (John 15:25).

Two further uses deserve note. In extra-biblical Christian use, *sermo* acquires the familiar sense 'sermon, homily', translating the Greek ἡ ὁμιλία 'moral discourse'. The noun *sermocinatio* appears just once in biblical Latin, but in an important context, at Proverbs 3:32: 'An abomination before the Lord is every mocker, and his conversation (*sermocinatio*) is with the simple.' Here the Greek has

---

[55] See 3 Regnorum 21:17 (Elijah), Jeremiah 13:3, and approximately 30 instances in Ezechiel. The same formula with *verbum* for *sermo* occurs in the Vulgate at Hosea 1:1, Joel 1:1, Micah 1:1; the two terms were probably interchangeable within the Old Latin traditions. The idiom is taken up in the New Testament at John 10. 35.

[56] Examples: Proverbs 2:1, 4:20, 7:4, 19:27; Wisdom 6:12, 6:27; compare also Psalm 118:16–17.

[57] The him/it ambiguity is present in both Greek and Latin.

ἡ ὁμιλία again, in its other sense of 'lifestyle, way of passing time'. While this is natural in Greek, the Latin *sermocinatio* would not normally bear that sense; it is counter-intuitive to read it as anything other than a word relating to language.[58]

SERMO IN THE *CONFESSIONS*

Augustine uses *sermo* and *sermocinari* in the *Confessions* with a frequency which reflects the influence of biblical Latin: 36 times and 5 times respectively, giving a combined frequency of 4.92 per 10,000. It is, therefore, considerably more prominent in this work than in classical Latin. As he turns towards Scriptural exegesis in the later books of the work, *sermo* becomes more common with reference to the Scriptures. Sometimes this is in reference to specific biblical passages: for example: 'Who will resist us, when the word comes to pass which is written (*sermo qui scriptus est*): "Death is swallowed up in victory"?' (1 Corinthians 15:54, quoted at *Confessions* 9. 4. 11); 'As for the fact that the "firmament" is said to have been made on the second day and "called heaven", this is an indication of which "heaven" the word spoke (*sermo locutus sit*) without reference to "days"' (*Confessions* 12. 13. 16, harmonizing the creation-narratives in Genesis 1:1 and 1:8). Sometimes this is in reference to the Scriptures in general, or to their typical language and style: 'You have "stretched out like a tent the firmament" of your book, your wholly-consistent words (*concordes utique sermones tuos*)' (*Confessions* 13. 15. 18); '[Had I been Moses] I would have wished to be given such a way of weaving language (*texendi sermonis modum*) that [my less sophisticated readers] would not reject my words... [Moses']

---

[58] Negative uses of *sermo* in biblical Latin are rare, and disproportionately common in the ablative plural; e.g. Psalm 103:3, 'they have surrounded me with words of hatred (*sermonibus odii*)'; Proverbs 6:2, 'if you have stood surety for a friend, you are trapped by your own words (*sermonibus propriis*)'; Proverbs 7:21, 'The harlot has snared [the youth] with many words (*multis sermonibus*).' On the interplay of singular and plural in the *Confessions*, see Chapter 5.

narrative bubbles up with a humble source of language (*parvo sermonis modulo*)' (*Confessions* 12. 26. 26–7).

These are enough to establish the broadly positive use of *sermo*. It is notable, though, that some of Augustine's biblical citations are either negative or at best neutral: 'The "word that comes forth from the mouth"... carries with it a temptation deriving from the desire for celebrity, which draws people into their own private position of prominence' (*Confessions* 10. 38. 62, citing Ephesians 4:29). This unfavourable analysis of language is a constant counter-current in the *Confessions*. It does not simply contradict the more favourable view which Augustine generally shows, but it does qualify it in two important ways. First, Augustine is critical of the merely external use of language as a form of exhibitionism. He does so by omitting a single adjective from his biblical source: 'Let not one *evil* word come forth from your mouth.'[59] The 'word' in question is now criticized not for its evil quality, but for the simple fact of being external. Augustine does not say that outward and public use of language is wrong; merely that it carries temptations. (For good measure, he adds that satisfaction even with one's inward use of language can lead to smugness). Secondly, there is the nature of this temptation: to use one's public position as a Christian exegete to boost one's own private standing. Here we may recall his quotation of John 8:44, discussed above: 'He who speaks falsehood, speaks of his own.' Since truth is common property, any special claims to private knowledge are likely to be false.[60]

Much the same is true of Augustine's final use of *sermo* in the *Confessions*. Commenting on the universal mission of the Church, and the universal authority according to the Scriptures, he quotes Psalm 18:4: 'There are no languages or dialects (*loquelae neque sermones*) where their voices are not heard' (cited at *Confessions* 13. 20. 26). This example of *sermo* in the sense 'dialect, form of

---

[59] Compare perhaps also Colossians 3:8: 'Put aside everything—anger, rage, malice, blasphemy, foul language—from your mouth' (*turpem sermonem de ore vestro*).

[60] The famous statement of Heraclitus, the first exponent of Logos-theology, seems ultimately to underlie Augustine's position: 'Although the Logos is common, most people live as if they had some private understanding' (fragment 2).

speech' is unique in the *Confessions*. Again, however, Augustine has modified the original context. Here the original is the Psalmist's classic statement of natural theology, a perfect epigram for the last three books of the *Confessions*: 'The heavens declare the glory of God, and the firmament announces the work of his hands.' The problem with this passage—as of all natural theology—for a Christian exegete is its tendency to abolish revelation. Why should a God universally apprehensible through nature need to manifest himself in other ways? Again, it is important to note Augustine's strategy here. We have seen already how he uses *loquor* and other verbs of speaking of objects in the created world in a way that is not so much metaphorical as an extension of the whole category of 'language' *in its literal sense*. The blurring of the distinction between literal and figurative senses is a key part of his Scriptural exegesis; while the *Confessions* as a whole celebrates the figurative mode of interpretation, the emphasis on the literal truth of Scripture is to be an increasingly prominent theme in Augustine's work in the new century. In this passage, the figurative 'sound' of the heavens proclaiming God's glory is equated with the literal 'sound' of the universal/Catholic Church preaching salvation throughout the known world. By equating literal and figurative senses of 'speech', Augustine turns Psalm 18 into a celebration of religion both natural and revealed. This revealed religion, however, is public and universal—'their sound has gone into every land'. We may see here an implicit contrast with particularist or esoteric groups such as the Donatists and Manichees. It is notable also that Augustine has no sense that differences of language might be a barrier to missionary work. The divine economy or management of the world does not restrict the truth to speakers of any given language—perhaps an undercutting of Jerome's project to translate the Old Testament Scriptures from their original languages.[61]

Particularly important in the *Confessions* is *sermo* in the sense '(philosophical) dialogue', a category which largely overlaps with that of conversation generally and which may also cover sermons. This important theme is treated further below (Chapter 3). In the sense 'Word, Logos', *sermo* is conspicuously absent in the *Confessions*,

[61] On economy and its relation to language, see Chapter 7, p. 177.

and is used only in reference to the Manichaean Logos-theology: the Manichee Logos is supposed to be sent by the Creator to rescue the human soul in its corrupted state, '.... though itself subject to corruption, since it came from one and the same substance' (*sermo... et ipse corruptibilis quia ex una eademque substantia*; *Confessions* 7. 2. 3). This use of *sermo* rather than *verbum* is presumably a distancing device.[62] The importance of language is underlined by Augustine's self-criticism not merely for holding these views but expressing them (*horribili sacril egio cordis et linguae sentiendo de te ista et loquendo*).

Augustine, then, prefers *verbum* to *sermo* to describe the pre-existent Word of God through whom the physical universe came into being and who became incarnate as Jesus of Nazareth. However, he retains the terms *sermo* and *sermocinari* to refer to the typically human action of using language. In the prologue to Book 1 of the *Confessions* he stresses it is the human nature of the Son which inspires his faith. His recognition of this humanity is a key step on the way back from Manichaeism to orthodox Catholic belief: from reading the Scriptures he learns that Jesus 'ate and drank, slept, walked, rejoiced, was saddened, talked to people (*sermocinatus est*)—and that his flesh did not cleave to your Word (*non haesisse carnem illam verbo tuo*) unaccompanied by a human soul and mind... for alternately producing rational sentences using signs (*proferre per signa sapientes sententias*) and keeping silent are properties of a mutable mind and soul' (*Confessions* 7. 19. 25). The importance Augustine attaches to Jesus' use of language is clear from its emphatic position at the end of the list, and from his glossing of the simple verb *sermocinari* in such formal terms.[63]

Finally, we have a remarkable comparison between language and the nature of the universe itself. This is invoked in different ways in

---

[62] Compare the retention of Greek terms in some early Christian Latin texts to refer to specifically Gnostic ideas, alongside the translation of the same terms when applied to Christian concepts; see Burton 2000: 145 note 11.

[63] Augustine's definition, and particularly his use of *proferre*, suggests specifically the Stoic-Neoplatonic λόγος προφορητικος or 'expressed word', as opposed to the λόγος σπερματικός or 'seminal word' (the universal human capacity for reason), and the λόγος ἐνδιαθετος ('internal word'), the inner conception formed by the mind before its expression in speech; see Winslow in Ferguson (1997) under 'logos'.

two passages. In Book 4 of the *Confessions*, Augustine is led through the account of his unnamed friend's death to contrast temporal pleasures with those eternal. Temporal pleasures, he writes, make full sense only when considered as part of the whole universe. This he illustrates with an analogy from language: 'It is the same also with the sentences we make using audible signs (*sermo noster per signa sonantia*). A sentence will not be a whole (*sermo non erit totus*) unless each word, once its parts have been uttered, makes way for another to take its place...for your Word (*in verbo enim tuo*), through whom they were created, [says] "Thus far and no farther"' (*Confessions* 4. 10. 15). In Book 11 he contemplates the means by which we measure time, taking as his model Ambrose's hymn 'O thou, the all-creator God' (*deus creator omnium*). When we pronounce this with its correct metre (iambic dimeter), he argues that this is because we have already premeditated in our mind the alternating short and long syllables; we don't pronounce it first and scan it afterwards. This is then generalized to any linguistic utterance (*quemque sermonem*; *Confessions* 11. 27. 36). In these two passages, language is arguably a metonymy rather than a metaphor for the created world. Temporal language, rightly used, partakes in the beauty of an ordered creation; but it is explicitly contrasted with the permanence and stability of God: 'These audible sounds pass away, so that others can take their place...But "Do I pass away somewhere?" says the Word of God' (*numquid ego aliquo discedo, ait verbum dei*; *Confessions* 4. 11. 16).

CONCLUSIONS

Language, then, is a prominent theme in the *Confessions*. It is in the nature of God to communicate with and through the created universe, though this communication is characterized by accommodation to the capacity of his various creatures, and—as we will see—requires interpretation by them. Humans too share this capacity for rational communication, with both each other and God; though as with all things human, this is likely to be abused or treated as an end in itself rather than a means to expressing truth. All human language is arbitrary and conventional, but this conventionality is two-edged. Where language is an end in itself, it may lead to mere linguistic snobbery; where language is used as a means to truth, then the coincidental associations that words have arbitrarily acquired over time may themselves turn out to indicate real truths.

2

Alternative Comedy: The Language of the Theatre

QUESTIONS OF GENRE

The *Aeneid*

Readers of the *Confessions*, ancient and modern, may well approach the work with the question more or less implicitly in mind: what genre does it belong to? This is a reasonable question, since ancient writers tend much of the time to identify early on in a work the genre to which it belongs. This in turn sets up a series of expectations in the minds of the readers, which may be then fulfilled, thwarted, or subverted in various ways.[1]

So much is obvious. But there is no work of ancient literature quite like the *Confessions*, and this does not help our understanding of it. Not only do we have no parallel for the structure of the work as a whole—nine books of autobiographical memoir, followed by a book of reflections on time and memory, concluded by three books of biblical exegesis—but each of the different elements itself subverts what expectations we have. Take Books 1 and 2. Accounts of the childhood and adolescence of notable characters are not uncommon in such works of historical fiction as Xenophon's *Cyropaedia*, or (on the Christian side) the *Infancy Gospel of Thomas*; but childhood reminiscences in an *autobiographical* work are rare indeed, and unlikely to reach their climax in the theft of some inferior pears.

---

[1] This is, of course, a very basic approach to a complex issue in the reading of ancient texts. For further discussion, see in particular Conte 1986.

Nor are they likely to contain speculation on the hero's or heroine's ante-natal existence, as the *Confessions* do.

If, then, there is no single genre which provides a framework for reading the work as a whole, we may reasonably ask whether any other ancient works provide at least a general model. The most likely candidate for this is generally recognized as being the *Aeneid* of Virgil. Augustine himself steers us strongly in this direction with some explicit references. As a boy he was 'forced to memorize the Wanderings of Aeneas, forgetful of my own wanderings, and to weep for the death of Dido... though all the while I could bear dry-eyed the fact that I was dying in my literary studies' (1. 13. 20). He hates his maths lessons, but finds the Wooden Horse of Troy, the burning of Troy, and story of Creusa's shade 'a most sweet spectacle of vanity (*spectaculum vanitatis*)' (1. 13. 22). He wins a prize for giving a prose rendition of Juno's monologue from the beginning of Book 1 of the *Aeneid*, 'the prize going to the boy whose show of anger and resentment was most suitable to the rank of his assumed character (*adumbratae personae*)' (1. 17. 27). The fact of his coming to Carthage in Book 3 is recounted in the plainest language—*veni Carthaginem*—and yet it is difficult not to remember Aeneas' arrival in Carthage (3. 1. 1). The Virgilian reminiscences are explicit when he leaves his mother Monica secretly in order to sail to Rome, as Aeneas had done to Queen Dido, a scene to which we will soon return (5. 8. 15). They are explicit too when we are told that Monica alone of all the mothers of Augustine's African coterie had 'followed' her son 'by land and sea' to Italy, just as Euryalus' mother had been the only Trojan woman to accompany Aeneas' men to the Italian mainland (6. 1. 1, quoting *Aeneid* 9. 492). And if much of the *Confessions* is concerned with Augustine's quest for his true, celestial 'homeland', that too may be paralleled in Aeneas' quest for his own true *patria* in Italy.

These facts are familiar enough, and have received some detailed and sensitive study in recent years.[2] And it is true that the *Aeneid* is

---

[2] Both Bennett's (1988) essay on the harbour scene at Carthage and MacCormack's wider study of 'Virgil in the mind of Augustine' (1998) have become classics of their kind; their influence on the views offered here is greater than a mere citation count would suggest. In particular, much of the material that follows is an attempt to explore the title-metaphor of 'the shadows of poetry'.

more important than any other secular work as an intertext for our understanding of the *Confessions*. Sometimes the differences are instructive. Monica follows Augustine to Italy at a time when he is spiritually dead, still stuck in his Manichee world-view; during the course of her time there, she sees him regenerate as a Christian and a Catholic. Euryalus' mother, in contrast, had gone to Italy only to see her son dead and dismembered. But at other times, the difference between the two works is too great to allow us to see the *Confessions* as being simply a 'spiritual *Aeneid*'. None the less, we have dwelt on the *Aeneid* so far not only because of its intrinsic importance, but because the way Augustine presents it may suggest a very different set of literary models.

Comedy and Mime

Augustine's account in the *Confessions* of his early reading of the *Aeneid* contains two repeated images. One of these is that of shadow and shade. In one of Augustine's favourite scenes, Aeneas while fleeing Troy is accosted by the shade (*umbra*) of his wife Creusa. Later Augustine wins the prize for best getting into the 'assumed character' (*adumbratae personae*) of Juno. The adjective *adumbrata* would normally suggest what was counterfeit or fictitious, which might make it superfluous here; it is, after all, in the nature of theatrical roles to be assumed. Assuming Augustine does not usually sprinkle redundant adjectives, we should consider the wider semantic range of the word, and its implications. Any reference to 'shadows' in the work of a Neoplatonist is likely to suggest the shadow-puppetry of the famous cave in Plato's *Republic* 514ff, where benighted humans are able to perceive only the shadows cast by what is truly substantial, and neither the true substances themselves nor the light-source which makes the shadow possible. Augustine imagines he is making progress as a Virgil scholar and a rising orator; in fact, he is a mere shadow-puppet. Yet this image may also allow poetry at least some value; provided a shadow is understood for what it is, one may infer from it the existence of some more substantial reality. Even the 'shadowy loves' (*umbrosis amoribus*, 2. 1. 1) in which

Augustine indulged as a teenager existed only in virtue of the legitimate pleasures of sexuality.[3]

Biblical references to shadow will also be important. One of Augustine's favourite anti-Manichee proof-texts is James 1:17, 'in you there is no change or shadow caused by motion (*obumbratio momenti*)' (cited at 3. 6. 10 and 3. 15. 25). This is a double hit: first against the Manichee notion of a Creator-God who was anything less than stable and transcendent, and secondly against the role that darkness and shadow played within the Manichee cosmic myth.[4] The phrase 'shadow caused by motion' would also suggest 'eclipse', particularly relevant given Augustine's doubts about Mani's astrological doctrines and his general failure to integrate his religion with the science of astronomy. The normal Latin term for an eclipse, *defectus* ('waning, lack'), in turn suggests Augustine's favourite definition of evil not as an entity in itself but as a 'lack of good' (*defectio boni*), and of the Devil as not a Manichee-style cosmic 'Prince of Darkness' but rather as a defector from the heavenly Civil Service (*caelestis militia*, 7. 21. 27).

The trail of allusions suggested by *umbra* could be traced further. Our main concern, however, is with Augustine's other repeated image in talking of Virgil: that of the theatre. Alongside his reference to his 'impersonation' of Juno, we have his reference to the *Aeneid* as a 'spectacle of vanity' (*spectaculum vanitatis*). Both *spectaculum* ('play') and *persona* ('mask, character') are most often found in Latin with reference to the theatre, which in practice means the traditional Roman comedy of Plautus and Terence, and the popular-culture genre of the mime. These may, of course, be dead or moribund metaphors; we can speak of 'backgrounds' or 'roles' in everyday English with no conscious reference to the theatre. There are, however, two reasons for thinking that Augustine is aware of the metaphor and expects his readers to be able to pursue its implications. First, there is the sheer inappropriateness of it in context. The idea of Aurelius Augustinus the young schoolboy

---

[3] Taking *amor* here in the sense of 'sexual pleasure' is probably too narrow; it is likely that Augustine is referring primarily in this passage to his adolescent sex-life, but *amor* could be taken more generally to refer to any strong liking or enthusiasm.

[4] For a general survey of the key Manichee doctrines and more specifically of Augustine's response to them, see Lieu (1985: 5–24, 140–3).

playing the part of the Queen of the Gods as she would have expressed herself had she been a Roman orator has a ridiculous quality of its own. Our second reason for taking seriously Augustine's theatrical metaphors in relation to Virgil is the sheer importance that the stage and the theatrical has elsewhere in the *Confessions*.[5]

The late-antique school curriculum was narrowly defined.[6] Greek schoolboys would typically study Homer as the model for epic, Euripides for tragedy, Demosthenes for oratory, and Menander for comedy. Latin-speaking boys would study Virgil as the great epicist, Cicero as the great orator, and Terence as the great comedian; for tragedy, the western school curriculum would generally substitute Sallust's fascinated accounts of the anti-heroes Jugurtha and Catiline. Individual teachers will have varied in their practice, but it is likely that Terence was often one of the first works studied; comedies in which young men generally emerged triumphant over their disapproving fathers were no doubt seen as works likely to arouse an interest in literature in the young.[7] Augustine himself describes his first experience of school in a phrase taken from Terence's *Adelphoe*: 'O God, my God, what miseries and what mockeries I knew there!' (*quas ibi miserias expertus sum et ludificationes*; *Confessions* 1. 9. 14, citing *Adelphoe* 867)—but in so doing he identifies himself not with either of the two young brothers of the play,

---

[5] The theatre is a major theme elsewhere in Augustine's work, most notably in *The City of God*; but a fuller study lies outside our present scope. For orientation, see MacCormack (1998: 198–200); Jürgens (1972) offers a broader study of patristic attitudes, with a useful index of citations.

[6] On Augustine's reading of classical texts, see the monumental work of Hagendahl (1967), especially 690–729. For his reading of earlier Latin, Hagendahl (377–83) demonstrates his awareness of Terence (with quotations in particular from the *Andria*, *Eunuchus*, and *Adelphoe*), which contrasts with a total absence of citations of Plautus. Hagendahl does not exclude the possibility that Augustine knew Plautus but simply chooses not to cite him, but in practice assumes that he simply did not know him. However, the rich manuscript traditions of Plautus if nothing else suggest fairly widespread awareness of his work; it may be easier to assume that Augustine simply found him less congenial to his tastes and purposes.

[7] We may perhaps recall Tom Sharpe's comic novel *Wilt*, in which a further-education lecturer tries in vain to interest his class of English provincial 1970s red-blooded day-release apprentice butchers in that alienated Eisenhower-era preppy Holden Caulfield. The present writer recalls William Golding's *The Lord of the Flies* and Alan Sillitoe's *The Loneliness of the Long-Distance Runner* being used in a similar way.

but with the sour old man Demea. This is followed with a more explicit comic reference, again to Terence. Reflecting on the way he was taught Latin at school, he states (rather implausibly) that he would not have learnt certain Latin words ('golden', 'shower', 'lap', and so on) had he not read the passage in Terence's *Eunuchus* (583–91) in which the young man contemplates a mural of Jupiter seducing Danae in the form of a shower of gold, and concludes that what is good enough for Jupiter is good enough for him. The passage in Terence is a classic example of the ecphrasis or literary description of a work of art, with the feature (frequent though not universal in ecphrases) of a viewer who sees in the artwork something of meaning for his own life.[8] But Augustine's representation of the young man before the wall-painting is itself an ecphrasis, with Terence's play as the object depicted and himself as the young man fatally demoralized by his reading of it. The problem lies not in Terence's words— Augustine is clear on this point—but on the way the educational system attempts to teach language and literature without reference to morality. It is presumably not coincidental that as Augustine gains a reputation as a brilliant schoolboy, he finds the world applauds him with the cry *euge euge* (1. 13. 21). This Greek exclamation ('bravo!') is in classical Latin overwhelmingly most frequent in comedy. Elsewhere it is most frequent in Christian writers, through citations of *euge euge* in Psalms 34:21–5, 39:16, and 69:4. Traditionally translated 'Tush' or 'Fie upon thee!', *euge* is here a cry of *dis*approval. As a junior lead in the human comedy, Augustine is applauded; but the same words have an ironic ring when cited from the Scriptures.

[8] The literature on ecphrasis has grown dramatically in recent years. The classic Latin examples of the ecphrasis-plus-viewer are, predictably, from Virgil's *Aeneid*: the Temple of Juno at Carthage in *Aeneid* 1. 453–93, in which Aeneas sees depicted the Trojan War; the doors of Apollo's temple at Cumae at *Aeneid* 6. 20–33, which Aeneas and Achates almost succeed in 'reading through' before they are interrupted by the Sybil; and the Shield of Aeneas at *Aeneid* 8. 608–731 which Aeneas marvels at without comprehending. A further refinement on the art-work-plus-viewer topos is the art-work-plus-viewer-plus-exegete, found e.g. in the proem to Longus' *Daphnis and Chloe* and (on the Christian Latin side) in Prudentius, *Peristephanon* 9. The class of ecphrasis may include a literary representation of another 'literary' work of art, such as the bard Demodocus' song at the court of King Alcinous (*Odyssey* 8: 499–534); Odysseus' response to this is a classic early example of the art-work-plus-viewer topos.

Alternative Comedy 41

So much for the more literary Roman comedy.[9] In addition to these, Augustine dwells at some length in the *Confessions* on the other forms of drama he watched as a student in Carthage (3. 2. 2–3), tragedy and (apparently) comedy and mime.[10] The attention he gives them is not simply a set of personal reminiscences of a youth which might have been spent better. Throughout the 380s and 390s both Church and the State, under successive emperors, were devoting massive resources to the putting-down of mime at least as a recreation for Christians. In 381, for instance, Gratian, Valentinian, and Theodosius had decreed that women actors might claim exemption from their trade on religious grounds, an exemption which would lapse irrevocably should they live less than fully Christian lives. In 394 Theodosius, along with Arcadius and Honorius, had followed this up by decreeing the tearing-down of pictures depicting scenes from the mime in public porticos, and forbidden Christian women and boys to consort with actors (*Codex Theodosianus* 15. 7. 12). In 397, an edict of Council of Carthage had prohibited the sons of bishops or clerics from giving public shows, on the ground that mere attendance at them was inadmissible for all Christians (*Acta III Concilii Carthaginensis* canon 11). Ambrose, Jerome, Paulinus, and Augustine himself had attacked the theatre with a frequency which suggests a spectacular lack of success.[11]

It is arguable, too, that theatrical motifs recur at key passages in the *Confessions*, and that an awareness of the theatrical background will help us understand these passages. The incorporation of dramatic motifs within another literary genre is not itself surprising; the *Aeneid* contains clear references to Euripides' *Hippolytus*, *Medea*, and *Bacchae*, along with Aeschylus' *Oresteia*. Particularly relevant to our present concern is the use of comedy and mime in the ancient novel. The importance of theatrical elements in the ancient novel was

---

[9] In practice, this means Terence, as Augustine never cites his less decorous older contemporary Plautus; Plautus is less highly regarded in antiquity as a model of good Latin, but the vastly superior manuscript evidence for his plays suggests he was at least as popular.

[10] Augustine does not refer to mimes as such in the *Confessions*, but his account of the theatrical lovers who 'enjoyed each other illicitly' (*sese fruebantur per flagitia*) may fit either comedy or mime, if indeed there is a meaningful distinction to be made at this date.

[11] For a full list of testimonia see Bonaria (1956: 124–41).

recognized in antiquity, and it has been persuasively argued that the Latin novelists Petronius and Apuleius incorporated many mimic and comic features in their work: stock scenes, characters, and names, plus a strong element of theatrical diction.[12] It may be worth our while to examine some passages where theatrical motifs are introduced, and to consider their effect for our reading of the work as a whole.

In identifying these theatrical passages, our emphasis will be in the first instance on the use of theatrical language, since this is relatively easy to identify. The classic Roman comedy of Plautus and Terence predates by a century or more the standardizing processes of the first century BC. Not only were certain features of their language obsolete by Cicero's and Caesar's day as the natural result of language change; some elements of them had been more or less consciously removed from the literary vocabulary. In addition to this, comedy and mime are the genre par excellence in which everyday situations and individuals are presented, making its language still more distinctive from the very public and masculine character of classical literary Latin. Aulus Gellius (*Noctes Atticae* 11. 7) has an anecdote about an opsimath orator who reduced his audience to bewilderment and laughter by using the words *apluda* 'chaff' (from Plautus and the late-third-century BC comedian Naevius) and *flocces* 'dregs' (from the Caecilius Statius, around 170 BC). Another achieves a similar effect by using the satirist Lucilius' *bovinator* 'timewaster'; satire is a non-theatrical genre, but one which shares language and situations with comedy and mime.[13] In the discussion that follows, it does not follow that any archaic word or word-formation in Augustine is

---

[12] The work of Panayotakis (1995) is of importance for both general background and for material on Petronius in particular. On similarities between the *Confessions* and the *Metamorphoses* of Apuleius, see Shumate (1988), Walsh (1988).

[13] Compare Quintilian's discussion of archaism in *Institutio Oratoria* (1. 39); the moderate use of archaism, he says, confers 'a certain authority which is not without pleasure', while their very unfamiliarity gives them 'a charm like that of a neologism'. However, he censures (among others) such museum pieces as *topper* 'forthwith', *antegerio* 'very much', *exanclare* 'to draw out', and *prosapia* 'lineage', words typically found in second-century tragic and comic writers. That comedy has its distinctive vocabulary, which may be over-fished by zealous students of archaism, is recognized also on the Greek side by Pseudo-Dionysius of Halicarnassus, *Ars Rhetorica* 10. 7–10. For an account of ancient theories of archaism, see Lebek (1970).

automatically a comic reference. As we have seen, some archaisms are rejuvenated in Christian writers through their use in biblical Latin.[14] Others are revived as part of the wider taste for archaism associated with authors such as Fronto (around AD 95–166), Apuleius (born AD 125), and Tertullian (around AD 160–240). Where archaisms are found in passages which recall comic and mimic themes in other ways, we may be justified in seeing them as comic touches. This does not exclude the possibility of other sources, and it will be suggested that an important element of Augustine's literary technique is his playing-off of comic and biblical senses of words.

THE STUDENT AND THE AXE

Our first example occurs in Augustine's mini-biography of his student and friend from Thagaste, Alypius (6. 9. 14). One day, while studying at Carthage, Alypius is apprehended as a thief by the market-wardens (*aeditimi*). It happens like this. He is mooning around the Forum, thinking over his latest rhetoric assignment. At the same time, another student is hacking away with an axe at some lead railing on a balcony overhanging Silversmiths' Street (or possible Bankers' Street; the Latin *argentarius* covers both). Alypius hears the noise, and idly goes to investigate. As he arrives, the other student comes running past him in the opposite direction. Alypius finds his axe, picks it up, and is wondering what was going on. Meanwhile, the silversmiths have heard noises, put their heads together (*submurmuraverunt*), and sent a party to investigate. The party arrives on the scene, and Alypius is dragged off amid general gloating (*tamquam furem manifestum se comprehendisse gloriantur*) from the silversmiths and the denizens of the Market Square (*inquilini fori*); this isn't the first time the lead had been stripped, and they themselves had been under suspicion. As they lead him away, they bump into the architect in charge of public works. This architect is a family friend of Alypius, so naturally knows he is innocent. A brief conversation is enough to get his side of the story. The party then

---

[14] See discussion in Burton (2000: 101–12).

descend on the home of the other student, where they find the young master's slave-boy (*pedisequus*) attendant by the door. They ask him if he knows whose axe it is; he, too young to know any better, says, 'Ours'. Tableau! The story has clear associations with the world of comedy, mime, and farce, and their relation the novel. The marketplace loiterer is a recognized class of waster from Aristophanes onwards.[15] The 'Swaggering Soldier' (*miles gloriosus*) is, of course, the eponymous hero of a Plautine play; the adjective is particularly common in comedy generally, and Cicero (*de Oratore* 1. 55. 236) cites the *gloriosus* as a stock character of the mime.[16] The 'Swaggering Silversmith' is a nice touch of bathos; while the involvement of the *argentarii* is a mere coincidence, Augustine is able to exploit its comic potential.[17] The use of the axe as a comically misinterpreted identity token belongs to a noble tradition. Best known perhaps is Cleostratus' shield in Menander's *Aspis* ('The Shield'), wrongly taken to mean that he had fallen in battle; the remains of Plautus' *Vidularia* ('The Travelling-Bag') attest a similar Latin tradition. Augustine's main model may, however, be not directly a mime, but rather Cicero's speech in defence of Marcus Caelius. In this speech the defence makes

[15] See Liddell and Scott under ἀγοραῖος II. Compare the Latin use of *forensis* to refer to idle and politically unstable elements in the state. In this connection we may cite also the ἀγοραῖος Alexander, a 'wicked man' who mocks the martyrs at Smyrna (*Martyrium Pionii* 6). Variously glossed as 'lawyer' or 'trader' (Robert 1994: 65), he is probably simply a loafer.

[16] Compare also *de Oratore* 2. 251, where Cicero lists the *gloriosus* also with the tetchy (*morosus*), the superstitious (*superstitiosus*), and the foolish (*stultus*) as types mocked by nature herself. Christian Latin follows the classical language in using *gloriosus* in both positive and negative senses ('glorious'/'boastful'). Augustine would be aware of Paul's theology of boasting, advanced at 2 Corinthians 9–12. This revolves around his citation of Jeremiah 9:23–4, 'Let not the wise boast of his wisdom, nor the strong of his strength, nor the rich of his riches; but let him who boasts, boast of this: that he knows and is acquainted with me, for I am the Lord (Vulgate *sed in hoc glorietur qui gloriatur, scire et nosse me*)'—a text which may itself echo Augustine's prayer to God at the beginning of the *Confessions*: *da mihi scire et intellegere*.

[17] *Argentarii* as bankers feature frequently in the comedies of Plautus. Various extant mimes feature the names of professions in their title; Bonaria (1953: 150–1) lists inter alia 'The Augur' (*Augur*), 'The Polisher' (*Colorator*), 'The Laundryman' (*Fullo*), 'The Weaving-Women' (*Staminariae*) (discussion in Wölfflin (1888)). 'In these plays either the trickster hero disguised himself as one of these professionals...or else, like the mimes of Herondas about shoemakers and schoolmasters, the story really centered on the tradesman and his lore' (Fantham 1989: 156).

an extended attempt to reduce part of the prosecution's case to the level of a mime (*Pro Caelio* 27. 65). At least two features of Cicero's account have their counterparts in Augustine's. Both involve a botched arrest:[18] Clodia's slaves fail to arrest Licinius, despite their ambush, the silversmiths arrest an innocent party, while letting the culprit escape. Both involve the possession of an allegedly incriminating object: in Licinius' case the *pyxis*, in Alypius' the axe. The motif of the innocent hauled off to trial also has precedent in Lucius' mock trial in Book 3 of Apuleius' *The Golden Ass*; possible overlaps with the novel will be a recurrent theme.

But there are specific linguistic clues also. The market-wardens are described with a word (*aeditumi*) which is identified by both Varro and Aulus Gellius as an archaism, compared to the current form *aedituus*. Gellius adds the further information that *Aeditumus* was the title of a mime by the Sullan dramatist Pomponius (cited by Augustine himself in *The City of God*). The silversmiths' hurried conference is described with a verb 'to murmur together' (*submurmuro*) apparently not attested elsewhere, but of a formation characteristic of earlier Latin. The preverb *sub-* is found in various classical compounds with the sense 'secretly' or 'rather' (as opposed to 'under'), but is especially associated with Plautus and the earlier dramatists and satirists: compare such Plautine words as *subausculto* 'to eavesdrop', *subblandior* 'to whisper sweet nothings', '*sublego* 'to kidnap', *suffuror* and *suppilo* 'to filch'.[19] The slave-boy is a *pedisequus*; this word occurs 7 times in Plautus (and once in Terence), but in the first century BC was already becoming rare except as a metaphor.[20] Although there are biblical instances of the word, which may have raised it again in the Christian literary consciousness, the archaic form of the word (as a noun+verb compound) marks it out as distinctly comic; new formations of this type become markedly

---

[18] On Augustine's citations from the *Pro Caelio*, see Hagendahl 1967: 43. Flight scenes seem to have been a standard feature of the mimic genre; see Fantham 1989: 158–9.

[19] These words are not all unique to Plautus, but are at least especially associated with his work. The existence of *submurmuro* in Augustine is not conclusively a comic reference, but this interpretation is at least consistent with the context.

[20] Compare the *Auctor ad Herennium*'s phrase (4. 14. 20) *pedisequae virtutis*, and Cicero's description (*de Oratore* 1. 55. 236) of jurisprudence as the *eloquentiae pedisequa*; Cicero's other two usages are literal.

rarer after the second century BC. The true thief is encountered 'carrying along' (*apportans*) an axe; even so apparently colourless a verb turns out to be particularly frequent in both Plautus and Terence.[21]

Finally, we note that the lead thief was carrying his axe 'secretly' (*clanculo*). This is a rather more problematic archaism. In earlier Latin the form *clanculum* is frequently found; in Plautus 26 times, in Terence 7 times, including the Danae passage invoked by Augustine in Book 1.[22] In classical Latin the word effectively vanishes from the record, until it is revived in the form *clanculo* by Apuleius (8 times). Apuleius is, of course, notorious for his code-switching tendencies, and for his promiscuous use of archaisms, colloquialisms, and features of other genres; it would be typical of him to favour a word both archaic and perhaps technical, modish, or bureaucratese. Certainly his use of *clanculo* heralds a mini-revival of the word in later Latin, from the *Codex Iustinanus* to Vegetius to Ambrose. In a late-antique context there is perhaps nothing distinctly comic about *clanculo* when used in isolation. Here, however, its comic associations may be activated by the presence of other comic words.

Not an archaism, but also strongly supportive of a comic-farcical interpretation of the passage, is Augustine's repeated use of *scholasticus* to describe Alypius and his fellow-student. Its basic meaning is 'student'; but it is much more than that. In the Elder Seneca, *scholastici* are 'people who thronged to declamations as though to athletic events, but who were not themselves students and not necessarily teachers' (Kennedy 1978: 175). It is applied to the heroes of both Roman novels: Ascyltos and Encolpius use the term of each other at *Satyricon* 10, and later have it used pejoratively of them by the freedman Niceros (61). The slave-girl Fotis in Apuleius' *Metamorphoses* (2. 10) addresses the hero (and her future lover)

[21] The absolute frequencies are 12 times in Plautus, 6 times in Terence. According to the Perseus Digital Library, these translate into a relative frequency of 0.73 and 1.18 per 10,000 words, higher than any other author on the database and notably above the average frequency of 0.12. Although *portare* and its compounds remain current throughout the classical period, the standardization process of the first century BC tended to favour rather *fero* and its compounds.

[22] *Eunuchus* 589, describing Jupiter's secret descent into Danae's lap. Augustine cites the passage at *Epistle* 91. 4 and *City of God* 2. 7, 2. 12 also. See Hagendahl 1967: 260–2.

Lucius as *scholastice*, emphasizing both the social gulf between them and his own status as an intellectual unversed in the 'real world'. Perhaps particularly relevant to the story of Alypius is the Greek joke-book known as 'The Laughter-Lover' (*Philogelos*), possibly from the fourth or fifth century. The first 103 of its jokes are all at the expense of dopey σχολαστικοί. One example will serve: 'A *scholasticos* found some gladiator's armour in the house and began to play with it. Suddenly, someone warned him that his father had returned. He threw down the shield and began to take off the greaves. But his father came in before he could finish, so he grabbed a book and started reading—with the helmet still on his head' (*Philogelos* 87, translation from Baldwin 1983). There is at least an overlap in the essential element of Alypius' story: a young *scholasticus* foolishly lets himself be caught in possession of something which undermines the tenuous social status his profession gives him. Alypius is acting in character. A joke-book is, of course, not a mime, but the two genres are related; one ancient source cites the mimographer Philistion as the author of the *Philogelos*.[23] Lastly we may note the admonition given to the young Gallus in Sulpicius Severus' *Dialogus* 1. 9: 'Seeing as you are a *scholasticus*, it's quite right I should caution you with the words of the well-know comic poet (*versu comici illius*), "Flattery breeds friends, truth hatred."' The exact force of this comment is hard to recover, but the connection between *scholastici* and the comic seems clear enough.

If we accept that there is a comic, farcical, or joke-book dimension to the story of Alypius and the axe, we may ask ourselves: why? The very presence of the anecdote has been perceived as obtrusive. In literary terms, this judgement is quite accurate, as the tone of the language is indeed lowered. The basic moral—that one should be slow to judge others—may seem less low-powered if we locate the *Confessions* within Christian debate about both State and Church as dispensers of justice. Alypius is a model of the Christian administrator, whose special capacity for this rests less on divine illumination in specific cases than on his own capacity for cautious judgement and for reflection on his own (God-guided) experience. It is notable also that Augustine is already ambivalent about State justice. Alypius'

---

[23] See Reich 1903: 426, 454ff. The work in question is the Suidas.

problems are not that he is treated illegally; the arrest-party do not mete out summary justice but take him off to the legitimate authorities, to face due process. The place where the incident occurs has strong links to the world of secular justice: in the *forum*, both marketplace and law court, in front of the *tribunal* or judgement platform. Modern readers may be uneasy at the way he is apparently rescued only by his social connections. For Augustine the apparently chance nature of the encounter with the architect itself underlines both divine providence and the contingent nature of all human justice.

More generally, the story illustrates how Alypius, like Augustine, is drawn by his literary studies into an unreal world. The nature of Alypius' set theme for recitation is not stated; at all events, it was both fictitious and engrossing. However, it is this obsession with one of the 'higher' literary genres of rhetoric which suddenly causes him to slide down several genres to the world of farce, where his forensic studies—which should have saved him—are useless.

AUGUSTINE ABANDONS MONICA

We turn now to the famous incident where Augustine, having decided to leave Carthage to pursue his career as a professor of rhetoric at Rome, abandons his mother Monica at the harbour:

Confessions 5. 8. 15. She refused to go back without me, but with difficulty I persuaded her to stay the night at the Shrine of S. Cyprian, which was hard by our ship. But that night I set out in secret, and she did not; she stayed behind, praying and weeping. And what was she begging of you, my God, if not that you should not allow me to sail? But in your deep counsels you hearkened to her true wish, and did not attend to what she prayed at that time, so as to make me what she prayed I should be always. The wind blew and filled our sails, and took from our sight the shore on which she stood, wild with grief and filling your ears with cries and reproaches. You stood aloof from her complaints, both because through my desires you were carrying me off to make an end of those same desires, and because you were chastising my mother's fleshly longing with your just and grievous scourge. She loved to have me present with her, as mothers do, but much more than most mothers, not knowing what joys you would bring her out of my absence. Not knowing this, she wept and wailed, and by her torments she was convicted of having in her the remnant of Eve, as she sought with groaning what with groaning she had brought forth. Yet even so, after charging me with deceit and cruelty, she turned back to praying to you for me. Then she went back to her usual life, while I sailed for Rome.

Et tamen recusanti sine me redire, vix persuasi ut in loco, qui proximus nostrae navi erat, memoria beati Cypriani, maneret ea nocte. Sed ea nocte clanculo ego profectus sum: illa autem remansit orando et flendo. Et quid a te petebat, Deus meus, tantis lacrimis, nisi ut navigare me non sineres? Sed tu alte consulens, et exaudiens cardinem desiderii eius, non curasti quod tunc petebat, ut in me faceres quod semper petebat. Flavit ventus, et implevit vela nostra, et litus subtraxit aspectibus nostris: in quo mane illa insaniebat dolore, et querelis, ac gemitu implebat aures tuas contemnentis ista; cum et me cupiditatibus meis raperes ad finiendas ipsas cupiditates, et illius carnale desiderium iusto dolorum flagello vapularet. Amabat enim secum praesentiam meam more matrum, sed multis multo amplius; et nesciebat quid tu illi gaudiorum facturus esses de absentia mea. Nesciebat, ideo flebat et eiulabat, atque illis cruciatibus arguebatur in ea reliquiarium Evae, cum gemitu quaerens quod cum gemitu pepererat. Et tamen post accusationem fallaciarum et crudelitatis meae, conversa rursus ad deprecandum te pro me, abiit ad solita, et ego Romam.

The similarities with Aeneas' departure from Carthage in Book 4 of the *Aeneid* have often been remarked. The similarities—and differences—have been traced in a classic study by Bennett (1988: 61–4). For Augustine, Bennett argues, literature can be useful as a means of self-discovery, provided you make the right discoveries, and identify yourself correctly with the fictive characters of whom you read. Augustine's failure lay in his excessive, literal-minded identification with the fictive Aeneas: 'Once again, he simultaneously thought that he was like a fictional person in a way that he was not and failed to recognize the way in which he was.'[24]

The major similarities between Augustine's abandonment of Monica and Aeneas' of Dido are beyond doubt. It is all the more striking, then, to find relatively little significant overlap in

---

[24] See also MacCormack (1998: 96–9), who is rightly more cautious about Bennett's stronger claims that Augustine consciously modelled both his life and his biography on Virgil's Aeneas, but offers a range of other verbal parallels between Augustine's self-presentation and Virgil's presentation of Aeneas.

the *language* used by Augustine and Virgil to describe the two scenes. Roots such as *navigare* (*Aeneid* 2. 237), *dolor* (547), *insania* (595), *gemitus* (667, 685), *querela* (677), *crudelis* (308), *lacrimae* (370) are common to both, but none of these words is especially unusual per se, nor does Augustine juxtapose them in ways that specially recall Book 4 of the *Aeneid*. Parallels have also been noted with the young Euryalus' failure to bid his mother farewell before the fatal night raid in *Aeneid* Book 9; as we have noted, Augustine does indeed link Monica to the anonymous *mater Euryali* by citing her willingness to 'follow him by land and sea'. But the one close verbal parallel between the *Confessions* and the *Aeneid* has gone generally unremarked. Augustine's account of how the wind 'took from our sight the shore' (*ventus... litus subtraxit aspectibus nostris*) recalls Aeneas' final encounter with Dido's ghost in the Underworld, with his desperate plea to her to 'halt your step and do not take yourself from our sight' (*Aeneid* 6. 465: *siste gradum teque aspectu ne subtrahe nostro*). Augustine has shifted the object of the verb from Dido to the African coast, so preventing any simple equation between Dido and Monica. But he invites the reading of himself as Aeneas—not the resolute Aeneas who slips secretly from Carthage to fulfil his destiny at Rome, but rather the shaken and pleading Aeneas of the Underworld, still lost—as we have seen him before—in a world of shadows (*umbrae*).

It is at least possible that the harbour scene may have associations with the world of comedy and mime as well as epic. Augustine's contemporary Servius, in the preface to his commentary on *Aeneid* Book 4, observes that the book is 'completely taken up with cunning plans (*consiliis et subtilitatibus*), for the style verges on the comic (*paene comicus stilus est*)—as one would expect when the subject is love.'[25] We have the testimony of Macrobius (*Saturnalia* 5. 17. 5) that the Dido story was a favourite subject of sculpture and painting, 'and not less celebrated in the constant gestures and songs of the dramatic profession' (*nec minus histrionum perpetibus et gestibus et cantibus celebretur*). This may refer to tragedy rather than comedy, though claims have been made for a tradition of mythological burlesque

---

[25] Servius goes on to detect comic elements in the diction of *Aeneid* 4. 534, 606, but elsewhere in the *Aeneid* only once.

under the Empire.[26] It is true generally that ancient comedy shifts away from mythological themes towards the everyday life of the solid citizen in New Comedy, to the scenes of contemporary low life in the mime. But these are never watertight divisions; Plautus' *Amphytrio* is the classical fusion of burlesque and New Comic realism, where Jupiter is the comic adulterer, nearly detected *in flagrante*, and Mercury the cunning slave looking out for the young master. We may note also that the motif of hurried embarkation and flight occurs in one extant Greek mime-fragment, the second-century AD *Charitium*, though of course it is not restricted to that genre.[27]

On the linguistic level, the passage is cast in language which may recall the world of the comic stage. Augustine leaves 'secretly', *clanculo*; as we have already seen, this word may mark a shift towards the comic mode. Monica departs complaining of her son's *fallacia*, the typical behaviour of the *adolescens* of New Comedy and vastly more frequent in Plautus and Terence than elsewhere in Latin literature; we have also Cicero's testimony that *fallaciae* are typical subject-matter of the mime.[28] She wails—*eiulat*—at his treachery. This too may be a comic touch: within classical Latin, this verb is found in Plautus to the near exclusion of other authors, though the picture is complicated by its revival in post-classical authors both Christian and pagan.[29] Her 'carnal longing' for her son is punished (*vapularet*) with a 'just and grievous scourge' by her true Master. Here again we may suspect input from the language of comedy, as

---

[26] See Fantham (1989: 157) and Panayotakis (1995: xv) for references.

[27] On the *Charitium*, see Panayotakis (1995: 140), who notes parallels with Euripides' *Iphigenia in Tauris, Helen*, and *Cyclops*; Odysseus' escape from the Cyclops is perhaps the prototypical version of this theme, but the variations are extensive. Escape scenes are also taken up in the novel, and from there come to influence the historical genre; see Marincola (1997: 201).

[28] *Fallacia* occurs 29 times in Plautus and 14 times in Terence. According to the Perseus Digital Library, these translate into frequencies of 1.75 and 2.76 per 10,000, as against an average of 0.29 for the rest of the database. The relevant passage of Cicero is *pro Rabiro Postumo* 35: 'thence springs all this skulduggery, thence, I say, all these ploys (*fallaciae*), thence all the subjects of the mime.' Although Augustine is by now himself teaching *adolescentes*, the term may still just be applicable to himself; it is not until the beginning of Book 7 that he notes that his *adolescentia* was 'now dead'.

[29] Plautus provides four of the six examples in the Perseus corpus of classical Latin; for the post-classical use of the verb, see *Thesaurus Linguae Latinae (TLL)*. On Augustine's description of *eiulatio* as 'shapeless noise' see Chapter 6.

Plautus and Terence supply nearly all classical attestations of the verb.[30] Again, however, this should be qualified by the modest revival of the word in biblical and Christian Latin, originally as a rendering of the Greek δέρω, also active in form but passive in meaning.[31] There is a biblical flavour also to the expression 'grievous scourge' (*dolorum flagello*); the use of the qualifying genitive (here *dolorum*) in an adjectival function is a well-attested Semitic idiom, even if there is no precise parallel for this phrase in the Latin Bible.[32]

There is scope, therefore, for seeing Augustine's account of his departure from Carthage not merely as epic but as mock epic, with the ambitious young professor playing the role of Aeneas and his uneducated old mother that of Queen Dido. There is some support for this reading in the language used, even though this evidence is not strong enough to require such a reading. Bennett's comments on Augustine's flawed self-identification may be recast: just as Alypius, aspiring to be a master-orator, finds himself a comic joke-book figure, so Augustine fails to be an Aeneas deserting Dido and risks being a mere burlesque instead.

MONICA *MERIBIBULA*

Our two final passages both also concern Monica—and her consumption of wine. Book 9 of the *Confessions*, sometimes described as the 'Life of Monica', contains a memorable flashback scene to her childhood (*Confessions* 9. 8. 17–18). The young Monica is brought up mainly by a decrepit old servant of the family (*famulae cuiusdam decrepitae*), much valued for her excellent character. This servant forbids the daughters of the house to drink even water with

---

[30] *Vapulo* occurs 38 times in Plautus and 5 times in Terence, out of a total of 46 attestations in the Perseus corpus. On the revival of archaic words to deal with difficulties of translation, see Burton (2000: 101–12).

[31] Two instances appear in the Gospels (Luke 12:47–8, Mark 13:9), but perhaps the most resonant for Augustine is Hosea 4:14: 'A people that hath no understanding shall be beaten.'

[32] On the 'Hebraic' genitive of quality, see García de la Fuente (1994: 176–7); more briefly, Plater and White (1926: 93–5). The metaphorical use of *flagellum* is also characteristically biblical (Burton 2000: 125–6)

Alternative Comedy 53

their meals, arguing that drinking of any sort was a bad habit to get into. Monica's parents, however, used to send her to fetch wine from the family barrel; and gradually she gets into the habit of drinking off whole cups of it neat there and then. Then one day she quarrels with the slave-girl who regularly goes with her to the barrel; the slave-girl taunts her by calling her *meribibula*, 'Little Miss Tipsy'. Monica is immediately ashamed and gives up her drinking habit.

Again, the language of the story has links to the world of comedy. The old woman is broken down, *decrepitus*, an adjective in classical Latin rare outside comedy; there is some evidence of its revival in post-classical Latin, but it is likely to have remained in part at least a conscious archaism.[33] She had once, however, carried Augustine's father on her shoulders, like other young girls (*grandiusculae*)—a word in classical Latin found only once, in Terence; though again there is some evidence of a revival in the later language.[34] Monica's actions are ascribed by Augustine to an ebullition of 'playful habits' (*ludicris moribus*)—but the Latin phrase may equally be taken to mean 'theatrical personality'. The slave-girl attempts to attack her young mistress secretly (*clanculo*, again). Two of the main *dramatis personae*, the old woman (*anus*) and the slave-girl herself (*ancilla*), are figures who regularly occur in Roman comedy. Lastly, there is the maidservant's cry of *meribibula*. This particular adjective does not, in fact, occur elsewhere in Latin literature; but we do find in Plautus (*Curculio* 77) a reference to an old bawd, 'much-drinking and neat-drinking' (*multibiba atque merobiba*).[35]

---

[33] Plautus and Terence together provide seven of the eight Perseus instances. Most of the later examples in *TLL* 5. 1. 217–8 are from Christian authors, but Apuleius and Symmachus also feature; Augustine once uses it in citing Job 15:10, but this passage does not appear to account for the relative frequency of the word in Christian writers.

[34] The Terentian example is from *Andria* 841, there also referring to a young girl; there is some variation in the manuscripts at this point, but this reading is known to Augustine's contemporary Donatus.

[35] Similar words, comic in the broader if not the stricter sense, are the satirist Lucilius' *vinibua* ('wine-glugger'), and the emperor Tiberius' nickname, as recorded by Suetonius (*Tiberius* 42), *Caldius Biberius Mero* ('Warm-Neat-Drinker', for Claudius Tiberius Nero). On the common phenomenon of adjectives used as terms of abuse in Roman comedy, see Lilja 1965: 19–25. The drunken older slave-woman is a stock character; Augustine's most-cited Terence play, the *Andria*, contains a reference (line 229) to a midwife who was a 'drunken, unreliable woman' (*temulentast mulier et temeraria*)—another overlap of vocabulary with this passage. For *temulentus* as a word found in comedy (and farce) mostly of women, see Adams (1984: 75).

But again there is a difference. Low-status female characters in New Comedy, especially old women, are often notable for their fondness for drink; here the old woman actively seeks to prevent Monica from getting a taste for it, and even the slave-girl unwittingly contributes to this. Former nurses have a reputation for giving their female charges moral advice which is captious, ingratiating, and self-interested. This old woman's prohibition on drinking has its basis in both authority and reason, the twin pillars of Augustine's approach to language;[36] while the usual Latin terms *auctoritas* and *ratio* do not occur, it is precisely these ideas that are invoked in Augustine's description of her 'venerable severity' (*sancta severitate*) in restraining the girls' behaviour (*in eis coercendis*) and her 'sober wisdom' (*sobria prudentia*) in instructing them (*in docendis*). Her speech, uncontrived as it is, has a certain rhetorical dignity, with simple but effective antithesis (*modo... cum autem*), and moderate use of homoeoteleuton (*sordebit... praevalebit*) and alliteration (*mos potandi praevalebit*). Even the rhythms may be deliberate; the stately double cretic clausula appears in the phrase *non habetis, cellariorum*, and *praevalebit*. In short, we have a scene which we are invited to view as comic in everything but the essentials.

Augustine's account of his mother's drinking-habits as a girl invite us to recall an earlier passage in the *Confessions*. When Monica first came to Milan, she continued her practice (normal among African Christians) of commemorative eating and drinking at the shrines of the martyrs—until informed by a minor church official that Bishop Ambrose had banned such activities, upon which she immediately desisted, criticizing herself for her habit rather than him for his ban. There is some overlap in vocabulary between the passages; related words for 'ban', (*prohibitio*), 'habit' (*consuetudo*), 'taste for wine' (*vinulentia*), 'little sips' (*sorbitio exigua*) are common to both.[37] No one of these similarities is specially striking, but

---

[36] See O'Donnell 1992. ii: 60, Law 1990: 191–207, Lütcke 1990, with further discussion in Chapter 7, pp. 176–7. Authority and reason are also, of course, of general importance in much ancient ethics and epistemology.

[37] *Sorbitio* is another typically comic word, but may also have a specific sense in Christian usage; Monica's contemporary the nun Egeria uses it of the little mouthfuls of flour-and-water paste eaten by the faithful at Jerusalem in Lent (*Peregrinatio Egeriae* 28. 4).

together they subtly reinforce the links between the two episodes. Ambrose's prohibition, like the old slave woman's, is made in virtue of his authority (and as such immediately obeyed by Monica); but, as she later finds out, it is based on reason: to avoid damaging comparisons with the pagan festival of the Parentilia, and so as not to give those so minded the opportunity to 'soak themselves' (*occasio ingurgitandi se*). This unusual verb has associations with the world of low drama[38]—Cicero notably compares Mark Antony to a character in a mime (*persona de mimo*), who, having 'soaked down' (*ingurgitasset*) somebody else's wealth, 'jumps up and down at having gone from rags to riches' (*Philippic* 2. 65). It should be stressed that the passage as a whole does not have the same strongly comic overtones as the *meribibula* scene. Even so, the two are linked by the common character of Monica and the common theme of wine-drinking. The *meribibula* scene, though narrated later in the *Confessions*, is chronologically earlier and acts as a sort of prequel to the scene at Milan; the Monica who had gone through it was the least likely person to gain the fondness for wine which Ambrose was seeking to prevent. Indeed, a comparison between the anonymous Christian serving-woman and Bishop Ambrose may be revealing. Both do essentially the same thing in essentially the same way; but it is the serving-woman who is given the more prominent and memorable scene in the *Confessions*.[39]

Before leaving the *meribibula* scene, it may be worth noting what comes next. Augustine follows this one incident from his mother's childhood with an account of her married life. Having cited Monica's repeated assertion that wives beaten by their husbands had only their own tongues to blame—further evidence of the power of language, however repugnant to our sensibilities—he goes on to

---

[38] In classical Latin, it is relatively rare; apart from the Cicero passage cited here, it occurs once in a fragment of the comic poet Naevius, once in Plautus, twice in Petronius (once metaphorical, once literally—of an old woman). In later Latin, however, it does become more frequent, beginning with the second-century archaists Fronto and Apuleius and taken up by the Christian authors; see *TLL* 7. 1. 1582.

[39] Note also how Augustine shortly afterwards portrays his mother as acting as peacemaker, reconciling feuding parties in a way which recalls to Augustine his own episcopal duties; another remarkable elision of the difference between a bishop and a relatively low-status woman. Compare Conybeare (2006) on the representation of Monica in Augustine's early dialogues.

note a distinctly non-comic aspect to her domestic situation: the remarkable harmony that obtained between Monica and her mother-in-law, despite the 'whisperings of the wicked maid-servants' (*susurris malarum ancillarum*; Confessions 9. 9. 20). Conflict between parents-in-law and children-in-law was doubtless a real-life phenomenon, but is also a stock comic situation,[40] and the maidservants here are acting in comic character. But again, we are invited to consider the discrepancy between comedy and life; Monica's husband Patrick succeeds in re-establishing the 'household discipline' (*familiae disciplinam*) which so often evades the comic *paterfamilias*, and the two women live happily thereafter.

COMEDY AND THE NOVELISTIC

We have now noticed on several occasions the overlap between the language of comedy and that of the novel. This overlap is to be expected, for two reasons. First, comedy and the novel (along with mime and satire) are the realistic genres par excellence of Latin literature. Features of real-life speech excluded from 'higher' genres are always more likely to be attested here. Secondly, both Petronius and Apuleius make allusion to the genres of comedy and mime, partly as a model for the representation of everyday language[41] and partly as a more general literary frame of reference for the understanding of their own work. Similarities between the novel (especially Apuleius' *Metamorphoses*) and the *Confessions* have long been noted,[42] and for now we will simply consider briefly some of the ways in which Augustine exploits the novelistic technique of

[40] A situation exploited—and to some extent parodied—in Terence's *Mother-in-Law* (*Hecyra*).
[41] The point will not be pressed here, but I am suggesting that later writers may persist in regarding the language of the comic poets as being the true everyday speech of the ordinary man or woman, even when 'ordinary language' might have subsequently developed in quite different ways. An obvious parallel for this is the persistence of Dickensian representations of non-standard English as late as the early twentieth century, even when (as Bernard Shaw argued) these had long ceased to be accurate.
[42] See above, note 12.

Alternative Comedy   57

incorporating language and motifs from various genres. Consider his account of his friends' warnings to him on the attitude of his new students at Rome towards their tuition fees. Compared with his former students in Africa, those at Rome are well-behaved; '"But suddenly," they told me, "a whole group of students will conspire to avoid paying their teacher his wages, and transfer *en masse* to someone else, betrayers of their trust and to whom honest dealing is cheap compared to their love of money"' (*sed subito, inquiunt, ne mercedem magistro reddant, conspirant multi adulescentes et transferunt se ad alium, desertores fidei et quibus prae pecuniae caritate iustitia vilis est*; *Confessions* 5. 12. 22). There is nothing here so gross as an allusion, but the whole tone of the passage is reminiscent of the historiographical style of the Sallustian tradition. This is most notable in the lengthy description of the students tacked on to the main clause, which falls into two unbalanced halves:[43] *desertores fidei*, a nominal phrase used in apposition, and *quibus...iustitia vilis est*, a longer relative clause. The supreme example of this sort of 'imbalance' or 'inconcinnity' (*inconcinnitas*) from Sallust is perhaps his description of the revolutionary Catiline's henchwoman Sempronia, 'learned in Greek and Latin literature, to sing and dance more elegantly than is necessary for a woman, and many other things which are the instruments of indulgence' (*litteris Graecis et Latinis docta, psallere et saltare elegantius quam necesse est probae, multa alia quae instrumenta luxuriae sunt*; *Catilinarian Conspiracy* 25)— another appended description, with the past participle *docta* construed in turn with an ablative case (*litteris*), the infinitive (*psallere et saltare*), and a direct object or accusative of respect (*multa alia*).[44] Sallustian too is the preoccupation with trust (*fides*) and the psychology of desertion. In particular, the phrase may echo Jugurtha's famous description of the corruption endemic in Roman public

---

[43] On this use of the 'historical period' in Sallust, see e.g. Wilkinson 1963: 184–6.

[44] Similarities with the Sempronia passage also subsist in the shared vocabulary of *fides* and *pecunia* (common to both), and in Sallust's *cariora* alongside Augustine's *caritas*; admittedly these are normal Latin terms to do with money and finance and the similarities may be coincidental. Less close verbally, but still suggestive, is Augustine's description of his students' 'conspiracy'. Sallust avoids *conspirare* in favour of *coniurare* in his account of the Catilinarian Conspiracy, but the two are synonymous; are we to see Augustine's Roman students as so many budding Catilines?

life in his day: 'This is a City up for sale, and ripe for destruction if once it find a buyer' (*urbem venalem et mature perituram si emptorem invenerit; Jugurthine War* 35).[45] The similarity here lies not in common vocabulary, but on the form of the two speeches—both are unusual interjection of direct speech into a narrative passage—and in the general theme of the venality of all things Roman. Jugurtha the African is commenting on the values of the supposedly more civilized Romans, Augustine is recording his impressions as an African newly arrived in Rome. Having read and no doubt taught Sallust, he should have expected no less.

In the same way, Augustine's use of comedy in the *Confessions* may be read as a literary game, but one with a serious purpose. We have noted Bennett's (1988) argument that Augustine's treatment of Virgil in the *Confessions* is marked by an awareness of his own failure to recognize the true resonance of the *Aeneid* with his own life, a failing especially grievous as he was at the time a professor of secular literature. We might modify this analysis and say that Augustine is also keen to point out how, with hindsight, he can see that literature does not always present a true picture of life. We have already considered three passages in which Monica is linked to the world of comedy, but there may be wider links elsewhere in the *Confessions*. One of the stock comic characters, as we have noted, is that of maidservant (*ancilla*)—often, from the point of view of the master (*dominus*), an unreliable character, complicit at least in schemes to undermine the household discipline. Monica herself, however, is also an *ancilla*. One of Augustine's most frequent self-characterizations in the *Confessions* is the biblical phrase 'the son of thy handmaid' (Psalm 85:16, 115:16, cited at *Confessions* 2. 3. 7, 5. 10. 18, 9. 1. 1). Monica, then, like the Virgin Mary (Luke 1:38), is a true 'handmaid of the Lord' (*ancilla domini*); these real-life handmaids of the true Master are far removed from their comic counterparts.

If Monica and her companions evoke stereotypical comic women only to reverse expectations, what of Augustine himself? We may

---

[45] Cited by Augustine in *Epistle* 138. 16 (Hagendahl 1967: 240). The Sempronia passage is not cited in his works, but may have lodged in his memory if, as Hagendahl (1967: 645) states, 'Augustine is, on the whole, more interested in [Sallust's] *dramatis personae* than in the events.'

even read much of the *Confessions* as a sort of alternative comedy. Monica's goal throughout the early and middle books of the work is a good marriage for her son. He, however, has an impediment to this, in the form of a concubine—a good comic motif. The unnamed concubine departs, in order to make way for the marriage. At this point the conventional comic thread starts to unravel; former lovers in Plautus and Terence do not retire to Africa to take up a life of vowed chastity. Moreover, the split is not followed by a marriage. Instead, Augustine takes another concubine while waiting for his intended to reach marriageable age, then abruptly renounces sexuality altogether, having seen the folly of his early self-identification with the typical young man of the stage.

This reading may be plausible, so far as it goes—but there may be a more sinister edge to Augustine's encounters with the world of comedy. It is time to return to that first quotation from Terence with which Augustine begins his account of his school days: 'What miseries and what mockeries I knew there!' (*quas ibi miserias expertus sum et ludificationes*; *Confessions* 1. 9. 14). But Terence's own words are different: 'I married, and what misery I knew there! My sons were born; another worry...' (*duxi uxorem: quam ibi miseriam vidi! nati filii; alia cura*; *Adelphoe* 867). Again we find the mismatch between life and art; the old man Demea's troubles come from his children, whereas the schoolboy Augustine's come from his parents. But Augustine's reference to 'mockeries' (*ludificationes*) is intrusive; though a good comic word, it doesn't occur in the Terence passage. This is the first of a series of words from this root which weave a tangled web of allusions across the early books of the *Confessions*. The young Augustine's leisure is ironically cut short when he is sent to *ludus*, 'play' or 'school'. There he is set to learning *ludi*, 'plays', because parents hope their children will be so successful as to be able to stage municipal games—*ludi* yet again. However, these ambitions are all too often choked by the children's playing around in class: *ludere* once more. But there is more to *ludificatio*. In comedy, the verb is often used to mean 'to seduce', 'to love and leave', or 'to rape'. Augustine, then, becomes himself a comic character—not the young lover he thought, but a victim of the rape/seduction scenario found in various comedies. And in Christian usage, *ludificor* is typically used of the activities of demons, a usage which may be well illustrated from Augustine himself; at *City of God* 18. 18, for instance, he suggests that 'Our readers may be waiting to see what we will say about all the seductive activity carried out by the demons (*de ista tanta ludificatione daemonum*)'.[46] Closely related to this activity of 'making a play' is that of open mockery or laughing at individuals (*irrisio*)—one of the forms of paralinguistic activity discussed in Chapter 6.

CONCLUSIONS

The theatre, for Augustine, is daemonic in at least two ways: plays are performed in honour of the pagan gods, whom he identifies as demons; and they often involve representations of immoral behaviour. Underlying all this is a classic Platonic anxiety about the seductive pleasure of these 'spectacular images'; not only because of their immorality, but because they aim to give pleasure through copies and representations, not through truth.[47] While actively sharing these intellectual concerns himself, he is also institutionally committed as a Christian bishop to the Church's attempts to marginalize if not to outlaw the popular theatre.

At the same time, Augustine is aware of the pleasure the theatre has given to many people, himself included. Since pleasure comes ultimately from God, there must be something in comedy and related literary genres which *ought* to give pleasure, however parodied and distorted it may be in individual comedies. Moreover, Plato's was not the only theoretical treatment of comedy in antiquity. As readers of

[46] For further examples, see *Thesaurus Linguae Latinae* 7. 2. 1766. 21ff. Within the *Confessions*, compare his statement that the 'mockery' (*illudere*) practised by the hooligan element in the Carthage student body was as close as could be to demonic activity; *Confession* 3. 3. 6.

[47] Within Plato's own work, key passages are *Republic* 394d ff. (on the inappropriateness of the Guardians' of the ideal state indulging in the mimetic arts of comedy or tragedy); 440a (on the man who could not resist the 'lovely sight' ($καλὸν\ θέαμα$) of the corpses of common criminals); 476b (on the distinction between the true intellectual and the 'lover of sights and sounds' ($φιλήκοο\ καὶ\ φιλοθεάμων$)). Notable also in this connection is *Republic* 606c (on the danger of taking excessive pleasure in the ridiculous, even in private matters, and so becoming a comedian in one's home ($ἐν\ τοῖς\ οἰκείοις\ κωμῳδοποιός$)).

Alternative Comedy 61

Eco's *The Name of the Rose* will remember, Aristotle had defended the moral value of comedy in the second book of the *Poetics*. Lost as that book now is, something of its substance may survive in the tenth-century manuscript known as the *Tractatus Coislinianus*.[48] Some of the elements of comedy identified in the *Tractatus* resemble those we have identified in the *Confessions*. Laughter may, for instance, arise from deception (as with Augustine's deceit of Monica), or from implausibility (as with Alypius' sheer bad luck in being caught in possession of the axe), or from the unexpected (as with the slave-girl's rebuke of Monica); there is, however, no evidence Augustine was directly influenced by Aristotelian theories, much less that he was consciously following these comic techniques. On the Latin side, Augustine was certainly aware of Cicero's lengthy discussion of the role of humour in oratory at *de Oratore* 2. 216ff.[49] There is the germ of an ethical theory of humour in Cicero's statement that its proper province is that which is 'morally debased or misshapen' (*turpitudine et deformitate*; *de Oratore* 2. 236), but despite the potential of this formulation, Augustine does not pick it up. A notable feature of Cicero's account is his acknowledgement of the similarity between wit in oratory and wit on the stage; one of the key tasks for an orator is to know how far the orator should go (*quatenus*) in this direction in order to be effective without lapsing into mere clowning. This Augustine does not do; but where he uses comic language and scenarios in the *Confessions*, we may read these passages as a form of alternative comedy, in which we are invited to laugh sympathetically at the plight of humans who misidentify their true place in the scheme of things.[50] It is tempting to call this a subversion of the comic impulse, but another word might be more accurate. As the fourth-century theorist of comedy Evanthius put it, the conclusion to a comedy 'consists of a complete turnabout of events (*conversio rerum*, glossing the Greek *catastrophe*), resulting in happy endings, with everyone made aware of what has happened

---

[48] English translation and commentary by Janko (1987).
[49] The passage in question is apparently not cited by Augustine, but there is good evidence of his familiarity with the work as a whole; Hagendahl 1967: 159–61.
[50] Compare, perhaps, the 'alternative comedy' offered by Cicero to jurors in the Caelius trial; see Geffcken (1973), a wide-ranging essay with many suggestive insights.

(*patefacta cunctis cognitione gestorum*)' (*de Comoedia* 4).[51] Repeatedly in the *Confessions* Augustine presents himself as driven by a similar desire for self-awareness or recognition (*cognitio*), a desire which he begins to fulfil only with his own turning-back (*conversio*) to God.[52]

---

[51] Whether Augustine knew the work of Evanthius, who 'worked in Constantinople during the 1st half of the 4th cent. AD' (*New Pauly*), is unknown. Our own knowledge of him comes through the preservation of the *de Comoedia* in the preface to Donatus' commentary on Terence (for the passage in question, see Kaibel 1899: 67); the fourth chapter may not be by Evanthius.

[52] We may here invoke the concept of the *eucatastrophe*, the resolution of human affairs for the good which has been identified by a more recent Catholic writer and theorist of language: 'The Birth of Christ is the eucatastrophe of Man's history. The Resurrection is the eucatastrophe of the story of the Incarnation.' See Tolkien (1975: 67–72).

3

The Vocabulary of the Liberal Arts

SECULAR GREEK

Most Latin works of any length contain a number of loanwords from Greek; the *Confessions* contain some 120.[1] These can be divided into two main classes. A large number of them occur either in biblical citations, or in contexts where a biblical allusion can plausibly be invoked. These are discussed in more detail in Chapter 5, where it is suggested that their Greekness is also a mark of their status as biblical words, and that most of them have broadly positive denotations or connotations. The others are those which are current in the wider language. Clearly some words will be common to both classes; these more marginal cases are discussed in Chapter 5, but will not be central to our discussion.

Of the words in this second class, many have negative associations. This in itself is unsurprising, since the use of Greek as a distancing device has long been recognized;[2] cases in point are *machinatio* and *machinamentum*, 'ploy', a familiar root, current in Latin since at least the second century BC, here given Latin derivational affixes, yet remaining to many readers at least transparently Greek in origin. A large number of the Greek terms in the *Confessions* belong to the field of classical education and culture, broadly defined. Examples of this include *agonisticus*, 'characteristic of (public literary) competition', *barbarismus*, 'barbarism, linguistic lapse involving a single word', *criticus*, 'critical (as a medical term)', *gymnasium*, 'place of

---

[1] For a full census, see Appendix.
[2] See e.g. Burton 2000: 141 and references. For fuller studies of Roman attitudes towards Greek, see Kaimio (1979), now supplemented by the excellent work of Fögen (2000); see also the observations in Adams (2003, especially 199–201).

civic education, school', *palaestra*, 'wrestling-ground, locus for civic competition', *rhetor*, 'teacher of rhetoric', *soloecismus*, 'solecism, linguistic lapse involving a group of words', *syllaba*, 'syllable'. Although most of these are purely technical and do not of themselves have any pejorative sense, Augustine often uses them in disparaging contexts. To anticipate our argument later in this chapter, we might consider his analysis of the false values that govern 'good' Latin. A would-be Cicero, he suggests ironically, has to know his rules of *grammatica* if he is to pronounce his *syllabae* properly and avoid *barbarismi* and *soloecismi* (*Confessions* 1. 18. 28–9). According to this account, 'good' Latin can be described only in Greek terms. Or consider again his description of his time as a young student at Carthage; a senior member of his *rhetor*'s *schola* (class, school), he is thoroughly conceited and full of *typhus*, 'pride' (*Confessions* 3. 3. 6). Or consider again the vocabulary of astrology, a practice soundly refuted in the *Confessions*: these include *genethliaca*, 'horoscope', (*Confessions* 4. 3. 5) and *mathematicus*, 'astrologer', (*Confessions* 4. 3. 4), a class of men Augustine describes as *plani*, 'deceivers'—another Greek word ($\pi\lambda\acute{a}\nu os$), and an apposite one, given the association of the same root with the 'wandering stars' or planets ($\pi\lambda\acute{a}\nu\eta\tau\epsilon s$). With the sole exception of *planus*, these terms are all notably Greek in their phonology, morphology, orthography, or all three.

The last set of words illustrates an important question of stylistics. It is arguable that *genethliaca* and *mathematicus* have no real Latin equivalent. Their pejorative content, on this view, rests entirely in the things they denote, rather than in the words used to describe them. The fact that these words are Greek may reinforce the sense of disparagement, but does not cause it, since one cannot easily discuss these matters in Latin without using these terms. *Planus*, on the other hand, is a relatively infrequent Latin word, besides being liable to confusion with the adjective *planus* 'flat' (Augustine himself puns on this). Latin has a variety of native alternatives to *planus*: *seductor*, *deceptor*, *errabundus* would all, in different contexts, be suitable. This, then, may be seen as an 'ornamental' Greek word, not essential to the argument. Further examples of this include *cothurnus* and *cedrus*. *Cothurnus*, 'tragic buskin', is familiar from classical Latin as a metaphor for the high style associated with tragic diction. Augustine uses it in reference to the arrogance of the Platonist philosophers who come close to acknowledging the truth of the Christian view of the universe, without making the final step of submission to Christ: they are, he suggests, 'carried away by the *cothurnus* of their supposedly higher doctrine' (*cothurno tamquam sublimioris doctrinae elati*; *Confessions* 7. 9. 14). Even if the allusion to tragedy is somewhat attenuated by this date, the word is still transparently Greek, and strictly extraneous here; it would be enough to say *tamquam sublimiore doctrina*.³ *Cedrus* is a rather more complicated case: his friend Alypius, even after his conversion, is reluctant to introduce the name of Christ into the writings of their circle, 'wanting them to smell more of the cedar-wood tablets of the schools' (*gymnasiorum cedros*—another mini-cluster of Greek)—these being, in the words of the Psalmist, the 'cedars which the Lord had laid low' (Psalm 28:5). While there are contexts where *cedrus* would be a fairly neutral term, that cannot be said here: where the term occurs elsewhere in the *Confessions* (7. 13. 19, quoting Psalm 148:9; *Confessions* 8. 2. 4, quoting Psalm 28:5), it is always in reference to a biblical passage, and presumably it is because of this association that it is chosen here.

We may, then, speak of a spectrum between the purely ornamental use of a Greek term, when it could easily be avoided altogether, and the purely functional, when it would be practically impossible to discuss the subject in question without the use of Greek. Between these two poles, there are those words for which both Greek and Latin terms were available. This chapter will take as a case study Augustine's handling of a small but important set of these terms in the *Confessions*, namely his terms for the Seven Liberal Arts of grammar, rhetoric, dialectic, music, geometry, arithmetic, and philosophy.

THE VOCABULARY OF THE SEVEN LIBERAL ARTS

It was the Seven Liberal Arts that provided the focus for Augustine's intellectual activity in the years following his conversion back to

---

³ The literary texture is more complex than that, since the metaphorical use of noun + other noun in genitive is well recognized as a feature of the biblical style (classical Latin uses this relatively infrequently, and tends to 'apologize' for its more obvious use of nominal metaphors with a word such as *tamquam, velut, quasi, quidam, quodammodo*).

Christianity in the Spring of 386.[4] We know this because he tells us so in the first book of his *Retractationes*:

Retractationes 1. 4: Throughout that time, when I was at Milan waiting to receive baptism, I tried also to compose books on the arts. I questioned those of my companions who were not averse to such studies, in my desire to arrive or to lead others by certain steps through things material to things immaterial. But of these arts I was able to complete only my book on grammar, which later I lost from my bookcase, and six books on music, touching the part known as 'rhythm'.[5] But these six books I wrote after my baptism and my return from Italy to Africa; at Milan I had only begun that art. Of the other five arts I had likewise begun there—dialectic, rhetoric, geometry, arithmetic, and philosophy—only the beginnings have remained, and even these I have lost, though I think some people have them.

Per idem tempus quo Mediolani fui, baptismum percepturus, etiam disciplinarum libros conatus sum scribere, interrogans eos qui mecum erant atque ab huiusmodi studiis non abhorrebant, per corporalia cupiens ad incorporalia quibusdam quasi passibus certis vel pervenire vel ducere. Sed earum solum de grammatica librum absolvere potui, quem postea de armario nostro perdidi, et de musica sex volumina, quantum attinet ad eam partem quae rhythmus vocatur. Sed eosdem sex libros iam baptizatus, iamque ex Italia regressus in Africam scripsi; inchoaveram quippe tantummodo istam apud Mediolanum disciplinam. De aliis vero quinque disciplinis illic similiter inchoatis, de dialectica, de rhetorica, de geometria, de arithmetica, de philosophia, sola principia remanserunt. quae tamen etiam ipsa perdidimus; sed haberi ab aliquibus existimo.

It has often been remarked that this interest in the liberal arts suggests a distinctly intellectual understanding of Christianity. Certainly Augustine had been influenced to reject Manichaeism by his discovery of incompatibilities between their cosmology and the laws of mathematics and geometry. His other early post-conversion works, such as the *Soliloquies* or the *de Magistro*, are philosophical

---

[4] The wider question of the origins of the canon are not touched on here. It is not even strictly clear that Augustine knows of a canon at all, though this seems a safe assumption. For a general discussion, see the work of Hadot (1984), with the criticisms of O'Donnell (1992, ii: 269–78), and now Shanzer (2005: 69–121).

[5] The *de Musica* survives, and there is some consensus around Law's (1984) argument that much of the *de Grammatica* is represented in the *Ars Augustini pro fratrum mediocritate breviata*. The *Principia Dialecticae* or *De Dialectica* is likewise generally held to be Augustine's work.

dialogues in form. The very verb he uses in this passage to describe his intellectual technique, *interrogare*, has a long history as a technical term of rhetoric and dialectic.[6] Augustine is clearly optimistic about the possibilities of taking the traditional view of the arts as a pathway from the physical to the incorporeal world, and of co-opting it within his own Christian Platonism.

Around 391 work on the project was abandoned. Certainly Augustine did not suddenly lose interest in Christian attitudes to education and science—as can be seen from the *de Doctrina Christiana*, begun around 395–7. We do not know why this work was not completed until some thirty years later. It would be tempting to ascribe this to a crisis of confidence in his views on the liberal arts, but this would mean overlooking the fact that there is no visible join between the two halves of the work; in truth, we do not know.[7] None the less, it is true that his later writings do betray an increasing pessimism about the possibility, or desirability, of a simple Christianization of the arts. I suggest we can see the beginnings of this pessimism if we look at the vocabulary Augustine uses to describe the arts in another work, closely contemporary with the *de Doctrina Christiana*, namely the *Confessions*.[8] In doing so, we shall also have occasion to note some ways in which Augustine combines classical *disciplina* with his own practice of Biblical interpretation.[9]

[6] As a general term for dialectical reasoning, from Cicero onwards: *de Fato* 28: *sic... interrogant: si fatum tibi est ex hoc morbo convalescere, sive tu medicum adhibueris sive non adhibueris, convalesces* (*TLL* VII. 1. 2272. 71ff.); also with the specific sense 'questioning requiring yes-or-no answer', *TLL* VII. 1. 2266. 28ff. Augustine is aware of both senses: *de Doctrina Christiana* 4. 25. 67, *... in collocutionibus* (i.e. philosophical dialogues) *est cuique interrogandi potestas*; *de Doctrina Christiana* 3. 6. 12, *ad percontationem multa responderi possunt, ad interrogationem vero aut non aut etiam.*

[7] For a lucid discussion of the issues see the edition of Green (1995: xi–xiii), who feels that it is 'unlikely that he forgot his work, or lost interest, or dropped it out of dissatisfaction'.

[8] The terminology of the *de Doctrina Christiana* will be mentioned marginally for purposes of comparison. The range of disciplines covered in this work is wider than that of the *Confessions*, and the intended audience may be more specialized. This question would deserve analysis of its own, the results of which may differ from those offered here.

[9] As background to this study, note the work of Marrou (1965: 561–83), who discusses first the technical senses of *scientia* and *sapientia*, before surveying the evidence for Augustine's different manuals.

The Greek terminology we have seen him using in the *Retractationes* goes back at least to the first century BC. 'I shall do my best', says Cicero in the *Academica*, 'to speak in Latin—except in the case of words such as "philosophy" or "rhetoric" or "physics" or "dialectic", which along with many others Custom now uses as if they were Latin words' (*nisi in huiuscemodi verbis, ut philosophiam aut rhetoricam aut physicam aut dialecticam appellem, quibus ut aliis multis consuetudo iam utitur pro latinis*; *Academica* 1. 7. 25). Again in the *de Finibus* he writes that 'we follow the example of our ancestors in using "philosophy", along with "rhetoric", "dialectic", "grammar", "geometry", and "music", even though they could be expressed in Latin, as being our own' (*Quamquam ea verba quibus instituto veterum utimur pro latinis, ut ipsa philosophia, ut rhetorica, dialectica, grammatica, geometria, musica, quamquam latine ea dici poterant, tamen quoniam usu percepta sunt, nostra ducamus*; *de Finibus* 3. 2. 5). The one notable absentee from this list, *arithmetica*, occurs as once a neuter plural in Cicero, who writes to his friend Atticus of one Vestorius, 'a man wholly conversant in matters arithmetic' (*in arithmeticis satis versatum* ; *ad Atticum* 14. 12. 3). The singular makes its first appearance in Vitruvius (admittedly an author freer than most with his loanwords), and is common from the first century AD onwards; the Elder Pliny, for instance, describes the sculptor Pamphilus as 'educated in every branch of literature, especially *arithmetica et geometria*' (*Historia naturalis* 35. 76).

By late antiquity, this Greek terminology, which we have already seen Augustine using, is clearly the norm. Martianus Capella uses a scheme based on *grammatica, rhetorica, dialectica, geometria, astronomia, arithmetica*, and *harmonia*; Cassiodorus has *musica* for *harmonia*, but is otherwise the same.

What were the alternatives? It is a commonplace of loanword studies that when a technical vocabulary is borrowed from one language to another, there is usually a period of experimentation, during which three things happen. Existing words are tried out as translations (a process sometimes called semantic extension); new words are coined (typically either descriptive of the referend, or calqued on the term in the original language); or words are borrowed from the first language into the second. As a very broad generalization, the loanwords often emerge as winners.[10] But the picture is not always so simple. Where the loanwords triumph, they often retain a foreign flavour—as for instance with *philosophia* and *rhetorica*, marked out as foreign by phonology, orthography, and general cultural association. As for the translations, where these were already current in the language they may retain a flavour of the word they were used to translate. Where they were novel coinages, they may vanish from regular usage, but still be referred occasionally by later authors—as happens with several of the terms discussed here.

One very important stylistic consequence follows from this. Much of literary stylistics rests on the twin notions of *substitutability* and *markedness*.[11] The principle of substitutability assumes that it is possible to say fundamentally the same thing in more than one way. At the lexical level, this substitutability is very similar to synonymy; at any rate, synonymy in the context in question. Now the very concept of synonymy is, of course, a major stumbling block for many semanticists; as we will see, with some reason.[12] The principle of markedness assumes that where two words or constructions may be substituted for each other, the less common of the two is more marked and so more interesting from a stylistic point of view. Marked terms may contrast with unmarked ones either by dialect (compare *faucet* versus *tap*), sociolectally (compare *napkin* versus *serviette*), or chronologically (compare *visual display unit* versus *monitor*). Other forms of contrast are possible, too, such as those by register (compare *partner* versus *other half*), or connotation (*socialist* versus *leftie*). In these cases, the speaker tends to have more conscious choice and control, and is more likely to adapt his or her use to the social circumstances of the utterance.

---

[10] See Coleman (1989) for this phenomenon in the field of philosophy and rhetoric, Langslow (2000: 127–30) (with caveats and qualifications) for the field of medicine; Burton (2000: 147–8) for the field of Biblical translation. Of course, it does not always happen like this. The Germanic Christian vocabulary has various examples of existing words pressed into new senses (Old English *god*, *gāst* (as in *Holy Ghost*), *hel*, *fēond* ('fiend', of the devil), alongside calques such as *godspel* (= *evangelium*), and outright loans such as *dēofol*, *mynster* (= *monasterium*), *biscop*.

[11] For definitions and examples, see Crystal (1991: 211–12, 340–1), Lyons (1968: 427–8, 451).

[12] For distinctly Latin perspectives, see in particular Biville (1994) and Fruyt (1994), with other essays in the same volume.

Let it be said that in all examples considered above, the synonymy is largely limited. In each pair, the two terms are substitutable in certain contexts only (*napkin* versus *serviette* is the most synonymous pair, and this is not entirely so). From this it might be concluded that true substitutability is so rare as to make the principle invalid. But this is to set too high a standard, for two reasons. First, native speakers are unlikely to produce utterances where a 'wrong' synonym is chosen: one might just be appointed *other half* in a very small legal firm, but not *milk visual display unit* anywhere. Furthermore, technical language such as the vocabulary of the Liberal Arts is a special case. By definition, these are special areas of the language where there is assumed to be a particularly intimate link between word and referend. While this does not exclude the possibility of a referend being indicated by more than one word, these words would normally be understood to be strictly synonymous within that register. The preference for one-to-one correspondence between word and referend, however, will tend to make one of the two synonyms the marked one. Secondly, in all these cases it is precisely the fact that the synonymy is not absolute which makes the linguistic choices interesting. What will interest us here is the intellectual possibilities which Augustine's choice of synonyms opens up for him.

Grammar

Let us consider first grammar and rhetoric. Throughout the *Confessions* Augustine is ambivalent about the mere existence of human language. The initial acquisition of language he enjoys, but it leaves him deeper in what he calls 'the stormy fellowship of human life' (*vitae humanae procellosam societatem*; *Confessions* 1. 8. 13).[13] And grammar as it is taught in schools merely reinforces this obsession with human values rather than divine ones: 'How carefully', he exclaims, 'the children of men observe the rules governing letters and syllables (*pacta litterarum et syllabarum*) that they have received from previous speakers, while ignoring the eternal rules that lead to everlasting salvation, which they have received from you!'

---

[13] On the importance of *societas* for Augustine's view of language, see Chapter 7.

(*Confessions* 1. 18. 29). At the heart of his critique is the Platonic belief that the conventional educational system is a fraud. Teachers and parents are 'grammar-mongers and their customers' (*venditores grammaticae vel emptores*; *Confessions* 1. 13. 23; compare 4. 2. 2, *docebam... rhetoricam, et... loquacitatem... vendebam*), but in fact knowledge cannot be imparted. Moreover, the *artes* of grammar and rhetoric are in any case concerned with fictions and plausibilities rather than with truth; the better educated your grammarian, the more likely he is to know that Aeneas did *not*, in fact, come to Carthage (*quia si proponam eis interrogans, utrum verum sit quod Aenean aliquando Carthaginem venisse poeta dicit, indoctiores nescire se respondebunt, doctiores autem negabunt verum esse*; *Confessions* 1. 13. 22).

Now, the usual word for grammar in the *Confessions* is *grammatica*, and usually it has bad connotations.[14] It is Greek *grammatica* that Augustine is forced against his will to study, and *grammatica* which teaches men to believe that a dropped aitch or incorrect case-ending is worse than a miscarriage of justice. Faustus the Manichee knows only *grammatica* of all the liberal arts—and had only an average knowledge of that.[15]

What were the alternatives? From an early date, the loanword *grammatica* had been used alongside *litterae*, itself a translation of τὰ γράμματα (an etymology known to Augustine) and such periphrases as *cognitio litterarum* and so forth. Cicero himself, although he allowed *grammatica* honorary Latin citizenship, preferred these expressions. And Augustine too uses them in the *Confessions*, alongside *grammatica*. So, for instance, where he criticizes *grammatica* for being concerned with solely human traditions, he goes on to observe that the zealous prosecutor's guilty knowledge (*scripta conscientia*) that he is doing unto others what he would not have done unto himself is no less deeply engraved on his being than is his *litterarum scientia* (*Confessions* 1. 18. 29). Elsewhere, *litterae* in

---

[14] For a less rhetorical presentation of Augustine's views on grammar, see *de Doctrina Christiana* 3. 87–9. There he declares that it is not his intention to teach the various literary tropes, in case he gives the impression of teaching the *ars grammatica*; useful as they are for the understanding of Scripture, they are also familiar to those with no formal training in grammar.
[15] *Confessions* 5. 6. 11, *expertus sum hominem expertem liberalium disciplinarum nisi grammaticae atque eius ipsius usitato modo*.

their broader sense may be good or bad. The Scriptures are as *sacrae litterare* (*Confessions* 12. 31. 42), but literalism is characteristic of Manichee exegetics; Augustine is freed only through Ambrose's reiteration of the principle that 'the letter kills, but the Spirit gives life' (2 Corinthians 3:6, quoted at *Confessions* 6. 4. 6). The term *litterare*, then, is not the positive counterpart of an intrinsically negative *grammatica*; in itself neutral, it may be used in favourable or unfavourable contexts. A basic knowledge of literacy is necessary, but not sufficient, for a true reading of the Scriptures.[16]

Harder to place, but apparently ambivalent, is Augustine's other word for grammar, namely *litteratura*. This term, as Augustine knew, went back at least to Varro, who uses it of higher literary skills as opposed to *litteratio*, 'basic literacy', though this distinction was already obsolete in Seneca's day.[17] Probably this is because both the *-tio* and *-ura* suffixes are characteristically deverbative, whereas there is no verb **litterare* from which to derive them. Yet despite the obsolescence of *litteratura*, Augustine uses it three times in the *Confessions*, twice in connection with another archaic translation, *oratoria* for *rhetorica*. Again, this translation has a good republican pedigree—one thinks of Cicero's dialogue, the *Partitiones Oratoriae*—but again, this time thanks to Quintilian, we know it was obsolete by the first century AD.[18] The three passages repay attention.

---

[16] This would seem to imply that the Christian exegete needed at least some basic, conventional education. Note that in the *de Doctrina Christiana* (*praef.* 4. 7) Augustine sidesteps even that minimal requirement, with his story of the barbarian Christian slave who learnt his letters after a three-day prayer session—the absence of any human agency (*nullo docente homine*) is stressed. It has to be borne in mind, however, that Augustine sees this example as an exception.

[17] The two key passages are Augustine, *de Ordine* 2. 12. 35: *Quibus* [*sc. litteris et numeris*] *duobus repertis nata est illa librariorum et calculonum professio, quaedam grammaticae infantia, quam Varro litterationem vocat*, and Martianus Capella, *de Nuptiis Mercuriae et Philologiae* 3. 229. Γραμματική *dicor in Graecia, quod* γραμμή *linea et* γράμματα *litterare nuncupentur . . . hincque mihi Romulus Litteraturae nomen ascripsit, quamvis infantem Litterationem voluerit nuncupare, sicut apud Graecos* Γραμματιστική *primitus vocitabar*. The distinction between *litteratio* 'basic literacy' and *litteratura* 'literary studies' has been painstakingly reconstructed by Kaster (1995: 86–93). For *litteratura* in both senses, and its obsolescence, see Seneca, *Epistle* 88. 20: *. . . prima illa , ut antiqui vocabant, litteratura, per quam pueris elementa traduntur*.

[18] Compare Cicero's use of the phrase *facultas oratoria* at *de Inventione* 1. 6, 1. 7; *de Oratore* 1. 245 . For the formation, we might compare Ovid's *Ars Amatoria*, clearly a parody of a technical handbook (Janka 1997: 31–4). For the obsolescence of the term,

The first is his description of his days at sixth-form college in Madaura, where he had gone *litteraturae atque oratoriae percipiendiae gratia* (*Confessions* 2. 3. 5). It is hard to know what, if anything, to read into this, though one is tempted to think Augustine is using the archaic expression to describe the provincial schooling available in Madaura in the 360s.[19] His second use is ambivalent rather than neutral: Simplicianus tells Augustine how he had taken the Emperor Julian's prohibition of Christians teaching *litteratura* and *oratoria* as the cue for his professional retirement (*Confessions* 8. 5. 10). Here Augustine's attitude is more complex. Simplicianus' decision will be one of the factors influencing Augustine's own retirement, but he does not approve of Julian's edict; elsewhere he equates it with persecution.[20] Augustine's focus in this passage is not on the evils of the conventional educational system, but on the uses to which it may be put.

More actively favourable is the third instance of *litteratura*, in a key passage for our present study. In Book 10 of the *Confessions*, Augustine discusses the arts not as they are taught in school, but in a more Platonic sense, as something accessible only to the intellect: *nam quid sit litteratura, quid peritia disputandi, quot genera quaestionum... sic est in memoria mea, ut non retenta imagine rem foris reliquerim...* (*Confessions* 10. 9. 16). Grammar in this more positive sense may fairly be described as *litteratura*.

Rhetoric

In the same passage Augustine refers also to rhetoric, and it is to this that we now turn. The *Confessions* contain seven examples of

---

see Quintilian, *Institution* 2. 14. 1–4: *Rhetoricen in latinum transferentes tum oratoriam, tum oratricem nominaverunt... et haec interpretatio non minus dura est quam illa Plauti essentia atque queentia.*

[19] Madaura, a centre of Romanization in North Africa in the second century AD, seems to have undergone something of a renovation programme around and shortly after Augustine's time there: Lepelley (1979–81, ii: 128–33) lists a series of public works on buildings *incuria paene ad interitum redactae* or *tot retro annis ruinorum labe deformes.*

[20] Augustine, *de Civitate Dei* 18. 52: *an ipse non est ecclesiam persecutus, qui christianos liberales litteras docere vetuit?*

rhetorica, all referring to Augustine's pre-conversion career. The one example we have encountered (4. 2. 2) speaks for all: *docebam in illis annis artem rhetoricam, et victoriosam loquacitatem victus cupidine vendebam.*[21] But in the key catalogue of the arts as they exist in the memory, Augustine again avoids this term: *numquid sicut meminimus eloquentiam?* (*Confessions* 10. 21. 30), he asks instead. There is every reason to think Augustine is using it in its technical sense; this sense goes back at least to Cicero, is solidly attested in Quintilian,[22] and most memorably of all appears in Eumolpus' introduction of himself in Petronius' *Satyricon* 88: 'Where is dialectic? Where astronomy? Where the well-tended path of philosophy? Who has ever come to a temple and paid his vows, having attained rhetoric?' (*ubi est dialectica? ubi astronomia? ubi sapientiae cultissima via? quis umquam venit in templum et votum fecit, si ad eloquentiam pervenisset?*) Elsewhere in the *Confessions*, Augustine's use of the term is similar to his use of *litterae* for *grammatica*. It is found both in pejorative contexts, as when he studies, 'with damnable purpose', the classics of rhetoric (*libri eloquentiae*) at Carthage (*Confessions* 3. 4. 7), but also in reference to the Scriptures: Moses is notable for his *facultas eloquendi* (*Confessions* 12. 26. 36), but never for his *facultas rhetorica*.

The *loq-* root appears also in another key passage of the *Confessions*. After describing his university education in Book 3, Augustine sums it up by telling God he learnt nothing: 'Whatever I learnt of the

---

[21] Note the description of rhetoric as an 'art', found also at 5. 12. 22; in the *de Doctrina Christiana* (4. 60) Augustine explicitly endorses Cicero's view that eloquence is not so much invented as discovered. Three of the other seven instances of *rhetorica* co-occur with *profiteri* or *professio*, to be contrasted with the *confessio* of the Christian Augustine. Note also how his own enterprise in the *de Doctrina Christiana* is carefully paraphrased as a 'means of presentation' (*modus proferendi*; 1. 1 and elsewhere), even though the closeness to rhetoric is obvious already from 2. 133: *sed haec pars* (i.e. *rhetorica* or *eloquentia*) *discitur, magis ut proferamus ea quae intellecta sunt*....

[22] Cicero does draw a loose distinction between untutored eloquence and rhetoric proper: see, for instance, *de Inventione* 1. 5: *civilis quaedam ratio est, quae multis et magnis rebus constat. eius quaedam magna et ampla pars est artificiosa eloquentia, quam rhetoricam vocant*, or *de Oratore* 1. 167: *non defuit... patronis... eloquentia neque dicendi ratio, sed iuris civilis scientia*. Quintilian, however, uses *eloquentia* as a straightforward translation: *Institutio* 2. 16. 2: *sequitur quaestio, an utilis rhetorice. nam quidam vehementer in eam invehi solent*... : *eloquentiam esse, quae poenis eripiat scelestos.*

art of speaking and discussing (*de arte loquendi et disserendi*), or about the measurements of figures and of musical matters and of numbers (*de dimensionibus figurarum et musicis et de numeris*), I learnt with no great difficulty—and with no human to pass them on. You know, O Lord my God, that even swiftness of understanding and sharpness of judgement are your gift' (*Confessions* 4. 16. 30). This, like the Platonic catalogue of the arts as they truly are in Book 10, is couched almost completely in Latin terms. Only *musica* is given a Greek name, on this its one appearance in the *Confessions*.[23] Here the relevant term is *ars loquendi*; the rest will be considered in their turn.

One other use or abuse of the *loq-* root we will consider later. For the present, we may note one other possible Latin translation of *rhetorica*, namely *facundia*. This is not a canonical translation in the way that *eloquentia* is, but there is some evidence that in earlier Latin it could bear this sense. Sallust uses it of the rhetorical skills of the second-century tribune Memmius, considered a great orator by the standards of his day (*ea tempestate Romae Memmi facundia clara pollensque fuit*; *Jugurtha* 30. 4), and Ovid of the Scythians' first faltering steps on the road to eloquence (*discitur innocuas ut agat facundia causas*; *Tristia* 2. 273). The Sallustian tag is recycled by Augustine in reference to his dedication of *de Pulchro et Apto* to Hierius, famous for his *Graeca facundia* (*Confessions* 4. 14. 21); it is used also of his early trips to hear Ambrose preaching in the basilica at Milan, where he is interested only in the style of Ambrose's preaching, not its content (*quasi explorans eius facundiam*; *Confessions* 5. 23. 13). Again, it is difficult to generalize on the basis of two examples. It appears, however, that this is an old-fashioned translation, not common in classical Latin, and that Augustine reserves it for rather unfavourable contexts; he is clearly critical of his pre-conversion preoccupation with rhetoric.

---

[23] In the *de Musica* Augustine repeatedly uses the phrase *peritia* or *ars (bene) modulandi*, also found in Cassiodorus' *de Artibus*; the first attestation of this formula is in the third-century grammarian Censorinus (10. 3). The phrase is not used in the *Confessions*, though it is notable that Augustine favours church music only if it is done *cum convenientissima modulatione* (*Confessions* 10. 33. 50). We should, therefore, be prepared to hear echoes of music in all *mod-* words in the *Confessions*: *modus, moderari, omnimodus, multimodus*, and so on.

Dialectic

We have noted that Augustine's attitude to the *artes* undergoes a major change between his conversion and the later decades of his life.[24] Nowhere is this more visible than in his use of *dialectica*. In his first post-conversion work, *Against the Academics* of 386, he observes that it was 'by adding *dialectica*, which is either the essence or the *sine qua non* of philosophy (*sapientia*), Plato is said to have perfected that art' (*Contra Academicos* 3. 18. 37). By the last decade of his life, he is not so charitable:[25] the first disciples, he writes in *The City of God*, 'were uneducated, not versed in grammar, not armed with dialectic, not puffed up with rhetoric' (*impolitos, non peritos grammatica, non armatos dialectica, non rhetorica inflatos*; City of God 22. 5)—three Greek words together. His works against Julian of Eclanum, also from his last decade, are full of sneers at Julian's pretensions as a *dialecticus*: where, he asks at one point, is Julian's vaunted grasp of Aristotle and the other tricks of the dialectical trade (*ubi est acumen tuum, quo tibi videris categorias Aristotelis assecutus, et aliam dialecticae artis astutiam*; contra Iulianum 3. 2. 7)?

But more than half of the 120 or so examples of *dialectica* in Augustine's works appear in a very different work—the polemic *contra Cresconium Grammaticum ex parte Donatistarum*, written in 405–6, and so chronologically quite close to the *Confessions*. Cresconius had accused Augustine of being a *dialecticus*. Augustine, however, is unrepentant—*dialectica*, he says, being 'nothing other than the art of disputation (*peritia disputandi*)'. A *dialecticus* is merely what in Latin is called a *disputator*; and, he says, 'to criticize under a Greek name what you have no choice but to praise under a Latin name is nothing other than to impose upon the uneducated, and to insult the educated' (*contra Cresconium* 1. 14. 17). For good measure, Augustine adds that the question-and-answer sessions we find Jesus practising in the Gospels was itself an example of *dialectica*.

---

[24] On matters relating to dialectic in late antiquity, including Manichee disputations, Christian deployment of the practice, and ultimately the growing preference for authority based on hierarchy, tradition, assent to formulas, and unanimous or at least univocal acclamation, see the groundbreaking study of Lim (1995).

[25] The turning-point can be clearly observed in *de Doctrina Christiana* 2. 117–31, where he cautions against an unbridled use of the *disciplina disputationis*, also called *scientia definiendi, dividendi atque partiendi* or *regulae conexionum*.

The Vocabulary of the Liberal Arts

A shrewd point—but his rather shrill defence of *dialectica* may lead us to suspect that Cresconius had touched a sore point. Augustine had, in fact, hardly used the word *dialectica* in his published works in the twenty years since *Against the Academics*. Certainly he does not use it in the *Confessions*—but he does have a range of alternatives. Two of his alternatives, *peritia disputandi*, we have encountered already, in his catalogues of the arts as they exist in the mind (10. 9. 16; 4. 16. 30). These are canonical translations; Cicero in the *Orator* (32. 113–14) links the *disputandi ratio* with *praecepta disserendi* as Latin versions of ἡ διαλεκτική. This preference for Latin words has one very important consequence; it enables Augustine to link the *artes* to specific Biblical passages, where the same words are used in a non-technical sense. The supreme dialectician, for Augustine, is God; it is God who teaches us, by forcing us to confront the inconsistencies and false values in purely human conventions. The link is provided by Isaiah 1:18, cited at 13. 19. 24: *venite, disputemus, dicit dominus*, 'Come, let us reckon up/do dialectic, says the Lord'—a passage to which we will return later.

Another important verb is *sermocinari*;[26] not, perhaps, so familiar a rendering of διαλέγομαι as *disputare* or *disserere*, but a rendering none the less. Both the *Auctor ad Herennium* and Quintilian use the term *sermocinatio* to refer to the rhetorical figure known as διάλογος, in which individuals referred to in a speech are made to converse in language appropriate to their character,[27] and *sermo* or *sermocinatio* can also be used of philosophical dialogue, whether Xenophontic, Platonic, or Ciceronian.[28] Indeed it is easy to see how *sermocinari*, a middle verb with a similar basic meaning to διαλέγομαι, could easily take on the sense 'to engage in dialectic'. Augustine himself is aware of

---

[26] Compare Conybeare (2006).
[27] *Rhetorica ad Herennium* 4. 52. 65. *Sermocinatio est cum alicui personae sermo attribuitur et is exponitur cum ratione dignitatis*; Quintilian, *Institutions* 9. 2. 31: *sermones hominum assimulatos dicere* διαλόγους *malunt, quod latinorum quidam dixerunt sermocinationem*.
[28] Cicero, *de Officiis* 1. 37. 134–5. *Sit ergo hic sermo, in quo Socratici maxime excellunt, levis minimeque pertinax; insit in eo lepos... habentur autem plerumque sermones aut de domesticis negotiis aut de re publica aut de artium studiis atque doctrina*; *Laelius* 1. 24. 38: *[Scaevola] exposuit nobis sermonem Laelii de amicitia... eius disputationis sententias memoriae mandavi... ut tamquam a praesentibus haberi sermo videretur*; Horace, *Odes* 3. 21. 9–10: *non ille, quamquam Socraticis madet/sermonibus, te neglegit horridus....*

this possibility. Cresconius the Donatist grammarian is pummelled mercilessly: if, Augustine asks, 'neither our Lord nor his interlocutors conducted dialectic in the course of their *sermocinatio*...what in your opinion *is* dialectic?' (*contra Cresconium* 1. 19. 23).

Of the five instances of *sermocinari* in the *Confessions*, all can, at a push, be classed under the heading of 'dialectic' or 'intellectual discourse'. On one occasion, Augustine fuses the double sense of *sermo* as a rendering both of ἡ ὁμιλία, 'homily' or 'sermon' in the English sense, and of διαλόγῳ—Monica goes to church to hear *not* the preacher, but *te [Deus] in tuis sermonibus* (*Confessions* 5. 9. 17). The notion of 'dialectic' is strongly present at this point—it is often been remarked that Monica is the classic untaught sage, and indeed Augustine refers to God teaching her in the 'inner *schola*' or lecture theatre of her heart. And at two other notable points in the later books of the *Confessions,* Augustine uses *sermocinari* again to refer to God as supreme dialectician: *audiat te intus sermocinantem qui potest* (*Confessions* 11. 9. 11); *tu me alloquere, tu mihi sermocinare* (*Confessions* 12. 10. 10). This special use of philosophical language in the later books is entirely appropriate.

Geometry and Arithmetic

We turn now to geometry and arithmetic. For geometry, we have already noted the list of the *artes* as they really are in Book 4, where Augustine uses the phrase 'measurement of figures' *dimensio figurarum*. In the catalogue of the arts in Book 10 we find a similar translation, *dimensionum rationes* (*Confessions* 10. 12. 19). Various other phrases also occur, referring to the measurement of shapes, of the earth, or of the cosmos more generally: *dimensiones figurarum* (4. 19. 30); *neque...siderum intervalla dimetimur vel terrae libramenta quaerimus* (10. 16. 24). The one expression we never find is *geometria* itself—even though it is one of Cicero's honorary Latin words. Augustine's alternatives are, in fact, reminiscent of some of the expressions Cicero himself tried and dropped.[29] But again, his translations both play up the radical sense of the words and allow

---

[29] Cicero, *Tusculan Disputations* 1. 5: *at nos metiendi ratiocinandique utilitate huius artis* [*sc. geometriae*] *terminavimus modum*; *de Senectute* 49. 6: *mori videbamus in studio dimetiendi paene caeli atque terrae C. Galum.* Compare also Horace, *Odes* 1. 28. 1–2, *te maris et terrae numeroque carentis harenae/mensorem cohibent, Archyta*....

The Vocabulary of the Liberal Arts

him to link the arts to the Scriptures: God, the Great Geometer, has 'arranged all things in measure and number and weight', and the humblest believer has a truer grasp of the source of geometry than the finest infidel professional (*fidelis homo... dubitare stultum est quin utique melior sit quam mensor caeli et numerator siderum et pensor elementorum et neglegens tui, qui omnia in mensura et numero et pondere disposuisti; Confessions* 5. 4. 7, citing Wisdom 11. 21).

Turning to mathematics, we may not be surprised to find that the word *arithmetica*, like *geometria*, is entirely avoided in the *Confessions*, even though it had been current in educated Latin for centuries. Instead, Augustine uses *numerus*.[30] This is the regular translation in Republican Latin—Cicero uses it twice in the context of Platonic philosophy[31]—and, like *disputare*, it enables Augustine to link the liberal arts to the Scriptures. The *Confessions* famously open with a reference to *numerus*, cited from Psalm 147:5: *magnus es, domine, et laudabilis valde. Magna virtus tua, et sapientiae tuae non est numerus*—and many of the forty instances of *numerus* and *numerare* in the *Confessions* appear in Biblical citations. So, for instance, Augustine can invoke Matthew 10:20, 'to you the hairs of our head are numbered' (*tu vero, cui numerati sunt capilli nostri!...; Confessions* 1. 12. 19), or the statement that Christ was 'numbered among us' (*et numeratus est inter nos; Confessions* 5. 3. 5, citing Isaiah 53:12, Mark 15:28)—this last in a passage concerned explicitly with the relationship between mathematics and theology. By choosing *numeri* rather than *arithmetica*, Augustine is able to portray God as the Great Mathematician.

Philosophy

Augustine famously encounters philosophy at the age of 18, through reading Cicero's lost protreptic *Hortensius*. Wisdom is with God;

---

[30] Compare *de Doctrina Christiana* 2. 136–7, where Augustine uses *numeri disciplina* (but elsewhere also just *numerus* or *numeri*) of the unchanging laws of mathematics, with relevance also for geometry and music, but distinguished from the arbitrary *numerus* of metre.

[31] Cicero, *Republic* 1. 10. 16: *cuius [sc. Platonis] in libris multis locis ita loquitur Socrates, ut etiam cum de moribus, de virtutibus, denique de re publica disputet, numeros tamen et geometriam et harmoniam studeat Pythagorae more coniungere*; compare *de Finibus* 5. 29. 87: *cur Plato Aegyptum peragravit ut a sacerdotibus barbaris numeros et caelestia acciperet....*

and the *Hortensius* teaches him that 'the love of wisdom has a Greek name: philosophy' (*apud te est enim sapientia. amor autem sapientiae nomen graecum habet philosophiam*...; *Confessions* 3. 4. 7–8). It is tempting to say that *amor sapientiae* is Augustine's, or Cicero's, gloss on *philosophia*. But Augustine does not present us with the Greek term, then with a Latin equivalent—or vice versa. Rather *philosophia* is presented as simply the 'Greek name' to describe the love of wisdom, in the same way that *amor sapientiae* is the corresponding Latin noun phrase. True philosophy, he suggests, is above and beyond linguistic particularism.[32]

It is true that this initial, positive experience is swiftly followed by a health warning, from the Apostle Paul: *videte ne quis vos decipiat per philosophiam et inanem seductionem, secundum traditionem hominum, secundum elementa huius mundi* (*Confessions* 3. 4. 8, citing Colossians 2:8). But this is bad philosophy, characterized by atheist materialism and an obsession with intellectual *diadochai*. This sort of philosophy is always *philosophia*, its practitioners *philosophi*.[33] The Latin terms are generally reserved for 'good' philosophy. In his catalogue of the arts in the memory in Book 10, Augustine talks of philosophy—that is, ethics—in purely descriptive terms; he speaks of the *affectiones* or *perturbationes animi*, but uses nothing we can call even a semi-technical translation of φιλοσοφία. Elsewhere, Augustine typically uses some locution involving *sapientia*. For the verb, Augustine avoids the pejorative *philosophari* in favour of the more positive calques *sapientiam colere* (6. 12. 20) or *diligere* (3. 4. 8), or simply *sapere*. For the noun, we find *studium sapientiae* (4. 14. 21), or just plain *sapientia*.

The rendering *sapientia* is familiar from Republican times onward. But again, Augustine blends this traditional intellectual discourse

---

[32] Once again, we find a more dispassionate treatment of this discipline in the *de Doctrina Christiana*, 2. 144–5. The nuances of his introductory phrase *philosophi autem qui vocantur* are hard to read. Like the use of quotation marks in English, the expression *qui vocantur* might imply a rejection of the claim of (all) philosophers to be friends of the truth; but such expressions are often used with Greek words, even familiar ones, with little more implication than the practice of putting (say) German loanwords in italics.

[33] In this respect he is following Cicero, who likewise in his speeches uses *sapientes* and *docti* as 'neutral' terms for intellectuals, *philosophi* as a pejorative: Adams 2003: 203.

with his new Biblical wisdom. Sixteen of the sixty instances of *sapientia* in the *Confessions* appear in Biblical citations, most notably the opening citation of Psalm 147: *sapientiae tuae non est numerus*. *Sapientia* is the quality par excellence of God; quoting Paul again, Augustine even identifies it with Christ (*ipse autem unigenitus factus est nobis sapientia et iustitia*; *Confessions* 5. 3. 5, citing 1 Corinthians 1:24, 30). And Augustine concludes his exegesis of the Creation story with the statement that God, the Supreme Philosopher, teaches us all these meanings through a process of dialectic (*haec nobis disputas, sapientissime deus noster*; *Confessions* 13. 18. 23).

WHY THIS DISTRIBUTION?

Having examined Augustine's practice, we should now enquire into the reasons for it. It is true that Latin writers often intersperse Greek and Latin technical vocabulary, especially in lists;[34] but that does not seem to be an adequate explanation here. Why are established words so regularly reserved for pejorative contexts, or else ignored altogether? Certainly Latin writers do frequently use clusters of Greek terms in order to distance themselves from their subject-matter. But Augustine himself explicitly warns Cresconius against criticizing in Greek what he approves in Latin, and in fact a high percentage of the Greek words in the *Confessions* are there precisely because of their occurrence in Biblical Latin. I would suggest it is true up to a point that Greek words may be used to indicate disapproval; I do not, however, think it explains the distribution of the liberal-arts terms we find in the *Confessions*.

A better explanation is surely the wider semantic resonances his translations possess. As we noted earlier, where existing Latin words are pressed into service to translate Greek technical terms, they may retain some of the sense of the Greek even if they do not become

---

[34] Compare, for instance, Petronius' catalogue of *dialectica, astronomia, sapientia,* and *eloquentia* (*Satyricon* 88, quoted above) with Quintilian's juxtaposition of *grammatice, musice, philosophia* (*praecepta sapientiae*) with *ratio siderum* and *eloquentia* (*de Institutione* 1. 4. 4–5).

the canonical translations; and if they do, they do not thereby lose all their original meaning. We have noted that within a technical register, close synonymy may occur between two or more words for the same thing. But it is hard to class the language of the *Confessions* as falling within a technical register. Technical uses there are, but in many cases—as with the biblical citations—the reader is left to choose how far to detect a technical sense. In such cases we should think of Greek words as having not a defined set of familiar Latin translations, but a penumbra of various translations. The extent of this penumbra is necessarily uncertain, and it may be worth while considering some borderline examples. Let us consider first *loquacitas*. We have already seen this word juxtaposed to *rhetorica*: 'Throughout those years I taught rhetoric, and sold the all-triumphant *loquacitas*, being myself a captive in Greed's triumphal procession' (*Confessions* 4. 2. 2). Augustine uses it also when speaking of his retirement from his rhetorical career, and his decision to 'remove the stooge that was my tongue from the markets of *loquacitas*' (*Confessions* 9. 2. 2). Shortly afterwards, this is put more prosaically: he seeks release from the *professione rhetorica* (*Confessions* 9. 4. 7).

These juxtapositions in themselves suggest an equivalence between the terms. Underlying them there may be an extension of the analogical principle by which many Latin translations are formed: ῥέω: *loquor*:: ῥητορική: x, x = *ars loquendi/eloquentia/loquacitas*. Augustine is not above making such loaded analogies explicitly: compare μῦθός *fabula*:: μυθικός: x, x = *fabulosus* (*City of God* 6. 5).[35] If we accept that *loquacitas* might be an equivalent to *rhetorica* in some contexts, we might draw the analogy for ourselves elsewhere; Monica, for instance, notably avoids the *loquacitas* of old women (*Confessions* 5. 9. 17)—primarily 'garrulity', but perhaps, for Augustine, qualitatively no different from empty rhetoric—pleasurable and persuasive speech, but void of substance? And should we think also of the smooth-talking Manichees, also typically loquacious?

[35] Disingenuously presented as the unfortunate outcome of the limited resources of Latin. The passage in full reads *latine si usus admitteret, genus quod [Varro] primum posuit, fabulare appellaremus. sed fabulosum dicamus; a fabulis eum mythicon dictum.* For this loaded use of the pejorative *-osus* suffix, we may compare *Confessions* 4. 1. 1, *contentiosa carmina et agonem coronarum faenearum*, where there seems to be an implicit analogy ἀγών: *contentio*:: ἀγωνιστικός *contentiosus*.

We may also see the penumbra principle at work if we consider again the case of dialectic. Both διάλογος and *disputatio* broaden their meaning in later usage, to mean not just dialogue but any intellectual disquisition, with or without other interlocutors; a dialogue may thus be a monologue. This is not, in itself, a problem for Augustine: in the *Soliloquies*, he openly acknowledges that dialogue may occur within one and the same individual.[36] So in the *Confessions* Ambrose's sermons at Milan are described as disputations, as is Augustine's own self-consolatory disquisition on the death of Monica. None the less, Augustine is never quite at ease with purely monologic dialectic: the term *disputatio* is also used of Faustus the Manichee's public talks, where Augustine is dismayed to find that no time is allowed for question and answer (*Confessions* 5. 6. 11). In this respect, he shares a widespread late-antique concern that dialectic could easily become mere verbal point-scoring, rather than an open search for truth. Some Latin terms for public debate—*altercatio*, *certamen*—virtually invite this understanding: Augustine notably avoids them in the *Confessions*.

We do, however, often find him using *colloquium*, *colloqui*, or sometimes *loqui cum*—not canonical translations of διάλογος to the same extent as *disputatio*, since they also have a wider use in the language, but translations just the same. The *loq-* root is common in the translation literature as a rendering of the Greek *log-*: as witness Augustine's own coinage *soliloquium* for μονόλογος.[37] And like his compatriot Cyprian of Carthage he may have known the text *venite, disputemus, dicit dominus* (Isaiah 1:18, cited at *Confessions* 13. 19. 24) in the form *venite, colloquamini*—'Come on, let's talk things over, says the Lord.' Indeed, we need only see a few examples to realize that he is using it in the sense *disputatio*. The sort of relaxed philosophical dialogue Augustine *hopes* to have with Faustus is a *colloquium* (... *cuius adventu collatoque colloquio facillime mihi*

---

[36] Augustine, *Soliloquies* 14: *Ridiculum est si te pudet, quasi non ob id ipsum elegerimus huiusmodi sermocinationes...soliloquia vocari et inscribi volo...cum enim neque melius quaeri veritas possit quam interrogando et respondendo, et vix quisquam inveniatur quem non pudeat convinci disputantem...placuit a me ipso interrogatum mihique respondentem, deo adiuvante, quaerere.* Note the various Latin terms for dialectic here: *sermocinatio, interrogare, disputare*.

[37] For further examples from the translation literature, see Burton (2000: 131).

haec... expedirentur; Confessions 5. 6. 10). His question-and-answer disputation on the drunken beggar in Milan is described in similar terms *(locutus sum cum amicis; Confessions* 6. 6. 9). So too are the philosophical discussions he enjoys with Monica before her death in Ostia (*colloquebamur ergo soli valde dulciter; Confessions* 9. 10. 23; *... cum quibusdam amicis meis materna fiducia colloquebatur de contemptu vitae huius et bono mortis*). Once we accept that *colloquium* may have this force of 'philosophical dialogue', we may sense its meaning in other, less expected contexts. For example, Monica's *amica colloquia* (9. 9. 19) to her fellow-housewives on how to avoid getting a beating counts as dialectic in two senses: specifically, because household management is one of the oldest themes in the dialectical tradition (dating back at least to Xenophon's *Oeconomica*), and generally, because any homely chat with a serious moral outcome may claim to be an inheritor of the original Socratic technique.

Or let us consider another example. Monica is peculiarly prone to visions, some of which turn out to be true, some false. She can always tell the difference, however, by 'a sort of taste, which she could not put into words' (*nescio quodam sapore quem verbis explicare non poterat*); this told her which were divine revelations and which were her own soul's imaginings (*Confessions* 6. 13. 23). Here it is at least arguable that *sapor* is meant to recall its cognate *sapientia*, 'wisdom/philosophy'. Taste is an important and recurrent metaphor in the *Confessions*. The apples Augustine and his friends stole from that orchard in Thagaste (*Confessions* 2. 4. 9) had no attractive *sapor*. The Manichee deity whom he devoured 'did not taste of God' (*nec sapiebas; Confessions* 3. 6. 10). The group at Rome who arranged for him to be offered the Chair of Rhetoric there gratified his secular ambition, but 'tasted of earth' (*terram sapiebant; Confessions* 5. 8. 14). God himself is repeatedly invoked as 'sweetness' (*dulcedo*). The reason for this seems to be that just as we instinctively perceive sweet things as appetible, so also we instinctively recognize truth and take pleasure in it; there may also be a latent allusion to Psalm 33:9, 'Taste and see that the Lord is sweet' (*gustate... quia suavis est dominus*). We would, then, be mistaken in putting the senses 'taste' and 'wisdom' in watertight compartments. When Augustine sees Ambrose in his atrium, intently pondering his books, he wonders what 'tasty joys'

The Vocabulary of the Liberal Arts

(*sapida gaudia*) he is extracting from them (*Confessions* 6. 3. 3); the joys are tasty *because* they are philosophic and religious. Monica's inexplicable 'taste' for truth can itself be interpreted as a sort of philosophy.[38]

Our penumbra, therefore, is hazy around the edges; we might expect to find the liberal arts in yet more passages of the *Confessions*, in some disguise or other. We might also need to look harder at apparently everyday words which also carry some intellectual or philosophical charge. One example will suffice. We began our enquiry by looking at the dialogical format of Augustine's early manuals of the arts, and in particular the word *interrogare*, 'to pose a philosophical question (requiring a yes-or-no answer)'. Once we are alerted to this technical sense, our reading of the *Confessions* is enriched at various points. Augustine interrogates, among others, his hypothetical grammarian (1. 13. 22), his soul (4. 4. 9), and himself (6. 6. 9); he is himself interrogated by Nebridius (9. 3. 6). Book 10 is a lengthy *interrogatio*, first of the created world, then on the senses, on the nature of God; Books 11 and 12 present Scriptural exegesis as dialectic (11. 12. 14, 12. 4. 6). The language of dialectic runs deep in the *Confessions*.

CONCLUSIONS

We have touched on the ways in which Augustine exploits Biblical language to support his argument, and this question deserves some further consideration. Augustine's detection of references to the liberal arts in the Book of Genesis or the prophecies of Isaiah strike us as far-fetched, perhaps even an abuse of Scripture. On this reading, the question how the Bible became the focus of Western culture could become a depressing one: the story of how intellectuals abandoned any search for first principles in favour of an ever-more-elaborate (and implausible) exegesis of a sacred text. It is true that Augustine does refer repeatedly in the *Confessions* to the

---

[38] On 'the flavour of God' in early Christianity, see now Fulton (2006).

auctoritas of Scripture, and take its inerrancy as axiomatic. We may congratulate him on his 'creative engagement' with Scripture, or some such quality—patronizingly, if it is to be silently understood that we would never venture to be quite so creative ourselves. More profitably, we might investigate the intellectual framework within which he describes his commitment to Scripture. This task must be postponed, yet it is clear that it must involve two things: first, an investigation into the terminology of *auctoritas*, and its intellectual pedigree; and secondly, a consideration of the importance of providence in Augustine's Scriptural exegesis. For if his discovery of dialectic, geometry, and so forth in the Scriptures is (on one level) the merest accident of translation, it is also clear that from Augustine's perspective these translations may themselves be seen as providential. The assertion of eternal providence as manifested in the authority of the Scriptures is rounded off with a Ciceronian phrase ascribing to God 'the stewardship of matters human' (*administratio rerum humanarum*; *Confessions* 6. 5. 7; compare *de Natura Deorum* 2. 1. 3). If Augustine's commitment to the Scriptures is ultimately an act of faith, it is at least one he attempts to rationalize within the recognized intellectual schemes of antiquity.[39]

In avoiding the traditional terminology of the arts, then, Augustine is attempting to revalorize them.[40] His alternatives are a mixture of established and familiar translations (such as *disputatio, numeri, figurae*), revived archaisms (*oratoria, litteratura*), and apparently novel usages of his own (*colloquium*). But in his distribution of these terms, Augustine goes beyond mere *variatio*. By avoiding Greek in his discussion of the higher arts, and by exploiting the

---

[39] On this matter, see the discussion by O'Donnell (1992 ii: 353-4) and its references.
[40] *Confessions* 10. 12. 19: *Audivi sonos verborum quibus significantur* [*sc. numerorum dimensionumque rationes*] *cum de his disseritur; sed illi alii, istae autem aliae sunt; nam illi aliter graece, aliter latine sonant; istae vero nec graecae nec latinae sunt, nec aliud eloquiorum genus.* Compare *Confessions* 10. 20. 29: *Nam hoc* [*sc. nomen vitae beatae*] *cum latine audit Graecus, non delectatur, quia ignorat quid dictum sit; nos autem delectamur, sicut etiam ille si graece hoc audierit; quoniam res ipsa nec graeca nec latina est.* In this respect, Augustine is closer than he would like to admit to Porphyry of Tyre: for Porphyry, 'the real barbarians are those who cannot, or will not, speak the language of the fatherland' (Clark 1999: 130).

nuances of his various Latin translations, he compels the willing reader to consider these *disciplinae* not as knack or trade or even profession that one learns at school or university. It is perhaps unfortunate for the later study of the *disciplinae* that Augustine himself did not persevere systematically with the demystifying terminology he explores in the *Confessions*.[41]

[41] Material in this chapter has been presented at Royal Holloway, University of London, at the NECROS seminar in Newcastle, at the UNED in Madrid, and at the Sixth International Conference on Later and Vulgar Latin at Helsinki, and at Villanova, PA. I am very grateful to all those who have offered helpful comments on it; I hope it will not be invidious to single out the late Bob Coleman.

4

Talking Books

INTRODUCTION

This book began with an outline of the importance of language within the spiritual journey of the *Confessions*. This is not in itself a wholly new observation. One earlier statement of the thought, however, is particularly suggestive. Flores (1975: 2) prefaces his useful account of reading and speech in the *Confessions* by remarking how the work 'shows a preoccupation with language, or more specifically with reading, as including the complementary activities of writing, speaking and exegesis'. Deconstructions of the polarity between orality and literacy have become familiar in recent years, and the primacy of the spoken word has been questioned on a variety of empirical and theoretical bases.[1] Flores's modest study, however, seems to have anticipated this trend, with his subsumption of speech, writing, and exegesis into a wider category of reading. It is a suggestion which deserves further consideration. Intimately linked to the question of reading, I suggest, is the question of the book as a three-dimensional physical entity. The following chapter will address these two issues.[2]

---

[1] Most notably, on the ground that while reading and (more especially) writing was clearly beyond all but a minority (usually estimated between 10 and 20 per cent) of the population; but the existence of professional scribes meant that this minority was 'not barred from the practical benefits of literacy nor from an acquaintance with the substance of texts' (Gamble 1995: 8).

[2] The goals are necessarily restricted, due to the highly influential study of Augustine the reader by Stock (1996), an indispensable work on these matters. As with O'Donnell's commentary, it would be necessary to footnote constantly all points of contact with Stock's book.

BOOKS AND READING IN CLASSICAL THOUGHT

Christian intellectuals such as Augustine inherited a set of mixed attitudes towards books and literacy. The earliest Christian writers, in close contact with Judaism, no doubt absorbed the Rabbinic preference for the spoken over the written tradition of teaching. But it is not easy to distinguish between Jewish and Hellenistic attitudes on this point. The superiority of the spoken to the written word was widely taken as a given, as has been ably demonstrated by Alexander (1990). Though this attitude rarely amounts to a prohibition, and is on occasions challenged, it permeates many levels of discourse, from the artisan's to the philosopher's.[3]

A special case must be made of the Platonist tradition. It is to the Platonic school that we owe the most familiar critique of writing in ancient literature, the key texts being Plato's *Phaedrus* 274ff and the pseudonymous *Seventh Letter* of Plato 344ff. In the *Phaedrus*, Socrates suggests that the technology of writing will 'produce forgetfulness' on the part of those who use it, as they will neglect to practice their memory. One might think that written words speak intelligently, but if questioned they only ever say one and the same thing. The 'true account' (λόγος), he says, is that which 'accompanied by knowledge is engraved upon the soul of the student' (ὃς μετ᾿ ἐπιστήμης γράφεται ἐν τῇ τοῦ μανθάνοντος ψυχῇ); it is this which may be held to be the legitimate brother of the written word. The *Seventh Letter* goes further. Here Plato is presented as denying that he ever has or ever will place his true doctrines in writing; anyone claiming to do so is either mad or lying. As Alexander shrewdly notes, although these two texts can be harmonized when read out of context, they are really aimed at different targets: the passage in the *Phaedrus* being a polemic less against writing than against the new genre of technical manual, whether of medicine or tragic composition. Other features too may deserve our attention. First, we may note also the typically Platonic use of myth as a distancing

---

[3] To Prof. Alexander I owe also the reference to Jaffee (2001), a suggestive study of 'Torah in the mouth' in ancient Palestinian Judaism.

device: Plato in the persona of Socrates places the conversation in question in the mouth of the Egyptian deities Thoth and Ammon. Secondly, there is the fact that the *Phaedrus* does not present writing as the bastard brother of speech, but of a rational, well-informed understanding of the issue at stake. Thirdly, this understanding is still in some sense 'written' on the soul, if this is the correct understanding of γράφω in this context (the word in its radical sense means 'scratch, delineate, incise'; Chantraine 1968–80: 235–7). These last two points will be particularly important for our discussion.

The evidence of the main second-century Christian writers points to a broadly similar attitude to that found in the philosophical schools. A recent study by Stanton (2004: 92–109) has revealed that while Justin Martyr and Irenaeus freely quote the Old Testament as Scripture, and while they are apparently aware of the four familiar Gospels and regard them as having some sort of special status, they tend to introduce the words of Jesus as viva voce utterances—'he said', 'he taught', 'he commanded'—even where there is little doubt the source is a written account. As has often been suggested, a comparison between the literature which did and which did not make it into the Christian canon of Scripture reveals that the 'proto-orthodox' of the second and third centuries tended to reject accounts of Jesus' life which relied on claims to insider knowledge, in favour of records of his public ministry such as found in the Synoptic Gospels.[4]

By the fourth century, then, the position of orthodox Christianity is a paradoxical one. It inherits on the Jewish side both the concept and the fact of a body of sacred Scripture, along with a sympathy for the spoken word as being the best means of transmitting teaching. It has developed also a sense of itself as an open, outward-looking church, rather than a select circle of like-minded higher thinkers.

---

[4] The fact that Mark and Luke are ascribed *not* to primary witnesses but to followers is turned round by Christian apologists to mean that their accounts rest on what is widely attested, rather than on some esoteric tradition. The Gospel according to John, with its more arcane teaching, is slower to be accepted, and indeed the Muratorian Canon (later second century) goes to some length to argue that John *should* be accepted, and that the author wrote with the authority of the other apostles also. On the march of proto-orthodoxy see in particular Ehrmann (2003).

Talking Books

This in turn commits it to a practice of public reading of and live commentary on its sacred texts.[5] Indeed, a consideration of the attitudes towards books current in Augustine's day cannot properly be made without attention to those which might be inferred precisely from the Christian Scriptures.

BOOKS IN THE BIBLE

While Christianity, like Judaism (and Manichaeism), is classically a 'religion of the Book',[6] the Scriptures themselves show a range of attitudes towards books and literacy. The Hebrew Patriarchs managed tolerably well without writing. The Ten Commandments, however, are clearly an example of the codification of religion. From the later seventh century BC at least, there is an increasing emphasis on the book as the record of divine revelation par excellence. Good King Josiah, one of the last kings of Judah, is presented as having instituted a programme of religious reform following the invention of a lost 'Book of the Law of the Lord' in the Temple at Jerusalem (2 Kings 22–3), a book whose content seems to have been close to that of Deuteronomy (itself a book with various 'metabiblical' allusions: 17:18, 28:58, 61; 29:20, 27). The prophet Jeremiah had a secretary, Baruch, responsible for recording and publishing his works (Jeremiah 32:12–16, 36:4–32). Ezekiel's prophetic ministry begins when he is invited by Yahweh to eat a scroll (Ezekiel 3:1–2). Second Isaiah prophesies that in the Messianic Age 'the deaf will hear the words of the Book' (Isaiah 29:18), a nice illustration of both the centrality of the book in nascent Jewish religious consciousness and of the difficulty of polarizing oral and literate cultures.

There is a peculiar sense in which the history of the book is written by the victors, but it is hard to escape the fact that Judaism in the early Hellenistic period becomes increasingly and self-consciously

---

[5] Augustine's own sketch of Ambrose reading the Scriptures captures perfectly the tension between public and private aspects of reading: his scanty leisure time Ambrose spends reading, silently, but with the public allowed to watch and in principle at least to question him on the text before him (*Confessions* 6. 3. 3).

[6] For qualifications to this description, see Stroumsa (2003).

a people of the book. In one tradition at least, this is true in the secular as well as the sacred sense. The new genre of 'Courtier Literature' frequently presents Jews as being a nation of secretaries and clerks, integrated to and able to exploit the bureaucracies of the Gentile kings under whom they live. Daniel and the 'three holy children' at the court of King Nebuchadnezzar are endowed by God with 'learning of every sort of book' (Daniel 1:17). King Artaxerxes the Great beguiles his insomnia by listening to 'histories and annals of olden times' (Esther 6:1), from which Jews emerge as remarkably good and loyal subjects. Likewise in the First Book of Ezra (chapters 4–6), Artaxerxes is persuaded to rescind permission for the rebuilding of the Temple at Jerusalem on the basis of the 'history-books of his ancestors', only to be counter-persuaded by the Jews following an appeal to the Royal Library—an institution which would seem less at home in fifth- or fourth-century Babylon than in second-century Alexandria.

However, it is in the religious sphere that Hellenistic Judaism becomes most strongly a bibliocentric religion, to the point where books acquire the status of sacred objects. The author of the First Book of Maccabees describes how King Antiochus Epiphanes burns all the 'books of the law of the Lord' and kills all those who possess a copy (1 Maccabees 1:59–60)—a sacrilege set on a par with the desecration of the Second Temple. It is an incident with a long afterlife. While there is no reason to doubt the general truth of the frequent Christian accounts of how persecution from the second to early fourth centuries began with the confiscation and destruction of the Scriptures, it was stories such as this which reinforced the sense of outrage felt by Christians at the physical destruction of their own texts. Augustine himself shared the horror felt by the Donatists at the *traditores* who had surrendered their copies of the Scriptures during the Great Persecution, even if his version of events was very different from theirs.

Yet within the Scriptures there are counter-currents. The Ten Commandments themselves exemplify how the writing down of a text does anything but guarantee its stability and preservation, let alone its observance. The Book of Exodus tells how Moses first descended Mount Sinai with the Ten Commandments written on tablets of stone, only to shatter them in fragments when on descending the mountain he found the Israelites roistering around the golden calf his brother Aaron had made for them to worship (Exodus 32:1–20). This powerful image for the apparent strength and actual fragility of the written code seems to have been too much for the final editor of Exodus; the subsequent account of Moses' second descent (Exodus 34) with a second pair of stone tablets seems designed to rectify this impression, as well as harmonizing the story of the first tablets with the belief that the Ark of the Covenant contained the tablets given to Moses. The story of the second pair clearly depends on that of the first, but also somehow weakens it; how much more solemn had that sole specimen of divine epigraphy perished as soon as it was brought down from the mountain. Surely secondary—and neglected now—is a *third* story in Exodus (24:3–8), in which Moses writes down 'all the sayings of the Lord' in a *scroll*, which the Israelites undertake to observe.[7] It is the image of the broken tablets which may underlie the prophet Ezekiel's insistence that the Lord will take away Israel's 'heart of stone', and give them one of flesh (11:19, 36:26). The author of the 'Court History' of David clearly understood the value of writing as a means of deception and betrayal. Having impregnated Uriah's wife Bathsheba, David sends Uriah himself off to the front with a letter to his commanding officer ordering him to engineer his death (2 Samuel 11:14–17);[8] we are left to speculate whether Uriah was too scrupulous to read the letter himself, reluctant to break the seal, or simply illiterate. Finally, there is for some the sheer ennui of the life spent in the library: as 'the Preacher' of Ecclesiastes (12:12) famously puts it, 'To the multiplication of books there is no end.'

Within the New Testament, these cross-currents become deeper. The Gospels clearly present Jesus as knowing the Scriptures and able to match his opponents citation for citation, in best rabbinic style. But the Devil too can quote Scripture (Matthew 4:1–11); and a consistent and clearly historical tradition shows Jesus himself impatient with the concerns of the professional scholar and exegete.

---

[7] I am particularly indebted to Goode (2005: 141–51) for the stimulating treatment of the Decalogue stories.

[8] Compare, on the classical side, the similar story of Bellerophon (*Iliad* 6. 166–70), sometimes claimed as the earliest reference to writing in Greek literature.

In the Gospel according to John (5:47), he asks how his Jewish opponents will believe 'Moses' letters' when they do not believe 'my words' (*meis verbis/sermonibus*). It is John's Gospel which contains Pilate's gnomic refusal to alter the *titulus* 'The King of the Jews' on Jesus' cross: 'What I have written I have written' (John 19:22), a fine illustration of the inscrutability of the written word. John indeed concludes, in the form we have it, with the editor's (despairing?) note that if all Jesus' deeds 'were written down one by one, I suppose the world itself could not contain the books that would be written' (John 21:25). The Apostle Paul, linking Exodus and Ezekiel, likewise contrasts 'the letter that kills' with 'the Spirit who brings to life' (2 Corinthians 3:6)—a key intertext for Augustine the reader, along with his emphasis on the 'Law that is written on [the Gentiles'] hearts' (Romans 2:14, cited at *Confessions* 1. 18. 29).[9] Paul indeed stretches his definition of a written text: the Corinthians, he writes, *are* his letter of introduction, 'written not with ink but with the Spirit of the living God'.[10]

The Scriptures, then, would offer Augustine no single view on the nature and relative values of the written and spoken word. What they offered was a range of starting points for meditation on the uses and abuses of literacy. This point is worth emphasizing, as it would by no means have been obvious to all his contemporaries. As Kaster has demonstrated, the idea that literacy and literary culture define what is civilized—which in Latin at least means what is *human*—was widely current in later antiquity, and far from unknown among Christians (Kaster 1988, especially 70–95). No doubt many would echo the Elder Pliny's curious epigram, that there was 'no book so

---

[9] The translation given here is the familiar one, down to the capitalization, but the phrase is equally translatable as 'the breath gives life'. Paul indeed may be 'spiritualizing' an existing saying on the relative status of oral and written accounts.

[10] Book imagery becomes even more developed in some Gnostic traditions. On the 'living book of the living', see *The Gospel of Truth* 19–20, 22–3: 'This is the knowledge of the living book which he revealed to the aeons, at the end, as [his letters], revealing how they are not vowels nor are they consonants, so that one might read them and think of the something foolish, but they are letters of the truth written by the Unity, the Father having written them for the aeons in order that by means of his letters they should know the Father' (Robinson 1990: 41–3). On the relationship between the elements of the alphabet and those of the cosmos in later antique mystical traditions, see Cox Miller (1986: 495–9).

bad one could not benefit from some part of it' (*Epistle* 3. 5. 2). The example of Augustine himself shows how this attitude could percolate through to lower social classes.

BOOKS IN THE *CONFESSIONS*

The vivid, impressionistic account Augustine gives of his early encounters with Virgil and Horace as a schoolboy do not include any reference to books as such; the emphasis is more on the inadequacies of his teachers. This changes when he describes how, as an undergraduate at Carthage, he came to read Cicero's dialogue *Hortensius*: 'I began to study the classics of rhetoric (*libros eloquentiae*)... and in the usual course of study I had arrived at a book by one Cicero (*librum cuiusdam Ciceronis*)... this book of his (*liber ille ipsius*) contains a protreptic to philosophy... this book changed my outlook (*ille vero liber mutavit affectum meum*) and redirected my prayers (*mutavit preces meas*) towards You, O Lord' (*Confessions* 3. 4. 7).[11]

The extent to which Cicero's *Hortensius* marks a turning-point is, I think, easily overlooked. This may be partly because, as the dialogue is lost, it is impossible for us to assess exactly which arguments of Cicero's Augustine may have found appealing. One suspects it may be partly also because of an unease among many readers at the idea that a religious conversion experience is an appropriate response to reading a work of Cicero's; such a response has too little to commend it either to classicists or to Christian readers of today. But Augustine himself appears to find it hard to overestimate its importance in his life. Indeed, the book is almost personified, actively changing his

---

[11] There is a problem in translation, as O'Donnell notes: should the sense be 'changed the character of the prayers I offered to you' (so Gibb and Montgomery) or 'turned my prayers to you' (Ryan, and most others)? O'Donnell argues for the former, on the ground that *mutare* does not mean 'to change *x* by turning it to *y*'. This is true, but it is hard to get away from the emphatic *ad te ipsum*. Probably *both* senses are intended: the *Hortensius* changed the nature of Augustine's aspirations *and* made God the addressee of his prayers.

outlook; the word *liber*, not found till now, suddenly occurs four times in succession. The impression is so strong that Augustine almost has difficult explaining why, when immediately afterwards he began to read the Scriptures again, he was repelled by their uncouth style—this being, he says, the result of his own arrogance.

Further encounters with books and reading continue to shape Augustine's career.[12] His dissatisfaction with Manichaeism is brought about partly through his extensive readings in philosophy (*multa philosophorum*; *Confessions* 5. 3. 3); the secular mathematicians and astronomers are able to give a more coherent account of the world than the Manichee myth-system. Characteristically, it is not the mere fact of reading that Augustine finds enlightening, but the fact he had 'committed their teachings to memory' (*memoriae mandata retinebam*), an important qualification given the Platonic anxiety about the spurious and the legitimate *logos*. Later, it is his reading of the classics of Platonism (*Platonicorum libri*) that persuades him, 'not in these words indeed, though the argument was the same', of the Christian truth that 'in the beginning was the Word, and the Word was with God, and the Word was God' (*Confessions* 7. 9. 13). From Plato, Augustine turns to Paul (7. 21. 27 to 8. 12. 30), culminating in a famous scene at Milan, where, disgusted at his own lack of spiritual resolution, he goes out alone into the garden of his rented house and opens his codex of Paul at random, to find the words, 'put on the Lord Jesus Christ and make no provision for the flesh and its lusts' (Romans 12:12–13; *Confessions* 8. 12. 29). In Book 9 he and his friends, along with his mother, go on retreat and read Psalm 4. Finally, Books 11–13 discuss at length the correct way to read the opening verses of the Book of Genesis. Rather than examine each of these in detail, however, we may take as a case study a story from Book 8, when Augustine is wavering on the brink of making a firm Christian commitment. It is the story of how Augustine's friend Ponticianus tells him about the conversion of two courtier friends from his time at the imperial city of Trier. In examining this passage, we will pay particular attention to the delicate counterpoint between written and spoken word.

---

[12] The examples given here are selective; for a fuller census, see Flores (1975).

Case Study: Ponticianus' Tale

Augustine is by this time working at the imperial court at Milan.[13] As he presents it, his life has come to a crisis: he has, by this time, renounced the Manichee religion, but has yet to commit himself to any other; engaged to a young girl of good family, he is keeping a mistress until his betrothed comes of age. Around him there is something of a coterie of fellow North African high-flyers. One of these, Ponticianus, comes in one day to find lying on a gaming-table a copy of the epistles of Paul, which Augustine had been studying. A Christian himself, Ponticianus is delighted to find that this is Augustine's chosen literature. From there the conversation turns to the phenomenon of Egyptian monasticism. Ponticianus is surprised to find that Augustine knows nothing of Athanasius' *Life of Antony*, the first great hagiographic work. He goes on to tell Augustine how, when he was at the imperial court in Trier, he and three fellow-courtiers were taking their afternoon stroll, the Emperor

---

[13] This passage too has been the object of a typically subtle discussion by Stock (1996: 95–102). On some questions of interpretation the account here differs. Stock regards the *casa* to which the courtiers go as a cottage inhabited by Christians, rather than (as suggested here) a hut inhabited by monks. Either interpretation is possible, though the fact that this encounter in the gardens 'next to the walls' follows immediately on from the description of the monasteries 'outside the city walls' does suggest the place is the same. 'Woodland pleasaunce' is enticing, and it would be nice to see in the courtiers' extramural wanderings a reflection of Socrates' and Phaedrus' meeting by the Ilissus; but what Augustine describes is probably no more than suburban market gardens. Stock is surely right in seeing the *casa* as being a 'spiritually pure locale': one thinks, for instance, of the 'hut of Romulus' on the Palatine, emblematic of Rome's primal humility, or of the cottage where Philemon and Baucis entertained gods unawares (Ovid, *Metamorphoses* 8. 633, 699; compare also Celeus' house where Ceres is harboured in *Fasti* 4. 516), or of the rustic idyll dreamt of by Tibullus (1. 10. 40, 2. 5. 26). Perhaps relevant too is Wisdom 11:1–2. Augustine labours the completely random nature of the encounter (*deambulare, spatiari, digredi, vagabundus, irruere*)—this is not a visit of inspection—and it is questionable whether the civil servants were surprised to find evidence of Christian inhabitation of the *casa*. As Stock's own translation makes clear, it is the content of the *Life of Antony* that inspires their wonder, rather than the presence of Christians in the area per se; Trier by this date already possessed a large basilica, and the courtiers are no more than an afternoon's ramble away. Finally, it should be said that the reading *turgidus* (*parturitione*), adopted by Stock, while attractive, is apparently a modern conjecture for the manuscripts' *turbidus*; it does not appear to be widely followed by modern editors.

being (suggestively) 'detained in the theatre'. Two of the party broke off, and came across a little hut occupied by some monks, in the symbolic 'desert' space outside the city walls. Within the hut they found a copy of Athanasius' *Life of Antony*. Reading it, one turns to the other and (the narrative breaks into direct speech) says: 'Tell me, if you would, where we hope to arrive with all our exertions?... Can we have any greater hope at Court than to be friends of the Emperor... But if I wish to be a friend of God, I can become one right away... If you are ashamed to join me, do not oppose me' (*dic, quaeso te, omnibus istis laboribus nostris quo ambimus pervenire? Maiorne esse poterit spes nostra in palatio quam ut amici imperatoris simus? Amicus autem dei si voluero ecce nunc fio. Te si piget imitari, noli adversari*; *Confessions* 8. 6. 15). His friend immediately joins him. At that point Ponticianus and the other courtier rejoin them. On hearing their story, they are delighted on their friends' behalf, but unable to share their resolution. Later, the fiancées of the two neophytes hear the news, and themselves take a vow of chastity.

Even from this summary, it is clear how carefully the alternation between spoken and written word is choreographed. Ponticianus enters; he and Augustine and their friend Alypius sit down and start talking (*consedimus ut colloqueremur*), in a verb which (as argued in Chapter 3) may refer to ordinary conversation or to the process of philosophical dialogue. Ponticianus happens to see the codex on the gaming-table; codices in the *Confessions* are intimately associated with the Christian religion, even though the context suggests that this could just as well have been pagan literature. The written book leads on a *sermo*, another conversation-cum-philosophical dialogue. Ponticianus is amazed that Antony's miracles are *inaudita* to Augustine and Alypius—literally 'unheard', thus collapsing the distinction between the word as heard and the word as read.[14] Their *sermo* then moves closer to home; Ponticianus' account of the monasteries outside Milan—unknown until that time to Augustine—is received in rapt silence. *Et intenti tacebamus*—the inset story is introduced in terms which may recall the reaction of

---

[14] The metaphorical use of *inauditus* is well attested from Cicero onwards, but it is hard to feel it is entirely a dead metaphor; as with the case of 'talking books', it is quite possible for familiar images to be reactivated.

Dido and her court at Carthage to Aeneas' inset account of the Fall of Troy; *conticuere omnes intentique ora tenebant* (*Aeneid* 2. 1). Ponticianus' tale of course both speaks to Augustine's own recent experience and anticipates his future, just as Aeneas' does for Dido. The two courtiers find another codex, that in which the life of Antony is written; one of them 'reads, and began to be changed inside' (*et legebat et mutabatur intus*), much as Augustine himself was 'changed' by reading Cicero's *Hortensius*. We are not told what passage of the *Life* they read, but given the context of a life-changing conversion experience, the reader of the *Confessions* may well at this moment recall, as Stock suggests, the critical moment in the *Life* when Antony himself renounces the world, having heard in the Gospel-reading the words, 'Sell what you have and give to the poor' (Matthew 19:21)—in other words, a reading out loud of a written record of a conversation. They are then able to give Ponticianus and his friend a clear account of their decision (*narrato placito et proposito suo*), to which Ponticianus and his friend can reply only by weeping—an action which, as we will see, may indicate a state of grace but may also indicate a breakdown of the ordered process of language. Throughout the scene, the spoken word leads to the written word and so back to the spoken word, eliding any sense of primacy of one other the other.[15]

TALKING BOOKS

To speak of books 'talking' is surely a familiar, even trite, metaphor in most languages that have a culture of writing. In particular, the use of the historic present of quotation—'Plato says that...'—would

---

[15] Two further uses of Augustine's, though not connected with reading, deserve note here. First, there is the courtier's complaint about the uncertainty of ambition (*quo ambire pervenimus?*)—*ambire* being not only the business of 'networking' (as we would say) but also literally of 'going round in circles', a key metaphor in the *Confessions*. Secondly, note the superficially surprising suggestion that the second courtier should 'imitate' the first in his conversion (*te si piget imitari, noli adversari*). The allusion here is ultimately to Paul's command at 1 Corinthians 4:16, 11:1, 'Be imitators of me, then, as I of Christ', an increasingly important text in the evolution of the hagiographical genre: courtier number two is to imitate courtier number one in imitating Antony in imitating Christ. *Adversari*, on the other hand, has diabolic associations in biblical Latin (1 Timothy 5:14, 1 Peter 5:8).

normally denote very little other than 'Plato wrote that...'.[16] But there are complexities: some verbs, such as 'to say' in English, λέγειν in Greek, and *dicere* in Latin, seem to indicate any rational expression of a feeling or opinion, in speech or writing, whereas others may be more specifically associated with the spoken word ('to speak' or 'to talk'; φάναι, λαλεῖν, εἴρειν; *loqui, aio, inquam, for*). My point is not that any native informant, if they could be asked, would immediately confirm the existence of such distinctions; but simply that they are generally observed in our existing texts and so may safely be taken to reflect popular usage. Alongside these verbs of direct speech, both Greek and Latin have one commonly occurring word, translatable in most contexts as 'say', which usually refers to the spoken word but which can refer to the written without any obvious or conscious metaphor.[17]

The metaphor of the talking book, however, is dormant rather than dead; it may easily be activated. Consider, for instance, the standard formula for proof-texts in the opening chapters of the Gospel according to Matthew: 'all this happened to fulfil what *was said by the Lord* through the prophet *who said*...' (τὸ ῥηθὲν ὑπὸ τοῦ κυρίου διὰ τοῦ προφήτου λέγοντος Matthew 1:23); 'then was fulfilled that which *was spoken* through the prophet Jeremiah, *who said*...' (Matthew 2:18); 'this is the one who *was spoken* (ὁ ῥηθείς) through the prophet Isaiah, *who said*...' (Matthew 3:3). This practice is not observed consistently, and it is true that in later chapters Matthew tends to preserve the phrase 'that which is written' where it is found in his source. But it is notable that the last of these three examples represents a rewording of Mark's opening words: 'As it is written in the prophet...'. Matthew's practice is at least consistent with a belief that he prefers to see the Scriptures not as a fixed, impersonal record,

---

[16] The connotations are subtly different: presenting someone's words or meanings in the historic present may tend to suggest that the author's or speaker's words have some continuing truth, interest, or relevance. This seems true in Greek, Latin, and English.

[17] Compare also the formulation in Duchet-Suchaux and Lefèvre (1984: 16): 'L'Ecriture...nous parle, elle ≪dit≫...'. These authors offer some telling illustrations of this use in mediaeval Latin.

but as God's speaking through human speech. For him at least, the talking book seems to be a more conscious metaphor.[18]

Augustine would concur with Matthew on this point. Something similar, indeed, occurs in the *Confessions.* Consider, for instance, his citation of Paul's words in 1 Corinthians 15:52 at 9. 4. 11: 'Who will stand against us, when "the word comes to pass which is written: 'Death has been swallowed up into victory'?"' (*quoniam quis resistet nobis, cum fiet sermo qui scriptus est: absorpta est mors in victoriam*). Again, in order to understand Augustine's meaning, we need to look more closely at the Latin. As noted in Chapter 1, the formula *sermo domini factus est ad aliquem*, 'the word of the Lord came to so-and-so', is common in biblical Latin to describe the process of prophetic inspiration. In such contexts, *sermo* usually stands for Greek λόγος, as it does here also. But as we have noted also, this is in many contexts an inexact translation. The Greek word can readily refer to any rational expression: a sentence, a speech, a piece of writing, even a mental concept. *Sermo*, on the other hand, is quintessentially the viva voce, living word of conversation. Used of a written text, its normal meaning would be 'philosophical dialogue', the written representation of a conversation. While paying due attention to the pansemanticist fallacy—the idea that every time a word is used, it is used with all its significations—we may suggest that Augustine is likely to look kindly on the idea that someone to whom the 'word of the Lord' comes is more likely to be engaging in a form of inner dialectic than acting as a sort of dummy for a divine ventriloquist. Beyond that, we may detect an element of paradox in the reference to the '*sermo* that is written'. What the phrase suggests is not that the process of writing pins down the living word like an entomologist's butterfly, and perhaps not even that the writing itself takes on the living quality of the spoken word.

We might at this point reject the idea of any conscious paradox on Augustine's part, on the ground that the phrase *sermo qui scriptus est* is simply a Scriptural citation; Augustine is citing a form of words

---

[18] Or, to take another example from Augustine's own day, consider Jerome's words to his friends Chromatius, Jovinus, and Eusebius (*Letter* 7. 2): 'But now I am chatting with your letter, hugging it, talking to it—it alone here knows Latin' (*fabulor... amplector... loquor*).

familiar to him, rather than devising an original phrase of his own. The question cannot be proven beyond doubt, but it is unlikely that so highly trained and careful a language professional as Augustine would miss the unusual collocation of *sermo qui scriptus est*. Moreover, he has already entertained the idea elsewhere in the *Confessions*. In Book 4, he describes the intense pleasures he shared with an unnamed friend in his home town of Thagaste, as a young graduate: 'talking together, laughing together, doing each other good turns, reading sweet-speaking books together (*simul legere libros dulciloquos*)...' (*Confessions* 4. 8. 13). The joys of laughter and dialogue we have already considered; it is notable that the joys of reading together are not only described in terms of viva voce speech, but that the adjective in question is attested only once before Augustine.[19] There can hardly be a clearer example of the talking-book metaphor being activated. Finally, we may note Augustine's vocabulary for referring to the Bible. The *Confessions* contain just one word which refers only to the Bible, namely *scriptura* (not uniquely a Christian word, but one with special associations in Christianity). Alongside this, we find *libri*, 'books', and *litterae*, 'literature', qualified in each case by some adjective ('sacred letters', 'books of God', and so on). These are not distinctly Christian terms, and indeed it is notable that *libri* is apparently shorthand for any canonical body of text.[20] Alongside these, we find also *eloquia*, literally 'sayings' or 'outspeakings'.[21] This again is biblical, being found frequently in the Old Testament to refer to some previous promise or saying of God's; for instance, the Psalmist's appeal to God to 'bring me to life according to your saying' (*propter eloquium tuum vivifica me*; Psalm 118:154). Though completely absent from the New Testament, the word is picked up by Christian writers and reapplied to refer to the Scriptures.[22] In quantitative terms, it is hard to assess the degree of

---

[19] Notable also is the repetition of Augustine's *Leitmotif* of sweetness, that which instinctively gives pleasure; see discussion in Chapter 5.

[20] For instance, *libri eloquentiae*, 'classics of rhetoric' (3. 4. 7), *libri Platonicorum* (more tendentiously) 'Platonist bible' (7. 20. 26).

[21] In classical use, often 'rhetoric'; in this sense, the Bible is God's oratorical performance. In Christian writers it is often translatable as 'oracle'. See *Thesaurus Linguae Latinae* 5. 2. 412. 44ff; 415. 38ff.

[22] For examples of the Christian usage, see *Thesaurus Linguae Latinae* 5. 2. 416. 19ff.

prominence this usage has in the *Confessions*. Such an assessment would involve not only measuring the frequency of the term per *x* words in this and in a range of other, comparable texts, but also an identification of the number of times it was used with distinct reference to the Scriptures (as opposed to any other sense), and arguably also a differentiation—in practice sometimes difficult— between uses in biblical citations and uses in free composition. But while a degree of subjectivity is inevitable, the word does seem to have had a special appeal for Augustine, perhaps to be explained in part by its etymological connection with the act of viva voce speech.[23]

Finally, we may note a series of images linking writing and speaking: first, the *Confessions* being offered as a 'sacrifice' to God by the 'hand of my tongue' (*manu linguae meae*; *Confessions* 5. 1. 1); secondly, the citation of Paul's words as having been 'made audible' through the Apostle Paul's 'tongue' (*per cuius linguam tua ista verba sonuisti*; *Confessions* 8. 4. 9); thirdly, again the picture of the *Confessions* as being the product of the 'tongue of my pen' (*lingua calami*). The last of these at least is a reminiscence of Psalm 44:2, 'my tongue is the pen of a swift-writing scribe' (*lingua mea calamus scribae velociter scribentis*), and it is likely that this has suggested the other images also. The biblical comparison of fluent speech to skilled penmanship is striking precisely because one would expect the opposite. Although Augustine inverts this comparison, the effect is not to contradict or undercut the biblical text. Rather, it is to blur the distinction between tongue and pen, through repeated superimposition of the one on the other.

HEARING READERS

If books talk, then, how do readers hear? A simple answer would be that the ancient reader did indeed hear the written word spoken aloud. We read the book, in many cases we murmur the words to

---

[23] The distinction was a living one. Jerome (*Epistle* 106. 82) uses *eloquium* and *verbum* to distinguish λαλία and λόγος. For a rough indication of the statistical prominence of *eloquium* in the *Confessions*, we may note it occurs there 1.80 times per 10,000 words, as opposed to 0.31 times in the mostly classical Perseus corpus.

ourselves, and in that sense the author speaks to us. But this cashing-out of the metaphor is too bland for our purposes. Indeed, the view of books as a representation of speech would quickly take us back to Plato's anxieties about how books are a mere copy or representation of something else. Such an analysis would force us to do a sort of balance sheet of the pros and cons of written versus spoken texts: written texts may be misunderstood through problems of punctuation, homographs, word-division, poor handwriting, physical wear and tear to the text, even poor lighting or bad eyesight on the part of the reader, whereas spoken texts may be misunderstood due to homophones, poor diction, unfamiliar accent, background noise, bad hearing on the part of the listener—to name the more obvious.

The unprofitability of this exercise is soon apparent. While Augustine does on occasion refer to some of these questions, they are not, for him, the real issue. While the written word may be secondary in time, it functions in effectively the same way as the spoken word. We have considered how in his early dialogue *de Magistro* Augustine compresses all forms of speaking to 'teaching' or 'explaining' (*docere*). This is clearly the case, he suggests, of statements, but true also of questions (which explain what we want to know) and commands (which explain what we want done). The strengths and weaknesses of this theory need not keep us here, except to note that it is not well adapted to dealing with the pragmatics of many real-life utterances, or indeed to many instances of religious language: it is hard to reduce such phrases as 'Good morning!' or 'Praise to the Holiest in the height' to the status of statements. What does matter here is that the words do not do the communication; as Augustine argues, words can only point to things (not always adequately), and things cannot ultimately be understood either in terms of their signs (as that is a circular argument) or in terms of themselves (as that is a tautology). Instead, all true teaching is the work of the 'one Teacher, who is Christ', who is also the 'Beginning, since he speaks to us' (*sermo quia locutus sum vobis*; John 8:25). Augustine's communication theory, then, does not rest on the primacy of the spoken word.

Alongside this collapsing of the distinction between the oral and literate, there is another striking collapse made in the *Confessions*: that between the speaker/writer and the hearer/reader as the source of meaning in any given text. Here the key words are the verb *velle* 'to wish, intend, mean', and the related noun *voluntas*, 'wish, meaning'. While these words are commonly used in the more general sense, there are various occasions where the stronger sense is required. Consider Augustine's appeal for sympathetic readers of his account of his response to his mother's death:

> *et requievit [cor in lacrimis], quoniam ibi erant aures tuae, non cuiusquam hominis superbe interpretantis ploratum meum. Et nunc, domine, confiteor tibi in litteris. Legat qui volet et interpretetur ut volet, et si peccatum invenerit, flevisse me matrem exigua parte horae... non irrideat, sed potius... pro peccatis meis fleat* (*Confessions* 9. 12. 33)

My heart found rest in tears, since it was there that your ears were—not the ears of some human who would be arrogant in their interpretation of my weeping. And now, Lord, I confess to you in writing. Let those who wish to read, do so, and let them interpret as they wish, and if they find it a sin that I wept the smallest part of an hour for my mother, let them not laugh but rather weep for my sins...

The paradox of 'confession in letters' will now be familiar. Obscured, however, in this translation is the paradox of *interpretetur ut volet*: this is, I suggest, not simply an affectation of indifference—'let other people interpret it as they like.' An element of indifference is there, but behind the subjunctive Augustine is also stating what is to him a fact: 'readers will put their own meaning on his words because that is what readers do.' What matters is not that their reading of Augustine should be the same as his own, but that it should be informed by Christian charity towards him. A similar theory is advanced in Book 12, where Augustine declines to reject any interpretation of the opening words of the Book of Genesis ('In the beginning God made heaven and earth'), 'except the carnal ones', while denying any exegete's claims to authoritative interpretation of Moses' meaning (the verb used here is *sentire* rather than *velle*, but there is little if any practical distinction). In this case, however, Augustine turns aside at the last minute from the possibility that Genesis might contain a true meaning *not* meant by Moses, in favour of the belief that Moses meant *all* the possible true interpretations (*Confessions* 12. 31. 42).

This theory may help explain other celebrated yet curious incidents in the *Confessions*. First, there is Monica's dream of standing 'on a wooden rule' and being approached by 'a young man, radiant and joyful and smiling at her':

> Qui cum causas ab ea quaesisset maestitiae suae quotidianarumque lacrimarum docendi ut assolet non discendi gratia, atque illa respondisset perditionem meam se plangere, iussisse illum, quo secura esset, atque admonuisse ut attenderet et videret ubi esset illa ibi esse et me... (*Confessions* 3. 11. 19)
>
> He asked her the reason for her grief and her daily tears—not in order to find out, but in order to instruct, as usual. She replied that she was bewailing my perdition. He then told her not to worry, and counselled her to wait till she saw me where she was also...

Augustine—still at this time the Manichee—suggests that his mother should not give up hope of being what he is. She immediately rebuts this: ' "It was not said to me, 'Where he is, you will be also,' but 'Where you are, he will be also.' " ' It is his mother's critical acumen in rejecting such a plausible (though false) interpretation and in 'seeing what was to be seen' (*vidit quod videndum fuit*) that impresses him more than the dream itself. This account brings into contact the two approaches to hermeneutics outlined above. The young man who asks 'for the purpose of teaching rather than learning' must be identified with Christ. It is clear from the sequel that Augustine *does* accept the idea that interpretation cannot be a wholly arbitrary affair; his mother's hermeneutic skills are better than his own, through her appreciation of a quality intrinsic to that which is being interpreted. O'Donnell notes that the 'wooden rule' in question is likely to be a kind of spirit-level containing a channel of water. This also is suggestive: it is a formal quality of water to find its own level, though ultimately one given by God, 'who has arranged all things according to their measure, number, and weight' (Wisdom 11:21, quoted at *Confessions* 5. 4. 7).

The second passage in question is that where Alypius, informally attending Augustine's classes at Carthage, is shocked to hear his lecturer illustrate some point with a satirical comparison with the practices of the Circus (*Confessions* 6. 7. 12). Alypius, a fan of the Games, takes this as a sideswipe at himself, and immediately mends his ways. Nothing of the kind had been intended on Augustine's part; though he does not say that Alypius interpreted his own words as he (Alypius) meant them, this seems to be a fair gloss. And yet there is no question that Alypius' interpretation is a right one; it is wholly correct in the sense of being level with the 'rule of faith'.

Lastly, we come to the case of Augustine's final commitment to celibacy, in the garden scene at Milan (*Confessions* 8. 12. 29–30). As this too has been explicated in fine detail by Stock (1996: 102–11), we will simply observe here the importance of Augustine's initial interpretation of the child's voice (if voice there was). Though recognizing that it might be part of some children's game, Augustine chooses to interpret it as a divine command to pick up his codex of Paul. In short, he interpreted the words as *he* meant them, the meaning he put on them being not that of the child. Claiming direct communication from God is, of course, dangerous for one's reputation for sanity; Augustine avoids this (perhaps) by claiming responsibility for his own interpretation of the words he has heard. Again, the notion of *voluntas* is not far off. Augustine 'did not mean' (or 'meant not') to read (*nec ultra volui legere*) further than he did. 'Interpreting as one means' is, then, not simply what one does to books, but potentially to any form of sign.

The theme of *voluntas* has deeper resonances in the *Confessions* than has been sketched here. But there are other examples of the more specifically 'linguistic' sense of the word. The first statement about humanity, in the third sentence of the work, is that we 'mean to praise' God (*laudare te vult homo*). This is not, of course, a statement about a casual wish of human beings (many, of course, are quite unaware of any such wish), but rather a statement about the property of what it is to be human. The quality of meaning is linked to that of being and knowing in Augustine's allegory of the Trinity: 'I am, I know, I mean: I am knowing and meaning, I know I wish and mean, I mean to be and to know. In the case of these three, let who can see what an inseparable life there is, yet one life, one mind, one essence' (*Confessions* 13. 11. 12). 'Unchanging meaning' (*incommutabilis voluntas*) is a quality of God—which, as we will see, needs a 'reading' of its own.

The topic of the *regula*, the yardstick or spirit-level of interpretation, also has further importance. The *regula* in Monica's dream we have already noticed. Augustine himself revisits this motif at *Confessions* 8. 12. 30, where he links his mother's 'wooden rule' with the concept of the *regula fidei*, the 'rule of faith' which offers (as we might say) a benchmark for belief or practice in the early Church. The expression is well established in Christian use, with attestations dating back to Irenaeus and Tertullian. Augustine himself exploits the concept in more developed form in the *de Doctrina Christiana* (3. 2ff) as a means of determining orthodox from heterodox punctuations (*distinctiones*) of the Scriptures. First, this is originally a set of basic values rather than an elaborated credal statement (Beinert 1999). The great Donatist exegete Tychonius had promulgated his own 'Book of Rules' for Scriptural interpretation. Augustine himself had noted Ambrose's hermeneutic *regula* that 'the letter kills', while 'the Spirit brings to life' (6. 4. 6). These are, however, principles rather than dogmas. Secondly, the 'canon of belief' is a guide to practice as much as to doctrine. Augustine's own call for his more critical interpreters to have the charity to pray for him should be interpreted in this light; their conduct must be measured against the standard of Christian charity. The implications of this concept are not systematically explored in the *Confessions*. It is easy to imagine a more prescriptive and authoritarian version of it than the English phrase 'rule of faith' would suggest. This does not, however, appear to be Augustine's understanding.

CODIFICATION: THE BOOK BETWEEN REIFICATION AND ABSTRACTION

Augustine's emphasis on the dialogical nature of reading needs to be set aside his attitude towards the book as a physical object. Here again we encounter the familiar tension in Augustine's thought, between belief, typically though not uniquely Platonist, in a transcendent God and a higher order of things, and his assertion, notably in anti-Manichee polemic, of the goodness of the physical, created world. In stressing that books are simply a medium for debate, he may be implicitly rebuking the practice of bibliolatry, the excessive regard for books purely as *objets d'art*. The Christian book by the late fourth century is at something of a crossroads. Of the Gospel manuscripts we possess, the one most likely to have been extant in Augustine's day—the *Codex Vercellensis*—is of competent but unremarkable workmanship.[24] Purple manuscripts and metallic inks make their first appearance in Augustine's lifetime. Our earliest Christian illustrated manuscript, the magnificent *Quedlinburg Itala*, is richly illustrated with scenes from the Books of Samuel and Kings by an artist skilled in the conventions of classical art; King Saul, for instance, appears in the dress of a Roman Emperor, carrying out the very Roman practice of officiation at a public sacrifice (Elsner 1998: 251–4). Most estimates are for the period 400–50, some slightly earlier; at all events, it is either from Augustine's lifetime or shortly afterwards. But such luxury manuscripts seem to have been atypical in Christian circles. For Augustine, it is the Manichees who are the great amateurs of the book as a physical object. The Manichee bishop Faustus he taunts for having 'many large and precious codices... with their elegant covers ornamented with fine leatherwork' (*contra Faustum* 3. 6, 18)—surely the Manichee God, he jokes, should be liberated from imprisonment in so gross a matter. Certainly extant Manichee codices are characterized by a very high standard of penmanship.[25] It is unlikely that Augustine's antipathy towards the high-quality Manichee codex was motivated purely by philosophical concerns over the nature of the book, or vice versa; but it is quite likely that each reinforced the other.

Yet he remains strongly aware of the consequences, both practical and intellectual, of the sheer physical nature of the book. For Christians, the physical form of the book has particular importance. It is now established that the rise of the codex as opposed to the scroll format was an overwhelmingly Christian innovation, probably from a very early date. Consider, for instance, the account in Luke (4:17–21) of how Jesus, having read in the synagogue at Nazareth from the scroll of Isaiah, 'folds up the book' and declares ' "Today in your hearing this scripture has been fulfilled." ' Here we should give full weight to the sheer physicality of the scroll in question: it is

---

[24] On the external decoration of Gospel books, see Lowden's paper on 'the Word made visible', in Klingshirn and Safran (forthcoming); see also, in the same volume, Clark's essay on the extent to which Rome was, for Augustine, a 'City of Books'.

[25] For a concrete example, consider the case of the *Codex Manichaeus Coloniesis* on the life of Mani; 23 lines of Greek per page are fitted on to a writing space just 3.5 × 2.5 cm (Lieu 1985: 30).

handed to Jesus, unrolled, read, rolled up, and handed back.[26] While this undoubtedly heightens the tension of the passage, it may have a more specific function. The 'book of the Prophet' is quite clearly a scroll, as one would expect of the Jewish scriptures. If we can date the rise of the codex to around or before AD 100, and localize it within a distinctly Christian environment;[27] and if, further, we may date Luke to the late first or early second century, then we may see in the passage an enactment of the supersession of the Jewish written code by Christianity—both in the person of Jesus Christ and in the form of codices such as Luke's own.

The physicality of the books, and the implications of the codex form, was something well understood by Augustine. We have noted above the importance of Antiochus Epiphanes' burning of the Jewish Scriptures in shaping the attitudes which led to the Donatist controversy in North Africa, a controversy which sprang from the Donatist claim that the Catholic church was the spiritual inheritor of the *traditores*, those who had handed over their copies of the Bible to the authorities during the Great Persecution of 303–11. One obvious Catholic line of apologetic would be to concede the fact but deny the inference: to admit that their ancestors had handed over the Scriptures, but to argue that Christians were nowhere commanded to preserve the Scriptures at the cost of their lives, and that the Christian religion enjoined worship of a living God rather than lifeless parchments. It is notable that in Augustine's polemics against the Donatists, roughly contemporary with the composition of the *Confessions*, this line of defence is nowhere attempted. From a later period, we have his detailed description of the practical problems involved in the publication of the twenty-two-book *magnum opus*, *The City of God*: it is too big to be bound in one volume; if it is bound in two codices, they should contain ten and twelve books each; if in five codices, these should consist of two codices of five books and

---

[26] The 'book' in question could in principle be a codex or a scroll, and in fact the early manuscripts readings and patristic citations offer good support for both Jesus' 'unrolling and rolling up' and his 'opening and closing' it. The latter is likely to be an assimilation to the more familiar practices of the Christian scribe.

[27] Both views which would command widespread consent. See Roberts and Skeat (1987), who believe its introduction into Christian use 'must date well before A. D. 100' (p. 45); for subsequent discussion, Stanton (2004: 165–91).

three of four (*Epistle* 1A, from AD 426).²⁸ Although in some contexts the codex may simply be a member of the wider set of books, the two terms are not identical. Though the point is not made in so many words, it is the portability of the codex which makes possible at least some of the encounters with books in the *Confessions*; it is also the codex format which facilitates the practice of opening a work at random and taking a lesson from whatever passage meets the eye—though in later works we may detect a move away from the apparently approving attitude to sortilege that we find in the *Confessions*.²⁹ Indeed, the imagery of the codex is remarkably persistent. Consider, for instance, the catena of biblical citations on the authority of Scripture near the conclusion of the work: 'Who but you, our God, has made for us the firmament of authority that is above us in your Scripture? "For Heaven will be rolled up like a book" (Isaiah 34:4), and now it is "stretched above us like a tent" ' (*sicut pellis extenditur*) (Psalm 103:2)—a catena made possible by the ambiguity of the Latin *pellis*, 'skin', 'sheet of leather', hence 'tent' or 'parchment'. This book, is, however, no more than a stopgap measure for fallen humanity, like the 'skins' in which God clothed Adam and Eve when they first saw that they were naked (Genesis 3:21). But for the angels, no such skin/parchment is necessary, since 'they see your face always, and read there without syllables of temporal duration what your eternal Meaning means' (*ibi legunt sine syllabis temporum quid velit aeterna voluntas tua*; *Confessions* 13. 15. 16–18; note that *voluntas tua* could also be taken in late Latin idiom as an honorific form of address, 'Your Meaning'). Having stated that angels do not need to read, Augustine immediately reinstates reading as the model for knowledge of God: 'Their codex is not closed, nor is their book rolled up, for you are that . . . ' (*non clauditur codex eorum nec plicatur liber, quia tu ipse illis hoc es*).³⁰ Even in his description of the most metaphorical of books, God himself, Augustine finds it hard to exclude the concrete artefact of the Christian codex.

[28] For further discussion, see the useful work of Gamble (1995: 132–40, 165–8).
[29] See *Epistle* 55. 20. 37.
[30] Identifying short biblical citations is notoriously difficult, but there may also be an allusion here to the scroll folded up by Jesus in the synagogue at Nazareth in Luke 4:17–21, discussed above.

5

Biblical Idioms in the *Confessions*

BIBLICAL LANGUAGE AND STYLE

Augustine's first conscious response to the Latin Bible was one of repulsion; or so at any rate he presents it in the *Confessions*:

> Therefore I began to apply my mind to the Holy Scriptures and to see what they were like. What I see is a thing 'not found by the proud, nor revealed to children'; humble in approach, but in its import sublime (*incessu humilem, successu excelsam*) and veiled in mysteries; but I was not such as could enter into it, or bend my neck to its steps. I did not feel then as I speak now, when I considered that Scripture; but it seemed to me unworthy of comparison with the dignity of a Tully. (*Confessions* 3. 5. 9)

The complaint against the language of Scripture is a well-worn one, and known better to us from Christian apologetic than from pagan polemic. It is a point often raised by Christians themselves—perhaps more often as an imaginary objection than as a real one—presumably because they felt it easy to counter (see Auerbach 1965: 30–81); as Paul had observed of his own preaching, 'we speak not in the learned words of human wisdom... for the kingdom of God consists not of language but of power' (1 Corinthians 2:13, 4:20).[1] Augustine's own account here, as has been observed (e.g. by Clark 2005: 70–81), exploits the classical notion of the *sermo humilis* or the *humile genus dicendi*.[2] This expression does not refer to slang or

---

[1] The translation given here is based on the Vulgate use of *sermo*, representing Greek λόγος. The original is better rendered in context as 'argument'—the Gospel is not simply a matter of smart debating tricks—but the Latin translation suggests the sense given here.

[2] For a fuller account of Augustine's views, and their context and influence on the evolution of the 'Christian plain style', see Auksi (1995, especially 112–26). Of pagan critics, it is Celsus and Porphyry who appear to have done their homework on the

non-standard speech, but rather to that which—at its lowest—
follows 'the most ordinary custom that belongs to the pure style'
(*demissa... usque ad usitatissimam puri consuetudinem sermonis*).
The phrase is taken from the first-century BC *Rhetorica ad Herennium* 4. 11, which describes this style as 'attentuated language'
(*oratio attenuata*); though it is clear that this is what others such as
Cicero and Quintilian call the *genus humile*.

Augustine's invocation of the *genus humillimum* is predictably
two-edged. Alongside the implicit argument that classical Latin has
always allowed for the representation of lower registers of speech
without any lapsing into vulgarism, there is, of course, the theological significance of humility. This is a key theme of several favourite proof-texts of the first half of the *Confessions*: for example, 'God
gives grace to the humble, but resists the proud' (Proverbs 3:34
quoted at *Confessions* 1. 1. 1, 4. 3. 5); 'a heart crushed and humbled
you will not despise' (Psalm 50:19, quoted at *Confessions* 4. 3. 4, 6. 9.
17); 'the bones that were humbled shall rejoice' (Psalm 50:10, quoted
at *Confessions* 4. 15. 27). The theme is picked up in his account of
how Ambrose persuaded him of the possibilities of allegorical
interpretation, and his own conclusion that the Scriptures were an
example of the 'lowest genre of speaking' (*humillimum genus
loquendi*; *Confessions* 6. 5. 8); the phrase is closer to that of the classical
humile genus dicendi, though Augustine's modifications of it are
meaningful: informal talk (*loquendi*) for public speaking (*dicendi*),
and the unexpected superlative, subtly inviting his readers to reconsider their familiar categories.[3]

To argue that the 'low style' was not incompatible with good
literature was, however, only one of two lines of argument open to
Augustine. In the first two books of the *de Doctrina Christiana*, on
which he had been working shortly before he began the *Confessions*,
he develops another theme, arguing that biblical language has its own

---

Scriptures best; and their attack is largely on the contents and on the Christian mode
of allegorical interpretation, rather than on the Greek style as such. For Augustine on
biblical Latin generally, see Evans (1984: 1–10).

[3] It is not suggested here that *loquor* can *never* be used of formal speech, simply
that it tends not to be used that way. The examples in *Thesaurus Linguae Latinae* 7. 2.
1662. 53ff. of *loquor* used of *sermo arte quadam compositus* are a mixed bag, and in
some cases at least there seems to be an actively metaphorical sense.

consuetudo or custom of speech. In so doing, he is exploiting another very familiar classical argument, namely that custom should be considered as one of the main guidelines for linguistic use.[4] By speaking of the *consuetudo* of biblical language, Augustine is using a classical argument to arrive at a distinctly non-classical conclusion: that the Latin of the Scriptures should be judged by its own standards, and not by those of a Cicero.

The *Confessions* is in many ways an enactment of this new manifesto. In his earlier works, notably the Cassiciacum dialogues, his style is broadly classical; Scripture is evoked and discussed, but biblical language tends not to spill over into his main, 'authorial' voice. In the *Confessions*, all is different. Let us consider the famous opening words:

'Great are you, o Lord, and very worthy of praise; great is your strength, and to your wisdom there is no number' (Psalm 47:2, 144:3). And to praise you is the will of man, a portion in some sort of your creation, and man, who carries around his mortality, who carries around the testimony that you 'resist the proud' (Proverbs 3:34); and yet to praise you is the will of man, a portion in some sort of your creation.

Magnus es, Domine, et laudabilis valde: magna virtus tua et sapientiae tuae non est numerus. Et laudare te vult homo, aliqua portio creaturae tuae, et homo circumferens mortalitatem suam, circumferens testimonium peccati sui et testimonium quia superbis resistis; et tamen laudare te vult homo, aliqua portio creaturae tuae. (*Confessions* 1. 1. 1.)

It is not surprising to find non-classical usages in the initial Psalm citation, though they should not be ignored: the unusual positioning of the adjective *valde* at the end of the clause; the extended sense of *virtus* to mean 'strength' rather than 'courage' or 'moral quality', the odd use of 'number' in juxtaposition to 'wisdom' (surely 'end' or 'limit', *finis* or *modus*, would be more natural). Outside the quotation, we have the repeated use of *et* ('and'? 'even'?);[5] the string of clauses in apposition to the subject *homo*; the distinctly biblical *creatura*. Then there is

---

[4] Alongside reason and authority (i.e. the practice of the 'best writers', with which it is sometimes conflated); see Law 1990. The content and origin of the idea is—as Law makes clear—still hotly debated.

[5] According to Verheijen (1949: 118–21) a feature of biblical style, in particular corresponding to the Hebrew *waw-copulativum*; even so, the sentence-initial position is unusual.

heavy repetition of *circumferens* and *testimonium*, not following the classical 'law of three', or the practice of using polyptoton in anaphora, or indeed the use of *inquam* after a repeated word, but with the imbalanced construction of *testimonium* first with the genitive then with a *quia*-clause. Even the prosaic *circumferens* is suggestively polysemous; the *Oxford Latin Dictionary* lists as well-attested senses 'to carry around in a circle', 'to carry around for purification', 'to take around for inspection', and 'to carry about with one (often ostentatiously)'. (How is the reader, opening the book for the first time, to choose?). The phrase in question illustrates two more important points. First, the boundary between biblical citation and free composition is often fluid. We have identified two citations in the passage above, but there is clearly an allusion also to 2 Corinthians 4:10: '...always carrying around in our body the mortification *of Jesus*'—not the same, then, as 'his own mortality'. Secondly, even a usage that occurs in a clear and direct citation, such as in the opening words, is still part of Augustine's style. Citations are a part of the texture of the work, not a superficial ornament.

A full analysis of more than a very short passage would be extremely long, and would throw up many linguistic usages which are not readily labelled. For this reason, we will concentrate on just two aspects of Augustine's use of biblical idiom, chosen as being easier than most to identify and quantify. A recent study of the language of the early Latin versions of the Gospels suggested that literal translation could be defined as 'the pursuit of exact correspondence between source- and target-language, with resulting distortions of natural usage and idiom' (Burton 2000: 85). While we are not in the *Confessions* dealing with translation literature as such, this definition is still useful for identifying biblical allusions and biblical-style language in the work. It should be noted from the start that distortion of natural Latin usage does not consist solely of individual novel phrases. Augustine is certainly capable of these. Twenty-two words into the *Soliloquies*, his first post-conversion work, we find the statement:

ait mihi subito sive ego ipse sive alius quis...
there says to me either I myself or someone else...

Here the juxtaposition of the third-person verb *ait* with the first-person subject pronoun *ego* is at first sight a shockingly ungrammatical use.

Though by the end of the clause the suggestion of ungrammaticality has been removed, the effect—a radical questioning of the identity of the subject—remains and informs the whole of the rest of the work. A similar effect is produced at *Confessions* 1. 4. 4, where God is invoked as *omnipotentissime*, 'most omnipotent'—often pointed out as a paradox, since logically there cannot be degrees of omnipotence. However, distortion can also be cumulative. As we have seen in Chapter 3, a cluster of unusual loanwords in a single passage will produce an effect of its own, more pronounced than if the words in question were used in isolation; the same is true also of other forms of interference.

The study cited identified several areas where distortions of language tend to occur in the biblical translation. Two in particular are of concern to us: the use of loanwords and the treatment of singular and plural forms of nouns and adjectives. With some modifications of definition, these three areas will also serve as useful starting points for our enquiry into Augustine's use of biblical Latin in the *Confessions*.

SINGULAR AND PLURAL

'Number is the most underestimated of the grammatical categories' (Corbett 2000: 1). Even within a single language, it is not always easy for most speakers to say why certain nouns are construed as singular or plural. The distinction between 'count-' and 'mass-nouns' is often made, and is useful. Thus *money* is a mass-noun (or non-count noun), whereas *coin* is a count-noun; we tend to talk of money as a mass or abstraction, whereas coins are concrete and countable. But even this example illustrates the fuzziness often found around the edges of such distinctions. The phrases *monies outstanding* or *coin of the realm* may be far less frequent, but both have some currency. It is even possible for the unusual use of a singular or plural form to become a linguistic in-group marker. The very phrase 'the gospel' (τὸ εὐαγγέλιον, in the singular) has recently been shown to be a distinctly Christian use: the 'Good New', contrasting with the far-more-idiomatic 'Good News' (τὰ εὐαγγέλια), typically employed in official proclamations of the Roman Emperor's latest feats of conquest or acts of munificence (Stanton 2004: 9–33). It is, indeed, a sound principle of sociolinguistics that the more arbitrary a feature is, the more it is liable to become a marker of group identity.

In translation, particularly where a literal approach is adopted, the singular/plural distinction is an area where distortion is likely to occur. One example is, in fact, noted by Augustine himself; at *Enarrationes in Psalmos* 50. 19, he comments as follows:

'*Erue me de sanguinibus...*'. *Expressit latinus interpres verbo minus latino proprietatem tamen ex graeco. Nam omnes novimus latine non dici sanguines nec sanguina; tamen quia ita graecus posuit plurali numero, non sine causa nisi quia hoc invenit in prima lingua hebraea, maluit pius interpres minus latine aliquid dicere quam minus proprie. Quare ergo pluraliter dixit, de sanguinibus? In multis sanguinibus tamquam in origine carnis peccati multa peccata intellegi voluit.*

'Deliver me from bloods...'. The Latin translator has conveyed the sense from the Greek using a not wholly Latin word. We all know that in Latin we do not say 'bloods' (*sanguines* or *sanguina*); but because the Greek translator put it in the plural simply because he found the same in the Hebrew original, his translator faithfully decided to say something not wholly Latin rather than something less meaningful. Why, then, did he say 'from bloods' in the plural? By a multitude of 'bloods' he intended that a multitude of sins should be understood, as if speaking of the origin of the sinful body.

This passage is of some importance for our discussion of biblical style in the *Confessions*.[6] It alerts us to Augustine's awareness of rare plurals as being a distinctly biblical feature, and to his willingness to see more in the phenomenon than plodding ineptitude on the part of the translator. In the absence of native-speaker intuition, it is important that the concept of rareness should be set on some sort of empirical basis. The procedure adopted here is as follows. Two derivational affixes have been selected for special attention, namely the suffixes *-as -atis* and *-tio -tionis*. For reasons given below, we are particularly, though not solely, concerned with the dative/ablative plural forms. The *Confessions* have, therefore, been searched for examples of the endings *-atibus* and *-ionibus*. Words occurring

---

[6] A similar point is made more briefly at *de Doctrina Christiana* 4. 10. 24, where Augustine observes simply that the translators 'perceived the relevance' of the plural form. Note in the passage from the *Enarrationes* the importance of the *translator's* 'meaning' or 'intention' (*voluit*) for the interpretation of the text; compare Chapter 4.

fewer than 10 times in any form are disregarded, on the ground that there are too few examples to allow meaningful inferences to be drawn. In the cases that remain, the distribution of singular and plural has been compared against a corpus of classical Latin prose texts, searched using the Perseus Digital Library database (as of January 2006). This corpus comprises all the available text of: Caesar, Cicero, Livy, Nepos, Elder and Younger Pliny, Sallust, Servius, Suetonius, Tacitus, Vitruvius, and the Duke University papyri databank.

A truly rare plural will be one whose frequency *relative to the singular* will be low, and one whose *absolute frequency* will also be low. The strongest case of this identified here is that of *suavitas* ('sweetness'), found 113 times in our corpus in the singular and only once in the plural. *Oratio* ('language, speech'), on the other hand, occurs 994 times in the singular as against 89 times in the plural; but though plurals account for under one in ten examples of the word, it is sufficiently frequent in itself that it is unlikely to appear especially rare.[7] Between these two is a word such as *iniquitas* ('iniquity'), found 66 times in the singular and 7 times in the plural. Though these relative figures are similar to those for *oratio*, the plural is still likely to have appeared more noticeable, simply because of its low absolute frequency. There is, then, a sliding scale of currency for many plural forms, and sometimes singular and plural may have different meanings. Both principles have, in fact, already been illustrated by our English example of *money* versus *monies*.

Which nouns may more readily take plural or singular forms is not, as we have suggested, wholly predictable. None the less, within the Indo-European family at least it is broadly true that nouns indicating concrete objects are more readily pluralized than those referring to abstractions. This binary division does not always work neatly in practice. It does not, for instance, predict well which 'abstract nouns' may refer to a quality or state, and which may in the plural refer also to (for example) the conditions, causes, symptoms, objects, or effects of that state. (English pairs such as *kindness/*

---

[7] The corpus used, with its heavily basis in Roman 'public' prose, is, in fact, likely to over-represent both the absolute frequency of *oratio* and specifically its frequency in the sense 'oration, harangue', the only sense in which it is common in the plural in classical Latin.

kindnesses, sight/sights, or *hearing/hearings* illustrate some of the sorts of semantic relationship that may exist, but the list could be greatly expanded.) For present purposes, it would be possible to avoid the terminology abstracts and concretes, by focussing on the formal rather than semantic properties of the two classes of noun which will be considered here: deverbative nouns with the suffix *-tio -tionis* suffix, and deadjectival nouns with the suffix *-tas -tatis*. However, as these are regularly associated with traditionally 'abstract' concepts, there is little to be gained by avoiding this terminology altogether.[8]

In distinguishing readily pluralized concrete nouns from less-readily pluralized abstracts, we are in danger of undermining the principle with which we began: namely, that the count/mass-noun distinction tends to be arbitrary and language-specific. It is this, we have suggested, which tends to cause distortion in translations. This is a common finding in the field of contrastive linguistics (the systematic study of the differences in modes of expression between different languages). In cognitive linguistics, on the other hand, these distinctions are often held to reflect something real either in the external world or in the ways humans have evolved to perceive it (or both).[9] It is not our purpose here to arbitrate between these points of view. For the present, we will make the more limited claim that within the languages with which we are dealing, abstracts tend to be singular, though Greek and Latin idioms are to some extent arbitrary and differ at times. In particular, it should be borne in mind that the biblical Greek on which biblical Latin is based is itself in origin a translation-language, and often reflects the Hebrew use of the plural to express states or qualities.

Finally—as we have indicated—we may note that inflectional class may also condition the acceptability of a given plural form. The Latin fifth declension, for instance, has genitive and dative/ablative plural forms such as *dierum/diebus* and *rerum/rebus,* but relatively few others in regular use. The nouns *species* and *facies* are not uncommon

---

[8] The use of unusual plurals has been noted before: see García de la Fuente (1994: 175) for examples and some older references. However, the assertion that most of these plural abstracts 'belong to the Latin current at all periods' is not corroborated, and appears questionable in many cases. On theoretical questions of defining the abstract in Latin, see Mikkola (1964–5).

[9] See, for instance, the discussion in Janda (2000: 6–7).

in the nominative/accusative plural, but for the dative and ablative—in Cicero's words—'I would be reluctant to say *specierum* and *speciebus*, even assuming it could be said in Latin... I would prefer *formarum* and *formis*' (*Topica* 30). Quintilian for his part wonders briefly whether forms such as the genitive singular of *progenies* or the plural of *spes* actually exist or whether they are just 'very awkward' (*praedura*; Institutio 1. 6. 26), before dismissing the topic altogether. But it does not go away. The grammarian Charisius (1. 9), Augustine's contemporary, is even undecided whether the fifth declension should form its genitive plurals as *materierum, luxurierum*, and so on, or *materieum, luxurieum*. Such anomalies are not confined to the fifth declension: Augustine's favourite text 'God gives grace to the humble' illustrates it again, since the dative/ablative plural *humilibus* is notably rare in Latin outside biblical translations.[10] In such cases, there is no single transparent synchronic explanation for the rarity of the rare forms. Euphony is probably a consideration, and certainly sequences of four or more short syllables seem to be avoided; *sonis* and *monitis*, for instance, are notably more common than *sonitibus* and *monitibus*.[11] But euphony will not account for absence of forms such as *specierum* or *facierum*, and in supposing that certain forms were avoided because they were felt not to 'sound nice', we may be confusing cause with effect. Similarly, nouns referring to abstractions may be comparatively rare in these forms, perhaps more logically.[12] The noun *confessio* itself is a case in point: very rare in classical (and even biblical) Latin in the plural, it occurs 13 times in the *Confessions* in the plural as against 11 times in the singular, but

[10] The Perseus corpus as a whole contains 268 examples of the word; of the 5 instances of *humilibus*, 4 are from are the Vulgate.

[11] The Perseus corpus lists 239 examples of *sonus*, 7 of *sonis*, of which 4 are in prose; and 579 examples of *sonitus* and 1 of *sonitibus* (in prose). It has no examples of *monitibus* at all. This is, however, a tendency rather than a rule; common words for which there is no obvious alternative, such as *hominibus*, can appear as tetrabrachs, and in any case the spoken language was probably always freer than the written in using them.

[12] The ablative case, for instance, may mark agency of a passive verb, or physical location or point of departure, all contexts in which an abstract noun is relatively unlikely. I am not concerned here with poetic plurals such as *gaudia* for *gaudium*. Even such cases, however, present issues of their own: the feminine gender of this word's French and Italian reflexes (*joie, gioia*, though not Spanish *gozo*) indicate a currency for *gaudia* in the spoken language, presumably for many speakers at least a plural.

never in the form *confessionibus*. Other rare dative/ablative plurals do occur, however; it will be suggested that these form part of Augustine's wider linguistic strategy in the work.

Examples

Our examination of the plurals of nouns of the -*as*-*atis* and -*tio*-*tionis* classes has generated a list of 17 words occurring more than 10 times in the *Confessions* for which the plural may require explanation. The full list is: *aetas* ('age'), *auctoritas* ('authority'), *cupiditas* ('greed'), *iniquitas* ('iniquity'), *infirmitas* ('weakness'), *necessitas* ('necessity'), *suavitas* ('sweetness'), *vanitas* ('vanity'), *voluntas* ('will'), *voluptas* ('pleasure'), *actio* ('action'), *cogitatio* ('concern'), *delectatio* ('delight'), *quaestio* ('enquiry'), *regio* ('direction, region'), *temptatio* ('temptation'), and *oratio* ('speech, prayer'). Of these, *aetas*, *auctoritas*, and *regio* are not significantly more common in the plural in the *Confessions* than in our comparative corpus of classical Latin prose.

Of the rest, two examples may be taken as paradigmatic for a wider group. *Quaestio* is particularly notable, since though the plural occurs fairly frequently in classical Latin (in our corpus, 180 times in the singular versus 59 times in the plural), its frequency is markedly higher in the *Confessions*, outweighing the singular by 3:10. Typically, the plural forms are found in unfavourable contexts. Nine of the ten examples are used either of Manichee dialectic, or dismissively of the party political wranglings of the philosophers, or of the undue respect accorded to Aristotelian logic by Augustine's professors at Carthage. Only in the description of Nebridius as a 'very keen investigator of the most difficult questions' (*Confessions* 6. 10. 17) is the word used in the plural without any pejorative nuance. This pattern corresponds very close to that found in biblical Latin. Twenty of the twenty-nine examples in the Vulgate are singular, and all broadly neutral ('enquiry, question'). The remaining nine are all, in their context, pejorative. Consider, for instance, 'the Preacher's' summary of the human condition at Ecclesiastes 7:30: 'God made mankind simple, and he has entangled himself in infinite questionings (*infinitis*... *quaestionibus*)'; or the pastoral advice given at Titus 3:9: 'As for foolish questionings (*stultas*... *quaestiones*) and genealogies and quarrellings and fights over the Law, avoid them.' *Suavitas*, on the other hand, we have already noted as an extremely rare plural in classical Latin, in both absolute and relative terms (singular:plural ratios in the *Confessions* and our wider corpus being respectively 11:4 and 113:1). Within the *Confessions*, there is a clear correlation between the plural use and the lower pleasures. As a schoolboy, Augustine finds that the difficulty of learning Greek spoils the 'sweetnesses' of Greek mythology (*omnes suavitates Graecas fabulosarum narrationum*; *Confessions* 1. 14. 23). As a sixteen-year-old, he finds no one attempts to confine the sweetnesses of sexuality within the bounds of wedlock (*Confessions* 2. 2. 3). As a young man, he finds his friendship with an unnamed friend at Thagaste 'sweet above all the sweetnesses of my life as it then was'—that is, as a Manichee. Newly converted back to Catholic Christianity, he finds it 'sweet to do without the sweetnesses of light literature' (*Confessions* 9. 1. 1). In this case, the use of the plural actually has no parallel in the Latin Vulgate (the singular is found some 29 times, usually in the positive phrase *odor suavitatis*, 'odour of sweetness, sweet-smelling sacrifice'). Old Latin influence, as a translation of αἱ ἡδοναί, may have given the plural some currency, but even αἱ ἡδοναί is not a prominent phrase in biblical Greek.[13]

The marked use of plural forms, then, is often correlated with words which are either negative in their denotations, or which have negative associations in their particular context. This is broadly true of *cupiditas*, *necessitas*, *iniquitas*, *vanitas*, and *temptatio*, in addition to the examples considered above. The use of plural forms which indicate attitude rather than strict number or deixis has been well documented over various languages by Corbett (2000: 219–42); he does not list pejorative uses separately, though some of his examples of 'intensificative' plurals come close. Even in classical Latin, there are—perhaps—examples of the phenomenon: *lautitia* 'elegance' and *munditia* 'cleanness, smartness' both seem usually to be pejorative in the plural, and only sometimes so in the singular; though nuances of this kind are by definition hard to capture now.[14] Rather than treat each case in the *Confessions* in detail, we will confine ourselves to a few further examples:

---

[13] Luke 8:14, Titus 3:3, James 4:1–3; four times in 4 Maccabees.
[14] The *Oxford Latin Dictionary*, for instance, lists the plural of *lautitia* as a separate subheading, though not that of *munditia*.

Cogitatio (21:13 and 149:66) and *voluptas* (29:12 and 217:64) can hardly be classed as rare plurals in classical Latin, but are still notably more frequent in the plural in the *Confessions* than they are in wider Latin use. *Voluptas* is, of course, often seen as morally questionable in classical Latin, perhaps especially in the plural. In biblical Latin the plural occurs just 3 times out of 23, but these three include an example in Jesus' exegesis of his Parable of the Sower at Luke 8:14 ('when [the shoots] come up, they are choked by the pleasures (*voluptatibus*) of life'); the familiarity of this passage may have contributed to Augustine's use. *Cogitatio*, while fairly neutral in sense in classical Latin, is frequently found in biblical Latin with unfavourable connotations.[15] One of Augustine's favourite proof-texts for and against the physical scientist in the *Confessions* exemplifies this: 'Though they know God, they do not honour him as God or give thanks, but waste themselves on their own concerns' (*evanescunt in cogitationibus suis*; Romans 1:21, quoted at *Confessions* 5. 3. 5, 5. 4. 7, 7. 9. 14). The association between the plural and the pejorative is all but explicit in his paraphrase of Proverbs 19:21: 'many were the concerns (*multae cogitationes*) in our heart, but your counsel abides for eternity' (quoted at *Confessions* 6. 13. 24).

Two words call for particular attention. *Voluntas* (67:16 and 708:31) is hardly a negative word in itself, but the high proportion of plurals in the *Confessions* is largely accounted for by Augustine's critique in Book 8 of the Manichee doctrine of the Two Wills that govern human behaviour, where 11 plural forms are found in a few chapters. Particularly striking here is the presence of four dative/ablative forms *voluntatibus*, a form found just 6 times in the whole of our comparative corpus.[16] The marginal nature of the language may be a rhetorical strategy to heighten the impression of bizarreness.

---

[15] Compare the first example, from Genesis 6:5: 'But the Lord, seeing that wickedness of mankind was great upon the earth, and that all the concern (*cogitatio*) of their hearts was inclined only to evil...'.

[16] All the terms considered here occur at least once in the dative/ablative plural in the *Confessions*. These forms are often very infrequent in the classical language. *Cupiditatibus*, for instance, occurs 4 times/32 instances of the word, as against 13/362 in the wider corpus; for *suavitatibus* the figures are 2/15 versus 0/114, for *cogitationibus* 7/34 versus 19/215, for *contentionibus* 2/3 versus 3/262.

Delectatio may seem to belong semantically with such 'negative' words as *voluptas* or *cupiditas*, which would account well for the high frequency of its plural. In fact, it is essentially a positive word, delight being the *Leitmotif* of the *Confessions* (*tu excitas ut laudare te delectet...*), being used both of the spiritual pleasure of contemplating the divine (as at 11. 22. 28, 11. 29. 39) and of the lesser pleasures to be had from contemplation of the created world (as at 2. 5. 10); it can even be used of physical pleasures which have become an end in themselves (as at 8. 3. 7, 8. 10. 24). We might expect a correlation between the plural and the lesser pleasures and the singular and the higher, spiritual ones. This does not, however, occur. An explanation for this may lie in the key verse from Psalm 15:11: 'In [God's] right hand are delights to the end (*delectationes in dextera tua usque in finem*).'[17]

Recapitulation

It has been consistently suggested here that Augustine often uses rarer plural forms as a distancing device, usually emphasizing pejorative connotations that already exist. Sometimes, however, the pejorative effect lies more in the denotation, as with the contrast between the Manichee doctrine of the Two Wills and Augustine's emphasis on the single, immutable will of God. The distortion which we have suggested is a crucial component of the biblical style is sometimes gross, but more often cumulative; having recognized the more strikingly unidiomatic uses, the reader is able to pick up the less striking but still unusual ones.

We should re-emphasize the fact that we are not necessarily dealing with forms that are felt to be *wrong* as such. As we have said, in the absence of native informants (or explicit statements by them) we cannot simply assume that every Latin-speaker would feel this way. What we can do is point to certain observable patterns of use, and try to account for them; it should be recognized that not all

---

[17] Here the *Corpus Christianorum* edition of the *Enarrationes in Psalmos* prints *delectatio* in the lemma, but lists early support for *delectationes*.

speakers would necessarily agree on the acceptability of any given form, or the nuances attached to it.[18] It should also be emphasized again that the unusualness of Augustine's use of plurals is cumulative. The *Confessions* contain many more unusual plurals than have been mentioned here. A fuller list covering also those rare plurals whose headwords occur fewer than 10 times would include, among others, *ebrietas* ('drunkenness'), *ambitio* ('(over-)ambition'), *contentio* ('strife'), *diremptio* ('rending'), *mutatio* ('change'), *seductio* ('misleading'). These rarer plurals are more likely to occur if they are particularly prominent in biblical Latin (as with *cogitatio* or *vanitas*, for instance), and in this respect Augustine's use may be paralleled in other Christian writers; but some of his favourite rarer plurals are rare even in biblical Latin (as with *voluptas*, *suavitas*, or *confessio* itself). No convenient term exists for such usages; for convenience, we may call them pseudo-biblical or biblical-style. The preference for unity, identified with God, over the plurality of the physical universe, is, of course, a good Neoplatonic theme. Augustine's linguistic use is largely an instantiation of his own description of how as a teenager he 'was torn away from [God], the One, and wasted myself upon the Many' (*ab uno te avulsus in multa evanui*; *Confessions* 2. 1. 1)—and, in passing, a pre-echo of his citation of Romans 1:21 (*evanescunt in cogitationibus suis*).

Plurality can even be used to set off positive reference against playful nuance. *Orationes* in the Christian sense of 'prayers' is essentially positive, if with qualifications: The singular occurs 4 times in the *Confessions*, while the plural occurs 9 times, 5 of which are in the form *orationibus*; for our wider corpus the corresponding figures are 1083:89:36. These plurals, and especially the dative/ablative, are especially associated with the activities of Monica, and tend to be in passages where her son seems at once respectful and faintly

---

[18] An exact English parallel for this is hard to find. In broad terms, the question whether e.g. *suavitas* has a plural in regular use may be similar to the question whether *little* has a comparative form in English: is it *lesser*, *less*, *littler*, or *smaller*? This question would (I take it) not normally occur to native speakers of English, but once posed is not easily answered. There are also similarities with the recent academic fashion for using pluralized abstract nouns (e.g. 'classicisms', 'masculinities') for the titles of books, conferences, modules, and so on. The linguistic politics are clearly not the same as in the *Confessions*, but there is a point of contact in the way unusual word-forms are used with a view to challenging existing perceptions.

patronizing towards her. At *Confessions* 5. 9. 17, for instance, she goes to church 'so she could hear you [o God] in your *sermonibus*, and you could hear her in her prayers (*et tu illam in orationibus suis*)'. The reciprocity has something of the comic (despite the lack of explicit allusion, it is hard not to feel that Augustine is presenting his mother as the Importunate Widow of the parable (Luke 18:3–5)).

We have noted how Augustine is prepared to see special theological significance in the use of specific non-idiomatic plurals like 'bloods' (*sanguines, sanguina*). But his coinage of pseudo-biblical idioms may allow him to mount an implicit challenge on the values of classical Latinity. Custom may require Latin-speakers to use some words in the plural only, while others are normally kept in the singular. But such a custom is often irrational; it is, if anything, inconvenient that nouns such as *arma* or *liberi* should not have a singular in current use. In Augustine's persistent use of rare and non-classical forms, we may see a challenge to the arbitrary rules which distinguish 'good' from 'bad' Latin. At the same time, he is not always above exploiting the sheer oddness of forms such as *voluntatibus* or *orationibus*—an oddness which rests on an acceptance of classical patterns as the norm.

GREEK WORDS FROM BIBLICAL LATIN

Identifying specifically 'biblical' loanwords is often straightforward: words like *evangelium, angelus, episcopus* are first attested in Christian authors, and even where the earliest attestations are not actually in biblical citations, it is reasonable to assume that they have entered the language through the medium of translations. At the other end of the spectrum, there are words which are common to biblical Latin and to the wider classical language. In extreme cases, these will effectively have ceased to be loanwords: items such as *gubernare* (Greek κυβερνάω) or *poena* (ποινή) are synchronically best regarded as Latin.

In the middle, there are words attested in both classical and biblical Latin. In such cases it is not always straightforward to assign them to either class. Take, for instance, the word *canistrum*, used at

Confessions 6. 2. 2 to describe the baskets used by Monica and her pious friends in Africa to take their offerings round the graves of the martyrs. This has good biblical warrant, being used 13 times in the Vulgate to refer precisely to baskets used for ritual offerings, though at the most prominent example of the word—Pharaoh's baker's dream of the three baskets at Genesis 40:17–18—it is used in a more general sense. But it is also found in various classical writers, again with reference to baskets used for offerings—and in any case the word may be felt to be so integrated to Latin, especially with its characteristic instrument-noun suffix *–trum*, that it hardly counts as a loanword at all. Despite its relatively high frequency in biblical Latin compared with the language as a whole,[19] it is hard to see *canistrum* as more than a 'weak' case of a biblical Latin Graecism. A strong case, on the other hand, would be *collyrium*, 'eye-salve'. This word is occasionally attested in classical Latin (with a metaphorical sense, Horace *Satires* 1. 5. 30, Juvenal 6. 579; literally, often in the Elder Pliny), and occurs just once in the Scriptures: 'rub eye-salve on your eyes, that you may see' (Revelation 3:18). But this verse is then taken up by Christian authors, as offering an explanation of false belief within the Church and of unbelief outside it: the truth is perspicuous enough, and humans are naturally capable of perceiving it, so any failure to do so is the result of poor theological eyesight, fortunately treatable. Augustine's use of the image at *Confessions* 7. 8. 12 ('the troubled and darkened sight of my mind was being healed... by a stinging eye-salve, painful yet salubrious') is only one example of many (see *TLL* 3. 1668. 73ff).[20] This word is best seen as an example of distinctly Christian usage, through its prominence in a single verse.

Putative examples of biblical Graecisms must, then, be weighed as well as counted. Clearly a loanword notably more frequent in biblical than in classical Latin is more likely to appear as a biblicism; the converse does not follow; a word need occur only once in biblical Latin to have a strongly biblical flavour, provided that occurrence is

---

[19] The Perseus corpus lists just 10 examples from extra-biblical sources, to set against the 13 from the Vulgate.

[20] *Collyria* are meant to be at least mildly irritant: Caelius Aurelianus *de morbis acutis* 2. 8. 35, Vegetius, *Mulomedicina* 2. 11. 3.

prominent enough. For this reason, it is not practical to draw up a definitive list of Greek words in the *Confessions* which have been transmitted from biblical sources. We can, however, identify a fairly clear core of biblical Graecisms. A notable feature of these biblical loanwords is the sheer range of semantic areas and associations they represent. In Chapter 3 we have suggested that outside biblical contexts Augustine tends to use Greek words to express disfavour. Within biblical Latin, the picture is different. Alongside such 'positive' words as *angelus, aroma, baptismus, catechumenus, ecclesia, eleemosyne, episcopus, evangelium, hymnus, margarita,* and so on need to be set terms such as *abyssus* (the 'depths of the sea', identified in Old Testament mythology with the forces ranged against Yahweh), *blasphemia, daemon, idolum, phantasma,* all obviously negative; and of course many loanwords do not of themselves fall neatly into either camp: *apotheca, cataracta, opsonium.* Indeed, there is, if anything, a slight preponderance of 'positive' words, which runs counter to what we have observed on non-biblical Greek words.

Central to loanword studies, as we argue in Chapter 3, is the concept of substitutability: the principle that a loanword is a special interest if a 'native' word is available as an alternative. Again, however, the question of whether a native alternative exists does not always admit of a yes-or-no answer. For many of the core group of biblical loanwords, alternatives had already been tried out in earlier Latin: *nuntius* for *angelus, senior* for *presbyter, misericordia* for *eleemosyna,* for instance. Such translations did not, as a rule, catch on; by Augustine's day it would no doubt have appeared very odd to start making such substitutions in familiar biblical passages (see Burton 2000: 144–6). Only in a few cases do the alternative translations remain genuine options. *Eremus* ('wilderness') has the alternatives *desertum* and *solitudo,* but Augustine uses all three.[21] To a more limited extent, *episcopus* may be substituted by *dispensator* (both words having the sense 'administrator, official in charge'; see *TLL* 5. i. 1401. 21ff). Though this is used twice of bishops in the *Confessions* (of Alypius, 6. 9. 15; of Augustine, 10. 30. 41), it is not

[21] *Desertum* only at *Confessions* 8. 6. 15, in the phrase *deserta eremi*; *solitudo* at 8. 12. 28 (where, however, *eremus* would be too specific), and 10. 43. 70. *Eremus* is found also at 10. 31. 46.

quite a true substitute, being used also of Moses and Paul as agents of God's word, and also of any future commentator on Scripture. While the Greek term can be used unfavourably—Faustus is the Manichee *episcopus*—it is still the more frequent and clearly not under pressure from *dispensator*.[22]

There is, however, another sense in which Augustine *can* choose whether or not to employ these biblical loanwords. It seems reasonable to suggest that his biblical references are not all equally integrated to the text. Clearly, when he has set himself to comment on the statement that 'God created the great whales' (Genesis 1:21), he is effectively obliged to use the loanword *cetos* (well-attested in Latin, but largely poetic). At other times, his biblical allusions are so brief and passing that they might be seen as little more than ornamental. The *collyrium*-metaphor we have already observed. Notable too are the terms in which he describes his career moves after reconversion to Christianity in 386: He has found the 'good pearl' (*bonam margaritam*; Confessions 8. 1. 1, citing Matthew 13:45–6), and has decided to renounce the 'Chair of Lying' (*cathedra mendacii*; Confessions 8. 2. 4)—a reminiscence of Psalm 1:1 ('Blessed is the man...who has not sat in the seat of pestilence'), ingeniously recontextualized.[23]

Why should it matter to Augustine whether a word is Greek? In principle it does not matter, for two reasons. First, there is his insistence—in the *Confessions* and elsewhere—that the 'word' that matters is the inward, 'endiathetic' word (to use the Stoic terminology), rather than the way it is formulated or expressed.[24] The argument

---

[22] As *dispensator* can also translate οἰκονομός and *dispensare* οἰκονομέω, the term may also allow Augustine to refer obliquely to the doctrine of divine economy (see Chapter 7, p. 177). In anti-Manichee polemic, this doctrine (that of the continuing management of the world's affairs by God) is clearly important, but the link with the word-family of *dispensare* is not pursued (*administratio* being used at Confessions 6. 5. 8).

[23] Roberts (1989: 97) draws a suggestive parallel between the reuse of *spolia* from classical buildings in late-antique public works and the reuse of classical poetic tropes in the literature of the period. We might extend this to the use of biblical *spolia* in new literary contexts, a practice which makes particular sense within Augustine's own theory of biblical hermeneutics; for him, the biblical citations are not so much wrenched from their original context as given a new meaning, or one previously only potential or latent.

[24] Admirably set out for a general audience in *Sermon* 288; see Law (2003: 105–8) for translation and discussion.

does not follow strictly; it is possible to maintain that some languages are better means of expressing ideas (as used to be said of Greek and Latin), or at any rate certain ideas—but Augustine does not come near suggesting this, even though in the case of loanwords it might be argued with some plausibility. Both intellectually and pastorally, Augustine had no interest in trying to establish a league table of different languages. Secondly, there is his continuing debate with Jerome over the relative place of Greek and Hebrew as the language of the Old Testament. Given his preference for the Septuagint over the Hebrew as enjoying most authority within the wider Church, it made little sense for him to express any criticism of Greek as such.

In practice, of course, it did matter. High levels of Greek borrowing—and different words from those accepted in classical Latin—mark out biblical Latin; to parade these words is a clear show of acceptance of Christianity as the most appropriate mode of discourse. A fuller study of Augustine's use of Greek words is outside our present scope, but given that the mid-390s marks the end of Augustine's earlier attempts at a sort of intellectual fusion of Christianity and Platonism, it may be that the *Confessions* marks a change in the way he deploys them. More actively, his use of Greek words—like his use of rare plurals—may challenge the conventions of classical Latin. If classical Latin can admit loanwords, why should Christians not possess also a similar 'custom of speaking' (*consuetudo loquendi*)?

Finally, a note on the Greek words used to describe Manichee doctrines. We have observed that a Christian bishop can be an *episcopus* or a *dispensator*, whereas only the former is open to the Manichee. Likewise, the term *paracletus* for the Holy Spirit occurs just once in the *Confessions* (3. 6. 10), where he describes the Manichees' constant talk of the Father, Son, and Holy Spirit, 'but only so as the sound and the noise made by the tongue'—in Augustine's Stoic terminology, a *vox* rather than a *Verbum*. Several other key Manichee terms are Greek. The 'Caves of Darkness' in the Manichee cosmology are the *antra tenebrarum*. In his late-Manichee period Augustine imagines evil as a volatile substance permeating the corporeal world 'like the physical nature of air' (*sicuti est aeris corpus*; *Confessions* 5. 10. 20). (Later, borrowing Stoic ideas on the identity of God and the world, he would visualize God as infusing the world as

Biblical Idioms

light does air (*aer*), or water an enormous sponge (*spongia*; *Confessions* 7. 1. 2, 7. 5. 7—more Greek words.) Admittedly these Greek words are not especially rare in Latin. More striking, however, is the repeated use of *phantasma*, 'illusion', to describe the God in which he believed as a Jesus the Messiah not as physical realities but as mere appearances (Lieu 1985: 126–7). In biblical Latin, however, the word is used by Jesus' disciples to describe the figure they see walking on the water (Matthew 14:26, Mark 6:49), usually translated as 'ghost'. Jesus' rebuttal of this (*'ego sum'*) can thus be read by Augustine as an exemplary rebuttal of *all* docetizing understandings of himself. The Greekness of the word, shown in its orthography and morphology, is hard to miss. Most notably Greek of all are the two theological terms *monas* and *dyas*, 'the Monad' and 'the Dyad', which Augustine used in his high-Manichee phase, 'not knowing what I was saying' (*Confessions* 5. 15. 24). Such imparisyllabic Greek nouns are particularly resistant to Latin borrowing, tending to be assimilated on the basis of their accusative to the first declension (thus *lampada* < λαμπάς, *sportula* < σπυρίς, eventually *aria* < ἀήρ). *Monas* and *dyas*, then, stand out. (By contrast, the Christian Trinity is always the familiar Latin *trinitas*, never Greek *trias*.) In using Greek terminology of Manicheeism, Augustine is probably doing nothing more than the Manichees did themselves. Subtly, however, he conveys the notion that Manicheism is as adventitious and recondite linguistically as it is doctrinally.

CONCLUSIONS

The use of both non-idiomatic plurals and unusual Greek lexical items allows Augustine to signal a switch into biblical quotation, or a generally biblical register. It is unusual for one of the rare plurals or Greek words to be absolutely confined to biblical use, but the effect is cumulative; the biblical features pile up until they are recognized as such. His approach, however, is not always consistent. Rare plurals and Greek words in general tend to be associated with 'negative' vocabulary, yet Augustine is capable of showing contempt for the linguistic conventions which dictate this. It is hard to avoid the sense that some of his use is rather opportunistic.[25]

---

[25] Compare also Law (2003: 102), who notes how Augustine rejects arguments from etymology on principle, yet deploys them when he finds it expedient.

6

The Paralinguistic

INTRODUCTION

Singing, weeping, groaning, and laughter, like language itself, would all seem to be universal human activities. If speech, the outward expression of language, consists of the imposition of form on the formless rush of breath—a favourite description of Augustine's, and one with strong Neoplatonic overtones—then singing may be said to refine it still further, while laughter, weeping, and groaning all represent the reversal or undoing of form. But, like other such universals of human behaviour such as food or clothing, they tend to acquire heavy symbolic value in most if not all societies. We may agree that laughter naturally proceeds from joy, or a desire to show pleasure (as Augustine notes, solitary laughter is a rare thing)[1]—but knowing who may laugh at what and when is an acquired social skill. And it is one in which one's own behaviour is frequently harder to judge than others'. The same is true of the other activities: musical ability, for instance, is generally highly valued in our society, but there are quite strict conditions on where, when, and how even a very able singer should sing. Augustine's attitude towards these 'paralinguistic' phenomena on the borders of language may help us understand his attitude towards language proper.[2] His views on these

---

[1] On the triggers for laughter, see Provine (2000: 23–53). Provine rebuts the general belief that laughter is necessarily or primarily the product of amusement or humour. For a stimulating combination of psychological and intellectual-historical approaches to 'the meanings of emotion', see Neu (2000, especially 14–40 on weeping).

[2] The definition of the paralinguistic assumed here will be: 'Any vocalized expression of an opinion, attitude, or emotion, either superimposed upon or apart from a purely verbal utterance.' This definition is not wholly satisfactory (where, for

matters do not, of course, spring entirely from his own head. He is influenced, more or less directly, by some eight hundred years of philosophical reflection, as well as by the less reflective traditions in Greek and Roman society, all of which has also fed into the thought and practice of the Christian church.

Particularly important for Augustine is the Christian doctrine of the Incarnation of the Son and Word of God in the human Jesus of Nazareth.[3] Augustine's implicit starting point is that any action ascribed to Jesus in the canonical Gospels is both accurately reported and fully and perfectly human. In practice, however, the Gospels' accounts of Jesus' behaviour do not offer the simple template that these axioms would suggest. There are incidents in Jesus' life which are nowhere described but which may be presumed (did he cry as a baby, for instance?);[4] incidents which are not described and on which presumptions are harder to make (did he laugh?); incidents where the evangelists' accounts are genuinely ambiguous (did he sing?); and incidents where his actions may have been appropriate only in response to certain conditions (as, for instance, when he wept at Lazarus' tomb). As we will see, there are also differences of emphasis between the various evangelists in their attitude towards emotional

instance, does the 'purely verbal' stop and the 'superimposed' element begin?), and it may be helpful to compare the formulation in Lateiner (1995: xix) on which it is based: 'Any communicable emotion or communicative event produced by the vocal apparatus except for the words themselves...'. I have dropped the element of 'communication', since one may laugh, cry, etc. to one's self; I have also modified Lateiner's clause 'except for the words themselves' on the basis that the manner of delivery of words may also be considered paralinguistic.

[3] For a discussion on how the Incarnation 'fell heir to both the tools and the difficulties with which philosophers had been dealing for centuries', see Miles (1979), especially 79–97.

[4] Popular piety remains divided on this. A typical English-language Christmas carol service may well contain the statements that Jesus knew tears and smiles and that he made no crying. Both statements are clearly intended to be in some sense theological as well as historical. At the other end of the intellectual spectrum, it may be instructive to consider the great biblical scholar G. B. Caird's observation that Jesus is portrayed as 'displaying the full range of human emotions. He suffered hunger, thirst, fatigue, anger, sorrow, disappointment, pity, joy, exhilaration' (Caird and Hurst 1994: 288). Of these nine, the first three are more physical sensations than emotions; joy and exhilaration are hard to distinguish, and Jesus' 'disappointment', while a plausible inference, is not quite directly warranted by the Gospel accounts. Caird no less than the hymnographers is clearly driven by theological motives.

display. And moreover, Christian exegetes had to deal also with various references towards displays of emotion outside the Gospels. One interesting case—to anticipate our discussion—involves the use of musical instruments in worship. Clearly this practice was frequent in Old Testament times; but was it still acceptable, at least in principle, in Christian times, or was it only ever a provisional concession to the weakness of the unregenerate flesh? Many Christian exegetes seem to have thought it was, but a definitive answer proved elusive.

But the Incarnation raises another moral issue. Alongside the question of whether and how far a human should ideally feel or express emotion is the question of how far a *god* should do so. Classical philosophers were broadly united in the view that gods should be exempt from, or above, emotion. Contrast, for instance, the account of how Zeus wept over his son Sarpedon's impending death in the pre-classical *Iliad* (16. 458–61), with Hercules' tears over the impending death of the young warrior Pallas (*Aeneid* 10. 464–72), for which he is rebuked by Jupiter; the deified hero retains his human emotionality, which the supreme god sympathetically rebukes.[5] This classical view is flatly at odds with the picture Augustine would have found in the Old Testament, where God is not infrequently represented as showing emotional states: love, even favouritism; anger; jealously; even changing his mind. This is clearly an important issue for Augustine in the *Confessions*, since he addresses it early on:

Confessions 1. 4. 4: You love, but do not seethe with passion; you are jealous, yet have no anxieties; you are angry, yet calm; you repent, but do not regret; you change your actions without changing your plan.

Amas nec aestuas, zelas et securus es, paenitet te et non doles, irasceris et tranquillus es, opera mutas nec mutas consilium.

---

[5] A more detailed comparison is instructive: Zeus is likewise rebuked by Hera, but only because his plan to snatch Sarpedon out of the battle might set a precedent to be followed by other gods in respect of their children; Jupiter does allude to the death of Sarpedon, 'my own offspring', but with no direct reference to its emotional effect on him. Hercules himself shows an interesting combination of paralinguistic responses: he 'suppresses a great groan deep in his chest, and pours out empty tears' (*magnumque sub imo/corde premit gemitum, lacrimasque effundit inanes*).

The rhetoric is, however, not entirely convincing, and Augustine does not make any concerted attempt to demonstrate how these different states can coexist.

First, a note on terminology. The Greek term for states such as anger, fear, hope, πάθος is traditionally translated into English as *passion*, following the Latin *passio*. But Latin itself has other translations also, notably *affectus, perturbatio, motus (animi)*. All of these words—or more usually their related verbs, *afficere, (per)turbare, movere*—are also in everyday, non-technical use, with the result that it is not always easy to identify whether a given usage is meant in the technical sense or not; any point on the continuum is possible. The same is true, in fact, of the Greek πάθος and its cognate verb πάσχω. The English word *passion* is, therefore, problematic, not only because in ordinary use it refers narrowly either to sexual love or (less often) to the crucifixion of Jesus, but also because such psychological states as anger, hope, and so on, are normally referred to as *emotions*. Yet *emotion* is not traditionally used as a translation of πάθος. This is probably the result in part of scholarly conservatism, and in part of a well-founded desire to keep the Greek notion of 'the passions' separate from the post-Romantic notion of 'the emotions' as something instinctive, even exalted (though the recent back-formation *to emote* is usually pejorative). The Greek πάθος and πάσχω, in contrast, always imply a degree of defeat; the human subject has 'had something happen' which compromises his or her free moral independence. If we admit that *emotion* is not an ideal translation of πάθος, we should also allow that *passion* is itself unsatisfactory in a different way. In the following discussion, the term 'emotion' will be used; not without reservation, but with the sense that in using an everyday word with a range of technical and non-technical meanings, we may be closer to both Greek and Latin practice.[6]

---

[6] In recent years some writers have started to use the words 'feeling' and 'to feel' as translations of Greek πάθος and πάσχω. These translations have much to commend them; they are ordinary English words, and the noun and verb form a transparent pair (whereas there is no obvious verb corresponding to the noun 'passion', and 'to emote' presents difficulties of its own); if they have a drawback apart from the fact they are not (as yet) current in this sense, it is the need to distinguish psychological 'feelings' from physical 'sensations'.

The Paralinguistic

Weeping and groaning may fairly be regarded as expressions of emotion, albeit with the distinction that weeping may proceed from intense feelings of grief or joy. Attitudes towards emotions in ancient philosophy have been extensively studied, though generally in isolation from the paralinguistic *expression* of emotion (a distinction which is often blurred); and many of the best studies still perpetuate the divide between 'classical' and 'Christian' thought-worlds.[7]

SINGING

Incidents involving singing, though not frequent in the *Confessions*, occupy some prominent positions in the work.[8] Augustine's attitude towards this particular paralinguistic phenomenon are complex, and need to be understood with the tradition of discourse on the role of music in the Christian life, especially in church.[9] This in turn is part of a wider discourse in the Graeco-Roman world on the social and psychological effects of music. Broadly speaking, the classical Greek tradition places a positive value on music as a suitable accomplishment for the male citizen. Guests at the elite symposium are expected to sing; young men of sufficient means are expected to study lyre-playing.[10] These views are, of course, open to qualification. Plato presents Socrates as believing that only uneducated guests at a symposium need professional musicians to make up for their own

---

[7] On the emotions in ancient philosophy, see the volumes of studies edited by Sihvola and Engberg-Pedersen (1998, with a useful essay by Emilsson on Plotinus), by Brunschwig and Nussbaum (1993), and by Braund and Gill (1997). The admirable essay by Erskine in Braund and Gill happens to illustrate the slippage between emotion and its expression perfectly. For an exemplary inclusion of Christian thinkers within the classical tradition, see Sorabji (2000).

[8] On singing as a human phenomenon, see now the fascinating work of Mithen (2005). Mithen broadly endorses the view of music and language evolving together as a 'musilanguage', with language preserving various features of their common origin.

[9] The literature on the history of church music is considerable. Useful orientation may be had from Ferguson in Ferguson (1997: 787–90); Quasten (1983) is a standard in-depth work; McKinnon (1987) is a valuable collection of sources in translation. On ancient music in general, see the essay and bibliography of Barker (1996).

[10] See, for example, the classic account of Marrou (1965: 206–17); see also references in Maas and Snyder (1989: 166, 241).

lack of intelligent conversation (*Protagoras* 347D–348A); admittedly not an argument against music as such, this still represents one end of a debate on the relative place of speech and music which continues down to Augustine's day. Most famously, Plato lays down that in his ideal state certain musical modes and instruments are to be banished because of their deleterious effect on the human psyche (*Republic* 397A–400E). This Platonic–Pythagorean tradition of speculation on the effect of music on the personality is not without its critics.[11] A third-century BC Egyptian papyrus preserves text, tentatively dated a century or more earlier, which is thoroughly scathing about professors of musical-ethical theories. The Epicurean Philodemus, a contemporary of Cicero's, is similarly dismissive. But notwithstanding such critiques, the intimate link between music and morality becomes something of a commonplace in later antiquity. The most fully worked-out account of the relationship between music and morality is found in Book 2 of Aristides Quintilianus' work *On Music* (perhaps around AD 300). Music, says Quintilianus, acts on the irrational part of the soul as philosophy does on the rational; it is, therefore, indispensable for the education of children, in whom the faculty of reason is still dormant.[12] The Neoplatonist Iamblichus (around AD 245–325) tells how Pythagoras practiced a regime of musical self-therapy every spring, sitting in the middle of a circle of skilled lyre-players and himself beating time for them (*Vita Pythagorae* 110–11). Similar therapy could even be used on others: meeting the young son of one Taorminian on a drunken rampage with his friends one night, Pythagoras instructed their flute-player to play a song with a spondaic rhythm (de *Vita Pythagorae* 111); they sobered up at once, and abandoned their plan to torch the house of the young man's rival in love. Christian intellectuals are no less keen than pagans to play up the link between the metaphysical, the natural, and the moral order. Basil the Great (around AD 330–379) repeats a version of the Pythagoras story (*Address to Young Men* 6), as does (on the Latin side) Boethius (around AD 480–524); Boethius indeed

---

[11] On the musical-ethical tradition in general, see Anderson (1966); on the Hibeh musical papyrus and on Philodemus in particular, pages 147–76.

[12] See Aristides Quintilianus 2. 3, with notes in the translation of Mathieson (1983).

goes beyond, beginning his work *On Music* with a defence of the moral value of music not only for children and young people but even for the elderly. As a thinker with strong roots in Neoplatonism and Pythagoreanism, Augustine inherited this sense of the link between mathematics and music and wider theories on the cosmos and the human condition. As a Latin-speaker, he inherited a culture which in practical terms valued music much less highly than it was in the Greek East; arguably, indeed, Latin has a stronger distinction between speech and singing, in that musical pitch is an essential component of the Greek system of accentuation, whereas in Latin its place is taken by the stress-accent.[13] Lyre-playing was not part of the standard Roman school curriculum; Macrobius cites the second-century BC hero and philhellene Scipio Aemilianus on the dishonourable nature of this accomplishment, 'which our ancestors decreed should be held reprehensible among the free-born' (*Saturnalia* 3. 14. 7).[14] The Roman elite dinner party was not a symposium in the Greek sense; Cicero (*Brutus* 75) could report the Elder Cato's account of how individual diners used to sing the praises of great heroes over dinner; but if this custom had ever existed, it had lapsed long before Cato's day.[15] Cicero's own *de Re Publica* seems to have contained a passage, now lost, in which one of the interlocutors railed against the influence of musicians on the body politic.[16] Some of the more famous passages in Latin literature touch upon the ambiguous cultural status (and gender politics) of singing. Sallust's Sempronia (*Catiline* 25) could 'sing to the lyre (*psallere*) and dance more elegantly than is necessary for a virtuous woman'—the obviously Greek verb (perhaps no more

---

[13] See Allen (1974: 106–8); though of course Latin sentence-patterns are likely to have had distinct pitch contours, according to the type of sentence (statement, question, command, wish, exclamation) and the pragmatics of the individual utterance.

[14] Reference from Marrou (1965: 363). This is the only reference in the 600-plus pages of Marrou's study of ancient education to music in the Roman world. Thomas Habinek's *Roman Song* (Baltimore, ML: Johns Hopkins, 2005) *non vidi*; this is a study of how *carmen* in its widest sense functioned to 'organiz[e] relations of power at every level of society'.

[15] Compare also Quintilian's comments on how boys should be taught to read poetry aloud: not like prose, but still in a suitably masculine way, 'not melting into a song and with an effeminate inflection' (*canticum dissolute nec plasmate... effeminate*); *Institutio* 1. 33. 8.

[16] Summarized in Aristides Quintilianus 2. 6.

than 'play the lyre') is striking. The Younger Pliny tells how his young wife Calpurnia had learnt several of his poems by heart and set them to the *cithara*—she had, he says, no professional instructor (*artifice aliquo*) but was taught by love, 'which is the best teacher' (*Epistula* 4. 19. 4); certainly better, one assumes, than a hired Greek. Pliny clearly regards this performance—amateurish, done by a woman, in private—with some complacency; but for a man to aspire to do the same, in public, to a professional quality, was quite another matter. And Pliny's contemporary Suetonius gives an account of the Emperor Nero's public performances as a singer and lyre-player; performances which were immediately recognized as conscious—and excessive—philhellenism. And *declassé* too; in his famous last words *qualis artifex pereo* ('what a loss to the profession'; Suetonius, *Nero* 49. 1), Nero's self-characterization as an *artifex*, though usually translated as 'artist', may equally suggest 'artisan, tradesman', a player rather than a gentleman.

And Augustine had inherited the Christian tradition also. Within this tradition, the Book of Psalms alone, with its frequent and unequivocal injunctions to sing and make melody on various instruments, might seem to put the propriety of all forms of music beyond doubt. Christian practice, however, followed that of the contemporary Jewish synagogue in encouraging singing, while eschewing instrumental music, which Christian writers, with few exceptions, tend to regard as belonging firmly to the pagan world. Jerome's advice to the mother of the infant Paula that she should be brought up not to know what the flute, lyre, and cithara are for (*Epistula* 107. 8) may represent an extreme statement of this point of view, but it is certainly the case that biblical references to the musical instrument tend to be allegorized rather than read literally.[17] Allegories, metaphors, and comparisons involving musical instruments are, in themselves, nothing new; according to one calculation, 'fully one-third of the fourth-century [BC] references to the [stringed] instruments are found in the context of various philosophical analogies' (Maas and Snyder 1989: 166). In Christian writers of the fourth century AD, however, the figure is probably higher still. Augustine himself in the

---

[17] On the anti-instrumental polemic, see Quasten (1983: 62–75). For a summary of the principal allegorizations, with references, see Ferguson in Ferguson (1997: 789).

Confessions exemplifies this, referring to the psaltery, the 'instrument of ten strings', as a metaphor for the Ten Commandments (*Confessions* 3. 8. 16), but never unequivocally in the literal sense.[18] This tendency is observable among both Greek and Latin writers, though the Latinists have the advantage that many of the terms for the various instruments occurring in the Old Testament—*cithara, cymbalum, lyra, organum, psalterium, tympanum*—are transparently Greek, and of themselves have an air of foreignness and (often) of undesirability.[19]

As we have noted, the Christian church is generally more positive about singing than about instrumental music. Church practice did indeed sanction singing as part of the public liturgy. It is recommended—as instrumental music is not—at various points in the New Testament.[20] But Augustine's anxious self-examination in the *Confessions* also may be seen as part of a wider debate, and one which was perhaps especially vigorous in his own lifetime. Augustine's older contemporary Nicetas of Remesiana (*circa* 335–414), a correspondent of Paulinus of Nola, found it necessary to write an eminently sensible essay on the benefits of hymnody, possibly motivated in part by the decision of the Synod of Laodicea of 360 to restrict singing in church to the 'regular psalms-singers' in the gallery.[21] In his preface, Nicetas sets out his opposition to those who think singing hymns and psalms is 'unnecessary and inappropriate to divine service'; 'they think that what is said in the heart is enough, and that to express it with one's tongue is self-indulgent' (*sufficere enim putant quod corde dicitur, lascivum esse si hoc lingua proferatur*; *de Psalmodiae Bono* 2).[22] Nicetas had grounds for his concern. Consider, for instance, how two other

[18] The *psalterium* seized by Evodius at Monica's death is almost certainly a psalm-book instead; see discussion below, and in Chapter 4. On Augustine's use of the *cithara* as a symbol, see van Deusen (1989: 201–51).

[19] On the cultural associations of Greek words, see Chapters 3 and 5. It was perhaps especially providential that all these words are *recognizably* Greek in their spelling or pronunciation.

[20] Most clearly at Ephesians 5:19, Colossians 3:15, James 5:13; for a fuller census, see McKinnon (1987: 12–17); useful summary of Western hymnody in Palmer (1989: 58–67).

[21] The standard work on Nicetas remains Burn (1905); on the Synod of Laodicea, see page xci.

[22] Even Nicetas allegorized David's *cithara*, though: it was 'a type of the Cross of Christ, being made of wood and having sinews stretched out upon it' (*de psalmodiae bono* 4).

contemporary writers treat the one reference in the Gospels to Jesus' singing. At Matthew 26:30 (Mark 14:26) the Last Supper party, having completed their meal, 'sang a hymn and went out towards Mount Olivet'. In his commentary on Matthew, Hilary of Poitiers glosses these words by saying that the disciples were 'borne up with common joy and exultation to the heavenly glory'. Jerome makes a similar observation in *his* commentary: 'he who has been filled with the Saviour's bread and drunk with his cup may in this way praise the Lord and climb up Mount Olivet, where there is refreshment after toil, solace after grief, and knowledge of the true light.' Neither writer denies that singing took place. But both tend instinctively to internalize the singing, with reference to the spiritual life of the singer rather than the outward sound. Jerome's interpretation, by focussing on the disciples as the praisers and 'the Lord' as the object of praise, even leaves open the question of whether Jesus himself joined in the hymn; the Latin *hymno dicto*, like the Greek ὑμνήσαντες and the English 'they sang...', leaves both options open.[23]

Augustine himself, though he does not comment on this passage, repeatedly shows in his exposition of the Psalms a similar tendency to spiritualize the act of singing. Take, for example, his exposition of the title of Psalm 94, 'the praise of a song' (*laus cantici*, as striking a phrase in Latin as in English). This, he notes, 'signifies both gladness, as it is a song, and devoutness, as it is praise... let us both praise, then, and sing; that is to say, let us praise with gladness and joy' (*cum hilaritate et cum laetitia laudemus*; *Enarrationes in Psalmos* 94. 1). The slippage from outward singing to inner rejoicing is very close to what we have seen in Hilary and Jerome. In commenting on the opening words of the following Psalm ('Sing to the Lord a new song; sing to the Lord, every land'), Augustine goes further: 'If "every land" "sings a new song", it is thereby edified as it sings; the singing itself is edification, provided it does not sing what is old... Suppose you love, and are silent: your love is the voice that goes to God, your love itself is the "new song"' (*Enarrationes in Psalmos* 95. 2).

---

[23] Note that *dicere* is often used of singing (with *carmen, numerus, hymnus* etc. specified as the object), and should not be taken to refer to spoken recitation; *Thesaurus Linguae Latinae* 5. 1. 977. 65ff.

The Paralinguistic 143

Analogues for such internalizations of the act of singing may be found in the Neoplatonist tradition. Porphyry (*de Abstinentia* 2. 6. 34) recommends silent contemplation as the most appropriate worship for the supreme god; for the lesser, 'intelligible' gods, 'hymn-singing in words' should be added.[24] In Christian circles, such internalizations may go no further than the Apostle Paul's injunction to 'sing with the spirit and with the mind, too' (*psallam spiritu, psallam et mente*; 1 Corinthians 14:15); but—as Nicetas notes—they sometimes did. Augustine, then, like Hilary and Jerome, do not criticize singing as such. Even the austere Jerome recommends that little Paula should sing hymns at set hours (while warning against allowing her a confidante 'able to warble sweet songs in a liquid voice').[25] But Augustine has his reservations. Although, as we will see, these do focus on the effect of music on the singer's or hearer's psychological balance, we should note first another concern of his: that singing may lead to the empty repetition of words without any thought for their content. The classic example of this is in his dialogue *De Ordine* of 386, where the enthusiastic young convertite Licentius scandalizes Augustine's mother Monica by his constant singing, 'in cheerful parrot-fashion' (*laete et garrule*),[26] of the psalm-verse, 'Turn us around, O Lord' (Psalm 79:8)—even when relieving himself (*De Ordine* 1. 8. 22). Licentius is allowed the last word, but Monica is clearly moral centre of the dialogue, and it is her authority which conditions our response.[27]

Within the *Confessions*, there are three main passages which cover singing.[28] Two of these occur in mini-biography of Monica in Book 9. The first of these is brief and uncomplicated. While Augustine is working at Milan, the Catholic community comes under threat from the Arian Justina, mother of the boy-emperor Valentinian. Bishop Ambrose counters this by introducing the oriental custom of antiphonal psalm-singing (with the two halves of the congregation singing

---

[24] Translation from Clark (2000: 69), to whom I owe—with much else—this reference.
[25] Jerome, *Epistle* 107. 9 (translation F. A. Wright).
[26] On Augustine's use of *garrire* to refer to mindless speech, see Chapter 1.
[27] See now the excellent discussion in Conybeare, *The Irrational Augustine* (2006).
[28] Our focus here is confined to the *Confessions*, but for a heartfelt account of Augustine's experiences trying to inculcate enthusiastic, intelligent singing into his congregation, see van der Meer (1983: 325–37).

alternate verses) (*Confessions* 9. 7. 15). This is a success as an emergency measure, and as a result becomes current throughout the west. The second passage is fuller and more complex. It comes in one of the great set-pieces of the *Confessions*, the death of Monica in Book 9. Augustine describes the scene:

Confessions 9. 12. 29–31: The child Adeodatus burst into tears and was silenced by the rest of us. In this way something childish in me, something which wavered on the edge of tears, was silenced also by the adult voice of my heart... Evodius seized a psalm-book and began to sing a psalm, to which all of us in the house made the response, 'Mercy and judgement shall I sing unto thee, o Lord'...I then gave a disquisition suitable to the occasion...

...*puer Adeodatus exclamavit in planctu atque ab omnibus nobis coercitus tacuit. hoc modo etiam meum quiddam puerile, quod labebatur in fletus, iuvenali voce cordis coercebatur et tacebat...psalterium arripuit Evodius et cantare coepit psalmum, cui respondebamus omnis domus 'misericordiam et iudicium cantabo tibi domine'...ego...quod erat tempori congruum disputabam.*

This passage is remarkable not least for its emphasis on the correct use of language and paralinguistic. Augustine's heart speaks with an 'adult voice', *iuvenali voce*; while the 15-year-old Adeodatus still has 'something childish' about him, *quiddam puerile*, and is compelled (rather than persuaded) by his elders to be silent. The word *auctoritas* is not used here, but the principle is clearly at work, and its ambiguity is nicely illustrated; it is not ideal, but it is the best restraint available given that Adeodatus had not reached the full adult exercise of reason.

Next, Evodius seizes the *psalterium* (*psalterium arripuit*); probably, as O'Donnell comments, a psalm-book rather than a psaltery.[29] The verb *arripere* offers a fascinating case study to students of Christian Latin. It seems to occur with particular frequency in the Christian authors; and whereas in classical Latin it may refer to good or bad actions, its connotations in Christian authors are almost

---

[29] As we have noted, the psaltery has a rich grammar of symbolic associations in Christian writings of this period, but our sources are unanimous that it is the figurative rather than the literal psaltery which matters. Incidents involving seizing on psalm-books, however, are more common; see following note.

universally good, denoting decisive spiritual actions. In the *Confessions* it occurs outside this passage four times, the object being once the contemplative life (8. 6. 15) and three times the Scriptures (7. 21. 27, 8. 10. 24). The nature of the singing is important, too. First there are the singers: the man Augustine and his friends, the young Adeodatus, and the consecrate virgins living in the house. It is almost an enactment of the Psalmist's admonition, 'Praise the Lord, men in your prime, virgins, old men, and boys' (*iuvenes et virgines senes cum pueris*; Psalm 148:12).[30] The responsorial nature of the singing also has its symbolism. A constant theme of early Christian writers on church music is the univocal (and presumably unanimous) response given by the congregation.[31] Augustine's own disputation, though a solo performance, has a similarly dialogic character (*disputatio* = ὁ διάλογος). The content of the individual psalm is, of course, important too. As O'Donnell (1992. iii. 141) points out, Augustine's citation of the response ('Mercy and judgement...') is meant to recall the whole of Psalm 100 of which it is a part. The words of the response themselves are self-evidently appropriate: the deceased Monica is commended to the mercy as well as the judgement of God. The main body of Psalm—the singer's assertion of his or her righteous way of life, whose influence ripples out from the domestic milieu (*in medio domus meae*) at the beginning of the Psalm to the wider public space of the city (*civitate*) by the end—could, as O'Donnell says, be put into Monica's own mouth, if humility permitted. But the opening words of the Psalm also merit attention: 'Mercy and judgement *shall I sing* unto thee, o Lord; *I shall sing and understand...*' (*psallam et intellegam*). It would be glib to describe

---

[30] There are similarities here with the account of Gregory of Nyssa (around AD 330–395) of his explicit choreography of the mourners at the death of his and Basil's sister Macrina (*Vita Macrina*e 33; McKinnon 1987: 73–4); though unlike Monica's wake, Macrina's is assimilated on the one hand to the burial customs of the martyrs and on the other to the Greek civic rituals of the chorus. On music in pagan and Christian death customs, see Quasten (1983: 160–7); on unison singing among mixed congregations of young and old, men and women, see Ferguson (1997: 787).

[31] See Quasten (1983: 66–72) for an extensive collection of references to univocal singing in the second and third centuries. This rhetoric of univocalism is apparently retained after the rise of responsorial singing. Indeed, the simple congregational response is an ideal vehicle for univocalism, making minimal demands on the singers' memory and musical talent.

this as pure literary self-referentiality ('a song about singing'). None the less, this introduction is a striking miniaturization of the widespread Christian concern, shared by Augustine, about the proper use of the human voice in liturgy.

But despite his disputation, Augustine is still grief-stricken. Not satisfied with the consolation of philosophy, he also seeks the consolation of bathing, having 'heard that baths are so called because in Greek they are called *balania*, on the ground that they drive cares from the mind' (βάλλει τὰ ἄνια) (*audieram inde balneis nomen inditum, quia graeci balanion dixerint, quod anxietatem pellat ex animo*). The appeal to etymology itself is reminiscent of those found in the older traditions of Latin linguistic theory, in particular Books 2–7 of Varro's *de Lingua Latina*.[32] But it is a remarkable aberration on Augustine's part to have thought that a visit to the baths would help, solely on the basis of a Greek etymology. Everything we have seen so far in the *Confessions* suggests a strong sense of the arbitrary nature of language, and a healthy disrespect for Greek cultural supremacists. At all events, it proves unhelpful: a misunderstanding not only of the nature of baths, but also of language: 'I bathed, and was the same as before I had bathed' (*Confessions* 9. 12. 32).

et nunc, domine, confiteor tibi in litteris: legat qui volet, et interpretetur ut volet, et si peccatum invenerit, flevisse me matrem exigua parte horae.... non inrideat sed potius... pro peccatis meis fleat ipse...

After his bath, Augustine sleeps, then wakes up to find his grief in large part soothed. At this point he remembers Ambrose's hymn:

> O God, creator of all things,
> controller of the sky, who clothes
> day with glorious radiance,
> night with the blessing of sleep,
> that rest may ease the limbs,
> restoring them to useful labour,
> might relieve weary minds
> and free the anxious from sorrow...

---

[32] Note in particular the Varronian technical use of *indere* 'to put a name' on something; originally a semantic extension on the basis of ἐπιτίθημι, and by Augustine's day apparently obsolete except in this sense.

> *deus, creator omnium*
> *polique rector, vestiens*
> *diem decoro lumine,*
> *noctem soporis gratia,*
> *artus solutos ut quies*
> *reddat laboris usui*
> *mentesque fessas allevet*
> *luctuque solvat anxios...*

Thoughts of Monica might in any case have prompted recollections of her time at Milan, of the respect she and Ambrose entertained for each other, and for her constant attendance at his anti-Arian psalm vigils. But this hymn is in other respects a key intertext for our reading of the *Confessions* more generally. The first line is both a straightforward Biblical citation, and a contradiction of the position Augustine had held as a Manichee; all creation is the work of a single good God. It is also a line which he had already discussed in the *de Musica* (6. 2. 2 and following). There it had served as the departure point for the classic Neoplatonic ascent from the world of the senses to the world of ideas. Our recognition, Augustine argues, of the regular iambic rhythm of the verse comes not through our physical perception of the sounds, but ultimately from an innate recognition of the mathematical ratios involved—a recognition which is not the peculiar preserve of those with a particular training in metrics, and which we naturally find pleasurable. This hymn, then, reminds us again of the picture Augustine has consistently painted in the *Confessions* of his mother as a natural intellectual in the true sense; her perception of the rhythm of Ambrose's hymn would have been no less genuine than Augustine's. Notable here is his emphasis on the form of verse and music as lying within the hearer's memory, rather than in the externals of their performance, a theme also pursued—with the same illustration—in Book 11 of the *Confessions*. The consolation Augustine derives from the hymn comes not from a performance of it (though that would require recollection), but from the recollection alone (*recordatus sum*).

In addition to these anecdotal accounts of the power of music, Augustine also offers in Book 10 a more cautious, theoretical analysis of its place in divine service. Here he cites his own experience of becoming too absorbed with the purely musical experience of church music—that is, singing—to the point where he ceases to pay attention to the words:

Confessions 10. 33. 50: From time to time, I am unduly cautious of this very fallacy, and make the mistake of being too austere... to the extent that I would have removed from my ears all the melody of the sweet tunes which accompany the Psalms of David, and from the ears of the Church itself. Then it appears to me safer to do what I remember being told many times that Athanasius of Alexandria did: he had his reader intone the psalm with such a moderate vocal inflection that he seemed to be reciting rather than chanting... I am increasingly led to profess the opinion—though not beyond reconsideration—that the custom of singing in church is a good one... but when it happens that the chanting affects me more than the subject-matter of the chanting, then I confess I have sinned and deserve punishment...

Aliquando autem hanc ipsam fallaciam immoderatius cavens erro nimia severitate... ut melos omne cantilenarum suavium, quibus Davidicum psalterium frequentatur, ab auribus meis removeri velim atque ipsius ecclesiae, tutiusque mihi videtur, quod de Alexandrino episcopo Athanasio saepe mihi dictum commemini, qui tam modico flexu vocis faciebat sonare lectorem psalmi, ut pronuntianti vicinior esset quam canenti... magisque adducor non quidem irretractabilem sententiam proferens cantandi consuetudinem approbare in ecclesia... tamen cum mihi accidit, ut me amplius cantus quam res, quae canitur, moveat, poenaliter me peccare confiteor...

The language here is carefully chosen. The art of music is often described formally as 'skill in modulation' (*peritia modulandi*) or similar, the standard formula in Augustine's own *de Musica*. *Modus*—metre, proportion, measure, due limit—is to be observed both in the 'moderate inflection' (*modico flexu*) of the voice and in one's wariness about the charms of music; one should not be 'unduly cautious' (*immoderatius cavens*) in one's attitude. And the unusual expression *melos cantilenarum* echoes, perhaps unconsciously, a similar phrase in Licentius' lavatory episode in the *de Ordine* (*cantilenae modum... melos inusitatum*). The Greek term *melos* is rather unusual in Latin.[33] While it can simply be an elevated synonym for ordinary Latin words for a piece of music, it also

---

[33] As indeed are Greek neuters in -ος generally, not lending themselves easily to Latin inflectional patterns.

The Paralinguistic

bears the semi-technical sense of 'melody' as opposed to 'rhythm'. In Neoplatonist musicology, the melody is the 'feminine' matter, 'lacking in energy and form' (ἀνενέργητόν... καὶ ἀσχημάτιστον; Aristides Quintilianus 1. 19), which is 'moulded and set in ordered motion' by the 'masculine' rhythm.[34] Augustine's language also suggests an uncertainty about the degree of conscious control he has over his response to music. Excessive delight in music for its own sake, he says, 'happens to me' (*accidit mihi*); it is the music that is the subject of the action (*moveat*), rather than Augustine himself. Ostensibly a rather crude piece of self-exculpation, this form of words may instead reflect Augustine's concern with the problem of self-knowledge and of identifying the true seat of his wishes; his response to music reflects in some way his true will, rather than the product of consciously formed resolution. This concern over alienation from one's self surfaces repeatedly in the *Confessions*; it is only God who is 'the Same'.

If Augustine often shows the same concerns as many of his contemporaries about the dangers of mindless singing, he is—in his own life, as recalled in the *Confessions*—drawn overall to a positive evaluation. Within a Neoplatonist context, one might expect the physical performance of music to be seen as a lesser, material rendering of the ideal mathematical proportions which constitute true music. While Augustine nowhere rejects this as a theoretical position, his endorsement of it seems in practice to be qualified by three factors. As a lapsed Manichee, he is always eager to emphasize the goodness of the created world; unheard melodies may be sweeter, but as physical creatures we may be led to perceive them through those we do hear. Secondly, there is apparently the influence of his mother. The three specific examples of singing in the *Confessions* are all associated with her, and are all positive in their associations.

Thirdly, there are the pastoral demands of the episcopate, which Augustine had assumed since writing the *de Musica*; music can, of course, both be an inducement to churchgoing and a source of moral instruction once there. Augustine is aware of how music can be used

---

[34] For a Latin formulation, compare Martianus Capella 9. 955: 'melody is the raw material, rhythm gives form to the sounds' (*melos materies est... rhythmus... formam sonis praestat*).

to inculcate certain messages or values, not necessarily with the rational assent of the person in question. We first encounter it in his description of his arithmetic lessons at school, where he observes how 'one and one are two, two and two are four' was an *odiosa cantio*, a nasty little song.[35] Augustine's chosen word for 'song', *cantio*, is probably by his day the ordinary current term (compare the ordinary Western Romance words: French *chanson*, Italian *canzone*, Spanish *canción*); this development may well have occurred concurrently with the specialization of the classical *carmen* in the sense of 'magic charm'. However, there is some evidence of a tendency among some Christian authors to reserve it for unfavourable contexts.[36] So alongside examples of *cantio* referring to the Psalms of David, we find also two examples of *obscaenae cantiones* in Arnobius, *meretriciae cantiones* in Eustathius, *vinolenta cantio* in Augustine himself. Later, his pupil and friend Alypius has great difficulty renouncing the path through the world which his parents had charmed into him (*incantatam*; Confessions 6. 8. 13). Though the verb *incantare* usually has unfavourable connotations—'to bewitch, charm'—Augustine himself occasionally uses it positively, with objects that are 'unmistakably divine and good' (O'Donnell 1992. ii: 365). The first martyr, Stephen, for instance, 'charmed the truth' (*veritatem incantabat*) into his persecutors, 'as it were to minds that were darkened' (*tamquam tenebrosis mentibus*). Similarly, Alypius attempts to 'sing into' Augustine (*cantans*; Confessions 6. 12. 21) his belief that their planned philosophical community will work only if women are excluded.

---

[35] The 'popular' character of *cantio* as opposed to *carmen* does not, of course, in itself mean that the word necessarily had pejorative connotations. However, the evidence of the relevant entry in the *Thesaurus Linguae Latinae* (III. 286. 75ff) suggests that alongside a neutral sense ('song') there was a tendency among some Christian authors to reserve it for unfavourable contexts. So alongside examples of *cantio* referring to the Psalms of David, we find also two examples of *obscaenae cantiones* in Arnobius, *meretriciae cantiones* in Eustathius, *vinolenta cantio* in Augustine himself.

[36] See *Thesaurus Linguae Latinae* (III. 286. 75ff). *Cantio* occurs only once in the Vulgate (Psalm 136. 3, where it might be interpreted as contemptuous). Biblical (and so Christian Latin) tends to use *canticum* or *psalmus* as the usual words for 'song', a word quite unusual in classical Latin (177 of the 192 examples in the Perseus corpus come from the Vulgate). This neatly avoids both the popular (and sub-literary?) *cantio* and the potentially ambiguous *carmen*.

The Paralinguistic

While these usages of *cantare* and *incantare* are obviously metaphorical, the metaphor does not seem to be a dead one. Moreover, the idea that music can instil moral habits can be seen as an extension of the view of music found in Aristides Quintilianus (2. 16): that it is the best medium of instruction of children, whose rational faculty is still dormant and who need to be taught by pleasure and habituation. Augustine's repeated emphasis on the importance of pleasure in education may be set within a Christian framework. As we have noted in Chapter 5, delight is the *Leitmotif* of the *Confessions*, and Augustine has his proof-texts to hand for this. It is also, however, a view with well-established Neoplatonist antecedents.

CLASSICAL ATTITUDES TOWARDS WEEPING

In Hellenistic philosophy, two strains of thought on the emotions become particularly influential. Stoic philosophers regard all πάθη as bad, things to be avoided by the wise man.[37] The Peripatetic school, however, maintained Aristotle's doctrine that with regard to the passions, it was best to preserve the mean between opposing extremes. This doctrine is later known by the name of *metriopatheia*, measured or proportionate passion, a term not found in Aristotle himself but readily applied to him by later writers.[38] It is a playwright rather than a philosopher who gives this theory its canonical statement. In the *Consolation to Apollonius* (130. c) ascribed to Plutarch, the third-century BC playwright Menander is quoted (fragment 740). A slave is addressing his young master:

---

[37] This is, of course, to put the matter very simply. For a valuable orientation in the subject, see Long (1999: 580–3).

[38] Compare, for instance, Diogenes Laertius' statement (5. 31), that Aristotle said that the wise man was 'not immune to passion, but moderate in passion' (ἀπαθὴς μὲν μὴ εἶναι, μετριοπαθὴς δέ). A full lexicographical discussion of μετριοπάθεια would be out of place here, but it is worth noting that while the two possible interpretations of the first element of the word offered here ('measured' or 'proportionate'), these are ideally at least closely related. A response should be proportionate to its cause, and can be so only if it is properly calibrated; this does not, however, rule out intense reactions to intense causes. In later Greek, μετριοπάθεια sometimes appears to be used in a less technical sense, to refer to a generally equable temperament.

The key point of my argument is this. You are a human, and no animal passes more quickly from humble status to pre-eminence and back again than one of those... In your case, young sir, the good things you have lost were not overwhelming, and the troubles you now suffer are only moderate (τὰ νυνί τ' ἐστι μέτριά σοι κακά). So bear your woe also according to some kind of mean (ὥστ' ἀνὰ μέσον που καὶ τὸ λύπηρον φέρε).

Roman ideals of reticence and self-control tended to favour an outward aspect at least of indifference to suffering, whatever one's inner feelings. Virgil's Aeneas is famously a man who 'feigns hope with his countenance, repressing his grief deep within his heart'.[39] Augustine's contemporary Servius, in his commentary on the *Aeneid*, at one point commends Virgil for having described only Aeneas' young son as weeping: it is possible, he says, to ascribe tears to a boy 'without any shame' (*sine pudore*); to strong men, however, he can ascribe only grief (*Commentarius in Aeneida* 9. 499). Cicero indeed writes to Atticus of the excellent moral character shown by his young nephew (*Q. Cicero puer*) in weeping when he received bad news of Atticus' sister (*ad Atticum* 6. 3. 1). On the question of weeping and groaning, Augustine inherited a set of complex ideas from both classical and Christian sources. Cicero had already laid down in the *Tusculanae Disputationes* (2. 55) that although groaning might on occasion be appropriate for a man, *eiulatus* was always inappropriate even for a woman (*ingemiscere nonnumquam viro concessum est... eiulatus ne mulieri quidem*); the archaic Laws of the Twelve Tables forbade such displays of emotion even at funerals.[40] Later Stoicism distinguished 'passion' (πάθος) from 'pre-passion' (προπάθεια), a distinction exploited by various Christian authors to explain Biblical references to apparent displays of passion by Jesus and others.

---

[39] Aeneid 1. 209: *spem vultu simulat, premit alto corde dolorem* (itself perhaps a Romanization of Theocritus' Aphrodite, λάθρᾳ μὲν γελάοισα, βαρὺν δ' ἀνὰ θύμον ἔχοισα; *Idyll* 1. 96).
[40] On the reading of the text here see Douglas (1990), who argues persuasively a) that the manuscripts' reading *fletus* is acceptable, and b) that even if the emendation *lessus* is adopted, it is *eiulatio* which is forbidden by the Twelve Tables.

CHRISTIAN ATTITUDES TOWARDS WEEPING

The Christian Scriptures contain numerous instances of individuals weeping and groaning, in various situations; but no clear single attitude emerges from these passages. A comparison between the treatment of the theme in the Synoptic Gospels is illuminating. Mark uses the verb 'to weep' ($\kappa\lambda\alpha\acute{\iota}\omega$) three times, in two separate incidents, namely the raising of Jairus' daughter (Mark 5:38) and Peter's denial of Jesus (Mark 14:72).[41] Matthew, while retaining both incidents, drops the verb from the first one, while introducing it in the Old Testament proof-text describing the slaughter of the innocents ('Rachel weeping for her children'; Jeremiah 31:15, quoted at Matthew 2:18). In Luke, however, the total rises to eleven, over six different incidents. But Luke modifies the motif in two ways. First, there are two incidents where Jesus is presented as twice telling people *not* to weep. The first of these stories (Luke 7:13) is unique to Luke, and in his version of the second (Luke 8:52) Mark has simply the question 'Why are you weeping?' Luke's second innovation is a pair of antithetical sayings: 'Blessed are you who weep now...woe to you who laugh now, for you will weep' (Luke 6:21–5), 'Daughters of Jerusalem, weep not for me, but weep for yourselves.' Luke, then, uses his inherited material in quite a different way from Matthew; he increases the dramatic intensity, whereas Matthew tends to lower it. Such redactional techniques may reflect no more than the individual literary tastes of the various evangelists; but they do provide later Christian authors with a range of different attitudes towards displays of emotion.[42]

---

[41] Mark 16:10 is treated here as a later addition. The question of the literary relations between the Synoptic Gospels is complex. For present purposes, it is assumed that Matthew had access to Mark and that Luke had access at least to Mark and quite possibly to Matthew also. Only the verb $\kappa\lambda\alpha\acute{\iota}\omega$ is considered, as $\delta\alpha\kappa\rho\acute{\upsilon}\omega$ does not occur in the Synoptics.

[42] Opponents of Christianity also found ammunition here. Origen cites the second-century anti-Christian writer Celsus as objecting to Jesus' 'crying and groaning' ($\pi o\tau\nu\iota\hat{\alpha}\tau\alpha\iota$ $\kappa\alpha\grave{\iota}$ $\dot{o}\delta\acute{\upsilon}\rho\epsilon\tau\alpha\iota$; the first verb may suggest a distinctly feminine action). Origen's response is narrow, if strictly accurate: the words in question are not found in the Gospel accounts.

However, the most familiar and influential example of weeping in the Gospels is probably the bald statement that 'Jesus wept' at the tomb of Lazarus (John 11:15). While the Gospels do occasionally record Jesus' emotional state (for examples, pity five times, anger three times in Matthew), this is the only time they record how he showed it. The passage is potentially very useful in polemic on the nature of Jesus, as it could be used to argue either something less than Jesus' full divinity (on the ground a god should be impassive), or Jesus' full humanity (on the ground that a solely divine being would not weep), or his full but imperfect humanity (the truly wise man would not weep in such circumstances). Tertullian, for instance, lists Jesus' weeping here as an example of the 'earthly' (not 'heavenly') quality of Jesus' flesh (*de Carne Christi* 9. 7). Augustine himself is notably silent on the question. Where he discusses the passage in his *Tractatus in Iohannem* 49. 21, he completely ignores the reference to Jesus' weeping. Likewise, he does not cite it in his list of Jesus' distinctly human characteristics in *Confessions* 7. 19. 25. Augustine might have argued that groaning represented a 'pre-passion', rather than a passion proper; but he does not. Indeed, it has been persuasively argued by Sorabji (2000: 343–56, 372–84) that he fundamentally misunderstood the distinction, and effectively rejected any difference at all. This left him with a problem explaining the instances of emotion in the Scriptures. By the time he wrote Book 14 of *The City of God*, he had resolved the problem by developing his own theory of emotions, according to which they were not opposed to reason, but ought rather to follow it:

But when these emotions are attendant upon correct reasoning, when they are employed when they should be employed—who then would venture to call them weaknesses or defective passions? This is why the Lord himself employed them when he judged they should be employed... but the Lord took these emotions into his human mind when he decided to do so, in the same way that he became human when he decided to do so. He did this for reasons of 'economy', as the phrase is...

Sed cum rectam rationem sequantur istae affectiones, quando ubi oportet adhibentur, quis eas tunc morbos seu vitiosas passiones audeat dicere? Quam ob rem ipse dominus... abhibuit eas ubi adhibendas esse iudicavit... Verum

The Paralinguistic

ille hos motus certae dispensationis gratia ita cum voluit suscepit animo humano, ut cum voluit factus est homo.[43]

Augustine's views need, of course, to be read against the context of other Christian thought on the emotions and how far they should be displayed. On the Latin side, an unusually positive assessment is given by Lactantius (around AD 240–320), *Fragmentum de Motibus Animi* (*Patrologia Latina* 7. 275):

Fear, love, gladness, sadness, lust, desire, anger, pity, jealousy, wonder—all these emotions or passions were set by the Lord from the very beginning of humanity, and so beneficially and healthily grafted into human nature that a man may, by controlling himself through them in an ordered and rational manner, be able through manly action to practice the good virtues through which he may rightly be found worthy to receive from the Lord eternal life...

timor amor laetitia tristitia libido concupiscentia ira miseratio zelus admiratio, hi motus animi vel affectus a domino ab initio hominis exsistunt conditi, et naturae humanae utiliter et salubriter sunt inserti ut per eos ordinate et rationabiliter regendo se homo virtutes bonas viriliter agendo exercere possit, per quas a domino perpetuam accipere vitam iuste meruisset...

Some writers re-interpret the concept of ἀπάθεια as immunity not only from the passions but also from sin altogether ('these senses are not always clearly distinguishable'),[44] even though the Stoic notion of the wise man's moral self-sufficiency is modified to make divine assistance a condition of it. With the rise of monasticism, however,—itself concomitant on the rise of Christianity as a default position for large parts of the population—ἀπάθεια tends to be regarded as an ideal for the monk and contemplative, rather than the ordinary brethren, for whom μετριοπάθεια is a more reasonable expectation. This is, in fact, simply a Christianization of an existing Neoplatonic view. Plotinus (*circa* AD 205–270) had similarly distinguished the 'civic virtues', which could indeed 'moderate the passions' (τὰ πάθη

---

[43] *City of God* 14. 9. We may note that Augustine makes emotions consistently the object of will and judgement (*iudicavit, voluit*); that (again) the notion of economy is invoked (*dispensationis gratia*); and that he implicitly evokes the classical notion of τὸ πρέπον/*decorum* (*ubi oportet, ubi adhibendas*).
[44] Lampe (1961) under ἀπάθεια. My dependence on this (and on Lampe's article on δάκρυον) is gratefully acknowledged.

156   *Language in the* Confessions *of Augustine*

μετροῦσαι), with the higher virtues which alone produced 'likeness to God' (*Enneads* 1. 2. 2–3).[45] The doctrine of measured passion has obvious appeal to the philosopher-pastors of the fourth century, seeking to promote moral reformation in a congregation where 'Christian mediocrity' is the norm.[46] Basil the Great, for instance, in his discussion of weeping, states that those 'who remain within the limits of nature' (τοῖς τῆς φύσεως ὅροις ἐμμένοντα] should observe a 'measure and strict rule' (μέτρον καὶ κανὼν ἀκριβής] there might be legitimate pleasure in 'shedding a little tear' over proper objects of grief, but 'roaring and wailing and tearing one's clothes' were definitely out (*Homilies* 2. 30B). These rules, he states explicitly, are equally binding on men and women. Jesus' weeping he understands as a 'natural property' (φυσικόν...σύμπτωμα; *Homilies* 4. 5). Basil's terminology here has affinities with the Aristotelian view of passions as natural and (potentially) rational.[47] However, the influence of Biblical models of weeping remains pervasive. Indeed, some writers go well beyond anything in the Scriptures; weeping is seen as a form of rebaptism, an ideal condition of prayer, even a special grace (χάρισμαι χάρις) of God. Augustine's contemporary Evagrius of Pontus even felt compelled to remind his readers that tears were a divine gift and should not be an occasion for pride.

The equivocal attitudes current in Augustine's day are perfectly illustrated in the two versions of a letter sent by his contemporary Sulpicius Severus to his mother-in-law Bassula, describing the death of Martin of Tours (*Epistula* 3, *PL* 20. 181–5). The Verona version of the text—probably the best—states that 'the chorus of virgins then abstained from weeping, out of modesty...and if faith forbade them to weep, their emotion still extracted a groan...you would forgive their weeping...' (*tum virginum chorus fletu abstin[uit] prae pudore...siquidem fides flere prohiberet, gemitum tamen extorquebat*

---

[45] On Neoplatonic philosophy and its interface with psychology in late antiquity, see the first chapter of O'Meara (2003), *passim*.
[46] The phrase and concept of 'Christian mediocrity' is taken from Markus (1990: 45–62).
[47] On the difference between Aristotelian and Stoic views of the passions, see Erskine (1997: 43), with references to Aristotle *Ethica Nicomachea* 1105b19–1106a13, 1108a31–b10.

affectus... ignosceres fletibus). Here weeping is treated as something to be abstained from; perhaps especially by religious, but venial even for them. Groaning is inevitable; perhaps especially for females, but one remembers how Paul regards it as the natural condition of the present world. However, the vulgate text of the passage adds a gloss: 'for it is a sacred obligation both to rejoice for Martin, and a sacred obligation to weep for Martin' (*quia et pium est gaudere Martino, et pium est flere Martinum*). The fact that someone at some point must have altered the text here points to a debate between an openly emotional Christianity and exponents of an outward impassivity. Martin himself, according to Severus, was 'never seen angry, never emotional, never grieving, never laughing'; his face, however, did express 'a sort of heavenly gladness', beyond what was natural for a human. When he weeps, it is only for the sins of his detractors. But Martin as portrayed by Severus is a sort of spiritual super-hero, a figure to be imitated yet remaining above imitation for the average Christian.

Christian intellectuals, then, have a range of possible positions to take on weeping. However, as our extract from Sulpicius Severus shows, the action of groaning could be interpreted in more neutral or even positive terms. Severus' own wording suggests that groans could be extracted even from the faithful, more or less irrespective of their will. This more positive evaluation no doubt stems from Paul's view of groaning as the characteristic condition of the world as it waits for the end of time: 'All creation groans and labours to this moment... and we too groan... the [Holy] Spirit intercedes for us with groans beyond telling... in this we groan, longing for our habitation... we who are in this tent groan...' (Romans 8:22–6, 2 Corinthians 5:2–4.)[48] This attitude—bolstered by other biblical allusions—gains such a currency that it is easily invoked in Christian literary circles, even where no explicit allusion is made.[49] It is capable of considerable elaboration. Consider the case of John Cassian's account of monastic prayer in Egypt (*Instituta* 2. 10): at

---

[48] Compare George Herbert's 1633 poem *Sion*: 'All Solomons sea of brasse and world of stone/ Is not so deare to thee as one good grone'.

[49] From the *Life of Martin* (3. 1–2) again, compare the response of the bystanders at Amiens to Martin's dividing his cloak with a beggar; some laughed, but the wiser ones 'groaned deeply that they had done nothing of the sort themselves'.

prayer-time, he says, the monks are utterly silent, refraining from spitting, throat-clearing, coughing, snoring, groaning(!), or any sound at all—'except perhaps such as through the mind's superfluity escapes the bars of the mouth, which creeps up unperceived upon the heart, afire as it is with overmuch fervour of spirit beyond all bearing' (*nisi forte haec quae per excessum mentis claustra oris effugerit, quaeque insensibiliter cordi obrepserit, immoderato scilicet atque intolerabili spiritus fervore succenso*). Here the ideals of hesychasm and *apatheia* enjoin restraint from all groaning, yet the groaner's piety proves too strong to resist—even if the result cannot be called a groan.

TEARS AND GROANING IN THE *CONFESSIONS*

At various key points in the *Confessions*, Augustine described himself or others weeping and groaning. This is rarely just a casual detail or an indication of emotional intensity; rather, we should understand it against the complex background of attitudes towards such emotional displays which we have just considered. Four examples in particular stand out.

First, there is Augustine's account of his weeping as a baby and as a schoolboy (*Confessions* 1. 6. 7, 1. 7. 11). The newborn Augustine knew just three things: how to suck, how to 'find rest in the pleasures of body and how to weep for its scandals' (*sugere noram et adquiescere delectationibus, flere autem offensiones carnis meae*). Such a picture of infant life seems simple to the point of naivety, but Augustine's language is highly charged with associations. First, there is the emphasis on 'rest' and 'delight'. This both echoes the opening theme of the *Confessions*—'you wake us up, so that we may take pleasure (*delectet*) in praising you... and our heart is restless till it finds its rest (*adquiescat*) in you'—and prefigures the eternal Sabbath-rest described at the end of the work. Note that the translation given here takes *carnis* with both *delectationibus* and *offensiones*, not just (as it might be) with the latter; the body is a source of legitimate pleasures and not only of discomforts, and our physical rest and pleasure matter in themselves. Augustine's attitude towards weeping in particular is ambiguous. While he links it closely to his putatively

The Paralinguistic 159

inordinate desire for milk (*flendo petere, inhiabam plorans*), it is not specifically made the object of criticism. The same is not true of his attitude towards his weeping towards the end of Book 1, when he wept for the death of Dido but not for his own spiritual death (*flente Didonis mortem et non flente mortem suam... et haec non flebam et flebam Didonem*). His earlier weeping, whether or not excessive, had in itself been appropriate for a baby lacking the resources of language. This weeping—the result of his acquisition of both language and literacy—was not so much excessive as misplaced, the result of a false consciousness instilled in him through language.

Secondly, there is the account of his weeping at the death of his unnamed friend from Thagaste in Book 4: 'Weeping alone was sweet to me, and took the place of my friend among my soul's delights' (*Confessions* 4. 4. 9). The paradox is obvious—weeping is psychologically not 'sweet'—but it is not mere paradox for its own sake. As we have noted in Chapter 5, images of sweetness and bitterness occur repeatedly in the *Confessions*, sweetness being one of Augustine's epithets for God himself: that which is in and of itself pleasurable.[50] Bitterness, on the other hand, is associated with the saltiness of the sea (and perhaps also of tears), itself the type of human inconsistency, whose surging tides (*aestus*) are held in check by God. This imagery is sustained in Book 4; the bereaved Augustine 'weeps bitterly and finds rest in bitterness' (4. 6. 11), he 'boils up (*aestuabam*), sighs, weeps, is emotional' (*turbabar*, perhaps with connotations of πάθος) (4. 7. 12). This is, in his own terms, all wrong; if rest and sweetness are qualities associated with God, how can 'the sweet fruit of groaning and weeping and sighing and moaning be plucked from the bitterness of life?' (4. 5. 10). Augustine's problem here again is not his weeping as such. There is no suggestion that he should have practiced impassibility (ἀπάθεια), but he does see his inability to accept his friend's mortality as indicative of a lack of μετριοπάθεια, measured passion: 'what a foolish mortal I was to suffer immoderately over our mortal lot' (*o stultum hominem immoderate humana patientem*; note

---

[50] I have not been able to trace a source for the Latin saying that 'there is no arguing about taste' (*de gustibus non est disputandum*), but Augustine would certainly have taken it in the opposite sense to the one usually meant; that which is sweet is sweet, and the person desiring sweetness cannot be satisfied with saltiness.

that *moderate pati* = μετριοπαθέω). The ideal of 'measured passion' can, however, fall foul of the frequent Christian objection to Aristotelian ideas; that they overemphasize the importance of humanity and human self-sufficiency in ethical matters, at the expense of God. Augustine himself is careful to point out that his excessive response to his friend's death is closely linked to his own theological deficiencies at the time; self-admonition to 'hope in God' brought no comfort, since the Manichee God he then believed in was 'a ghost' (4. 4. 9).

Next, we come to the scene in Book 5 of the *Confessions* where the young professor Augustine, fed up with his rowdy students in Carthage, leaves Africa to go to Rome. To avoid an emotional farewell with his mother, he leaves her at the shrine of S. Cyprian by the harbour in Carthage, pretending he has an appointment with a friend. He then slips away secretly by night before his mother can see him off. Monica is distraught:

Confessions 5. 8. 15: *[mater] me profectum atrociter planxit... sed fefelli eam violenter me tenentem... et evasi... illa autem mansit orando et flendo... Flavit ventus et implevit vela nostra et litus subtraxit aspectibus nostris, in quo mane illa insaniebat dolore et querelis et gemitu implebat aures tuas... flebat et eiulabat atque illis cruciatibus arguebatur in ea reliquiarium Evae, cum gemitu quaerens quod cum gemitu pepererat...*

The passage is a famous one, not least for the invitation it gives for a reading of the *Confessions* as a 'spiritual *Aeneid*'.[51] We have considered elsewhere the links between this passage and Aeneas' parting from Dido in *Aeneid* Book 4 and his encounter with her shade in Book 6. The closest biblical parallel is not an obvious one, but there may be echoes of the story of how the young Tobias' mother wept at his departure from Nineveh for the city of Rages in order to recover some family monies: '[Tobias'] mother began to weeping with incurable tears, and his parents' spirit was tormented' (*flebat igitur mater [iuvenis] irremediabilibus* **lacrimis**... *et* **cruciatur** *spiritus [parentum]*; Tobias 10:4). Tears are an important device for structuring the narrative of the Book of Tobit. If we are right in discerning

---

[51] For a discussion of the Virgilian background to this passage, see Chapter 2. For secondary literature, see Bennett (1988), MacCormack (1998: 96–100).

The Paralinguistic

echoes from this book, it may be apposite to quote Tobias senior's rebuke to his wife, 'Be quiet and don't get emotional' (*tace et noli turbari*); reticence and self-control go together. Monica is given no such salutary advice. Her reaction is characterized by various paralinguistic activities—lamentation (*planctus*), inarticulate moaning (*querela*), groaning (*gemitus*), weeping (*fletus*), and ululation (*eiulatus*) —and is clearly portrayed as excessive, even unhealthy (*insaniebat*). Augustine makes clear his view that his mother's grief here was purely at the loss of his physical presence. This is reinforced through his emphasis on her role as his physical parent, with his allusion to God's description of the woman's lot in the world outside Eden: 'multiplying your groaning, and with sorrows bearing your children' (*multiplicans... gemitum tuum et in tristitiis paries filios*; Genesis 3:16).[52]

If groaning is in some circumstances acceptable, we have seen how Augustine was at least familiar with traditions in which wailing (*eiulatus*) was not. Again, the language is gendered: *eiulatus* might in Cicero's (or Severus') formulation be improper even for a woman, but it is presumably more likely from a woman also. It is also distinctly non-human, or at least not the sound of anyone past infancy. Like the sound of a crying baby, it is characteristically 'shapeless' or 'unformed' and irrational; in Augustine's own words (*Sermo* 288. 3), wailing is 'a sort of shapeless sound... without any rational interpretation' (*informis quidam sonus est... sine aliqua ratione intellectus*). As we have noted, the imposition of form on formlessness is typical of God's activity in creating the world. The parallel with the way speech imposes form on sound is unlikely to be coincidental. Indeed, another religious mystic of Platonist bent had already made it; the author of the first essay in the *Corpus Hermeticum* describes his vision of a primal moisture, giving off an 'unspeakable groaning noise' (ἦχον ἀνεκλάλητον γοώδη) and an 'inarticulate shout' (βοὴ ἀσυνάρθρως ἐξεπέμπετο)—formless, pre-linguistic sounds which are finally succeeded by a 'Holy Word' (λόγος ἅγιος).[53] Likewise, Monica's moaning (*querela*) may be seen as a sort of

---

[52] Genesis 3:16 is variously translated in the Latin traditions; the form cited here is apparently the form most familiar to Augustine. See Fischer (1951–4).

[53] The *Corpus Hermeticum*, the Nag Hammadi library, and the Greek magical papyri reflect a rich mystical tradition on the relationship between language and the divine; for discussion, see Cox Miller (1986).

shapeless noise; the word often used of the sub-linguistic sound of birds or other 'irrational animals'. If Monica was Augustine's first teacher of the *ars loquendi*, then it is his pursuit of a rhetorical career which has reduced her to literal speechlessness.

These two dramatic scenes—the death of Augustine's friend and the nocturnal departure from Carthage—are played out against a background of tears and groaning of another sort: from Monica, and then from Augustine himself, over his spiritual state. This theme is worth tracing. It begins in Book 3, after his conversion to Manichaeism (only Book 2 of the *Confessions* has no reference in it to weeping), where Monica weeps 'more than mothers weep for the physical death of their children' (*Confessions* 3. 11. 19). But tears have their effect. The unnamed bishop whom she consults gives her the prophecy (*responsum*) that 'it is impossible that a son worth all those tears of yours (*filius istarum lacrimarum*) should perish' (3. 12. 21). The phrase in question is here translated according to classical Latin syntax, but Augustine is also availing himself of Christian Latin idiom, where *filius* plus qualifying genitive is equivalent to 'an (adjective) man'; for example, *filius iniquitatis* = 'wicked man'.[54] On this reading, Augustine becomes 'a man characterized by tears'. In Book 4 all the weeping is over the death of the anonymous friend, discussed above. Book 6, in which Augustine takes the decision to move from Manichaeism back to being a Catholic catechumen, begins with an evocation of the religious value of tears addressed to the true God: 'you are in the heart of those who make their confession to you and throw themselves on you and weep on your bosom ... you are merciful and wipe away their tears, and they cry all the more and rejoice in their tears...' (*Confessions* 5. 2. 2). The theme is not immediately developed, however. Book 6 opens with Augustine 'not yet groaning in prayer' for divine help (6. 3. 3), though in the course of the book he and his friends do come to groan over their spiritual state. If not yet to God; even the gift of continence which Augustine craves would have been given 'if I knocked at the door with inner groaning' (6. 11. 20). In Book 7, the groans start to be directed towards God, though the tears do not

---

[54] For this idiom, see Plater and White (1926: 19–20), García de la Fuente (1994: 176–7).

yet come (Augustine is too busy posing as the philosopher; 7. 20. 26). By Book 8 he is finally ready to make the commitment to life as a Catholic intellectual and celibate: in the famous garden scene in Milan, he takes up 'the business of weeping' (*negotium flendi*); at the point at which he forswears the procreation of children which his parents had destined for him, his voice is 'pregnant with weeping' (*fletu gravidus*; Confessions 8. 12. 28–9). Monica, on hearing the news, is delighted that 'more had been granted her than she had been wont to ask in her pitiable and tearful groaning' (8. 12. 30). *Miserabilibus flebilibusque gemitibus*; the phrase is an enacted renunciation of the aesthetic values of the classical rhetorician, with its disfavoured homoeoteleuton or jingle (*-ibus...-ibus...-ibus*), the rare dative/ablative plural,[55] the non-classical adjectives, and the arrhythmic sequence of five short syllables at the end.

Thereafter the theme of groaning and weeping does not end, but it is firmly directed towards God and is firmly focussed on Augustine's sense both of his own unworthiness and of the future delights of union with God. This leads to some paradoxical language: at *Confessions* 12. 16. 23, for instance, Augustine expresses the wish to 'go into my bedroom and sing love-songs to you, groaning with groans beyond telling', a striking superimposition of Matthew 6:6 (Jesus' recommendation that prayer should be private) with Romans 8:26 (Paul on groaning), fused with the erotic imagery of the Song of Songs. Augustine in the course of the *Confessions* moves from crying because he is unable to speak, through a career as a language professional, back to groaning at the inexpressibility of God.

Although Augustine's attitude towards weeping is not set out systematically, it is clearly an important theme in the *Confessions*, and an index of his spiritual development. We may identify two main attitudes towards it. In purely human matters, Augustine does espouse a version of $\mu\epsilon\tau\rho\iota o\pi\acute{a}\theta\epsilon\iota a$, proportional passion; this he fails to realize after the death of his anonymous friend in Book 4, but after the death of his mother in Book 9 he is able both to 'hold in

[55] For further examples of this phenomenon, with discussion, see Chapter 5. Monica's groans are literally pluralized, in accordance with Genesis 3:16; the plural *gemitus* is fairly common in classical Latin (more so in poetry than prose, though not distinctly poetic); however, the form *gemitibus* (a rare tetrabrach, like *sonitibus* and *monitibus*) is found in the entire Perseus corpus only in the Vulgate.

check' the tears at her funeral, then consciously to 'release the tears [he] was holding in check (*continebam*)' (*Confessions* 9. 12. 33). Again, the language can be interpreted in philosophical terms: Augustine's emotional continence is the ideal ἐγκράτεια of the classical sage. While accepting that not all Christians will think tears acceptable even in such circumstances, he is prepared to defend his own position against any 'arrogant mortal exegete' of his words. Alongside this espousal of μετριοπάθεια in human affairs is a quite different attitude towards tears and groans addressed towards God; there can be no question of proportionality where one of the terms is infinite.

LAUGHTER

Laughter is perhaps the hardest of the various paralinguistic phenomena to discuss. Certainly it is hard to describe as purely 'an expression of emotion'. Even if we regard it as an expression of amusement prompted by the ridiculous—a definition which itself risks tautology—we are left with the facts that laughter seems to be prompted by other psychological states as well as amusement (typically joy, but also despair), and that it is associated also with purely physiological actions such as tickling. It is pre-eminently a social activity, since (as Augustine himself observes) people rarely laugh alone,[56] but while being a universal human activity it is also one which has potential to cause division. 'We used to laugh quite a lot, didn't we?' muses Basil Fawlty to Sybil, on their failed marriage. 'Yes, dear, but not at the same time,' she replies. As a fascinating recent study suggests, 'the social circumstances that most favor laughing and smiling are similar to those that favor talking... solidifying friendships and pulling people into the fold' (Provine 2000: 46–7). But, the same author continues, 'laughter has a darker side, as when group members coordinate their laughter to jeer and exclude outsiders.'

---

[56] We may note two particular exceptions to this: laughter arising from reading, and laughter from the memory of something which caused laughter before. Both cases would interest Augustine enormously, for reasons suggested in our conclusions.

This theory has a long pedigree. Homer's *Iliad* and *Odyssey* assume a rich social grammar of laughter—who laughs at/with whom, in what circumstances, tone, and order, as Lateiner (1995, *passim*) has richly shown. This grammar is increasingly theorized and debated in the high-classical period. Socrates is famous for his εἰρωνία, a knowing dissimulation which relies for its effect precisely on the existence of insiders and outsiders; this irony itself is no doubt a response in part to the ridicule with which he was represented on the comic stage.[57] Plato himself, and his contemporary Xenophon, distinguish laughter entailing pure amusement and that which contains an element of bad feeling or deliberate affront. The latter variety is sometimes called consequential laughter, characterized by 'its direction towards some definite result other than autonomous pleasure...its deployment of an appropriate range of ridiculing tones...[and] its arousal of feelings which may not be shared or enjoyed by all concerned' (Halliwell 1991: 283). To Aristotle we owe the observation that 'humans are the only animals who laugh' (*de Partibus Animalium* 3. 10. 673A. 8),[58] an observation which may have been familiar to Augustine through Porphyry's definition of humankind as 'a rational mortal animal capable of laughter'. Latin writers on the subject tend to concentrate on the role of jokes within rhetoric, rather than on the nature of laughter itself. According to Quintilian, for instance, the 'good man'—that is, the orator—will not evoke laughter at the cost of his dignity and modesty (*Institutio* 6. 3. 25). But relatively little is said on the wider theoretical aspect of laughter. Cicero indeed not only states that a general description of its nature, origin, and pathology is beside the point—'a matter for Democritus', as he puts it—but also dismisses those who do profess a knowledge of it (*de Oratore* 2. 235).[59]

Laughter, like weeping, features in various well-known Scriptural passages (though not, as we have noted, in the Gospel accounts of

---

[57] See the essays by Rossetti and Narcy in Desclos (2000), a stimulating set of accounts of laughter in (mainly classical) Greek culture; a similar study of Roman laughter may soon be supplied by Conybeare.
[58] For discussion, see the essay of Labarrière in the wide-ranging volume edited by Desclos (2000).
[59] On the whole topic of pagans and Christian laughter, see the very useful collection of references and discussion in Curtius (1953: 417–35).

the life of Jesus).[60] Most intriguing, perhaps, are the two accounts of how Abraham and his wife Sarah are foretold of the birth of their son Isaac ('Laughter') (Genesis 17–18). In the first account, Abraham laughs when told the news. In the second, it is Sarah who laughs, and Abraham who rebukes her. The fact that the story is preserved in two forms almost certainly reflects a change in theological perspective on laughter, with Sarah's laughter (and Abraham's rebuke) being a later, 'antigelastic' superimposition. Various later passages describe how God or the righteous will laugh at the sinner's end (Psalm 2:4, 51:8). The wisdom literature of the Old Testament emphasizes the importance of appropriate object, timing, and degree of laughter. 'The Preacher' of Ecclesiastes notably observes that 'there is a time for weeping and a time for laughter' (Ecclesiastes 3:4) and that 'a fool's laughter' is 'like the crackling of thorns under a pot' (Ecclesiastes 7:4). These sentiments are elaborated by Jesus ben Sirach, one of the latest Old Testament authors: 'the fool lifts up his voice in laughter, but the wise man will hardly laugh silently' (Ecclesiasticus 21: 23).

Ben Sirach is perhaps already influenced by Greek views on the observance of due measure in expressions of emotion, and on the impassivity of the sage. Certainly Jewish and Christian commentators feel compelled to find a broadly classical intellectual framework for some of the less tractable biblical passages. The first-century Jewish commentator Philo of Alexandria, for instance, was at pains to find a philosophical context for the story of Sarah and Abraham; Abraham's laughter was 'not the physical variety, related to mockery (*or* amusement; Greek παιδίαν)... but the considered rejoicing and good disposition of the emotions' (ἡ κατὰ διάνοιαν εὐπάθεια καὶ χαρά; *Abraham* 36. 201). Augustine's conclusion is similar; that Abraham's laughter was 'the exultation of one who rejoices, not the derision of one who doubts' (*exultatio est gratulantis non irrisio diffidentis*; *City of God* 16. 26). While the ideas are similar, the emphasis is different. Philo's argument is that laughter comes from God, the source of all happiness for the wise man. Augustine

---

[60] A statement which needs some qualification. In one Gnostic-Docetic account, Jesus is held to laugh at those who crucified Simon of Cyrene in his stead (Simon and Jesus having been transformed into each other's likeness); in another, the Christ laughs at those who crucify the mere body of the human Jesus. See Stroumsa (2004) for a full discussion.

would—as we will see—concur, but not all his fellow-believers would share his view. Clement of Alexandria (around AD 150–215) was 'appalled' by the 'uncontrolled guffaw', but 'liked to dwell on the slow, melodious chuckle of the saints, "harmoniously relaxing the austerity and over-tension of our serious pursuits"' (*Stromateis* 2. 5)[61]—a view which, with the substitution of 'sage' for 'saint', could have commanded wide assent outside Christianity. Lactantius gives a charming account of how animals too appear to have a sort of laughter, sharing with their partners and children (and even humans) 'something like mutual love and understanding'.[62] But with the growth of asceticism in the fourth century, the earnest Christian was increasingly required to police his laughter. John Chrysostom (around AD 347–407) inferred from the biblical silence on the matter that Christ never laughed (*PG* 57. 69; see discussion in Kuschel 1994, especially 45–8).[63] Martin of Tours, according to Severus, was never seen to laugh (*Vita Martini* 27. 1), though the burgeoning genre of hagiography can still find room for edifying witticisms.[64]

Augustine's treatment of the subject within the *Confessions* may best be understood in terms of the antithesis between benign, edifying laughter and its malign counterpart.[65] Laughter, Augustine

---

[61] Paraphrase and translation are taken from Brown (1991: 134); in fact, Clement is rather less positive about laughter than this would suggest; the 'melody' of the laughter he commends is essentially metaphorical, and the ideal expression of it does not go beyond a smile.

[62] See the discussion in Sorabji (1993: 90).

[63] So far as I am aware, Kuschel's work is a unique attempt to summarize previous Christian thought on laughter and to evolve a modern response. His discussion of Augustine should, however, be qualified on one point (page 43): While Augustine does state (*Sermo* 31. 4) that 'people laugh and people cry, and the fact that they laugh is worth crying over', this is a *general* statement about humanity *in its fallen condition*; the saints, he says, 'pass from weeping to laughter'.

[64] Curtius (1953: 425–8), to which add the rather odd jests in the *Vita Rhadegund* of Fortunatus. For a subtle case study from the *Peristephanon* of Prudentius, see Conybeare (2002).

[65] The importance of laughter in the *Confessions* is a point of contact with that other great first-person narrative by a North African Neoplatonist, namely Apuleius of Madaura's *Metamorphosis*, the hero of which, having been the butt of the Festival of the God Laughter at Hypata, is promised that the divinity will thereafter 'lovingly and propitiously accompany you' (3. 11). The use of *amanter* may be echoed by Augustine at *Confessions* at 5. 10. 20; the adverb is unusual and the juxtaposition with reference to laughter is notable. See Lateiner (1995: 244–8) on laughter at games in Apuleius.

points out, does not come naturally to a new-born child;[66] he himself begins to laugh shortly before his first attempts at communication using signs (*Confessions* 1. 6. 8). (His suggestion that babies laugh in their sleep before they laugh when awake is surprising, in view of his later observation that no one laughs alone—but the point is not pursued.)[67] It is the laughter of those around him (*ioca arridentium*; *Confessions* 1. 14. 23) which gives him his first incentives to learn language. The implication is that such expressions of joy and solidarity are good and proper to humans—a point which should be noted, in view of the debate about whether Jesus *qua* human would naturally have laughed. But this laughter is soon followed by a kind which, though not malign, is at least unsympathetic: his parents' laughter at the beatings he received at school, 'an evil which was great and burdensome to me at that time' (*Confessions* 1. 9. 14–15). Striking here is his use of the word *malum*. Translatable simply as 'problem' or 'trouble', it should probably be given the full force here of 'evil', the origin and nature of which is a recurrent theme of the *Confessions*.[68]

The moral force of laughter in the *Confessions* generally can hardly be overstated. It is, as we have seen, God who is the ultimate mocker—but with a qualification. Augustine's prayer, as we have seen, at the beginning of the work is that God should 'allow him to speak':

since it is to Your Clemency that I speak, not to man, my mocker. Perhaps you too mock me, but you will turn back and have mercy on me. (*Confessions* 1. 6. 7)

sine me loqui, quoniam ecce misericordia tua est non homo irrisor meus cui loquor. Et tu fortasse irrides me, sed conversus misereberis me.

---

[66] Compare *City of God* 21. 14. 18, where he notes that only Zoroaster was born laughing, 'and that portentous laughter did not augur him at all well'.

[67] 'Modern medicine ascribes the apparent smile of a sleeping newborn to flatulence' (O'Donnell 1992. ii. 37). See also O'Donnell's note, with references, on 1. 6. 7; his tripartite analysis of laughter in the *Confessions* is here reduced to bipartite division, on the basis of Augustine's own repeated antithesis.

[68] Notable also is the use of *plaga* to describe these blows. A loanword established in Latin from an early date, it typically refers at first to the beating administered to a slave; it is canonized of schoolroom beatings through Horace's reference to his master, 'Whacker (*plagosus*) Orbilius'; and gains fresh currency in Christian use to refer to illnesses and other afflictions. All these senses may be in Augustine's mind.

It is God who laughs at his worldly ambitions for promotion and marriage (*Confessions* 6. 6. 9). But divine mockery is often mediated through human agency, a point stressed repeatedly. If he showed the same greed as an adult that he thinks he showed as a baby, Augustine notes, he would be 'laughed at and rebuked, and quite rightly' (*deridebor atque reprehendar iustissime*; *Confessions* 1. 7. 11). When he becomes interested in astrology and divination, it is his young friend Nebridius' mockery which helps put him off. Augustine himself, while still a Manichee, is capable of administering a salutary reproof to his student Alypius' enthusiasm for the games—a particularly interesting passage for Augustine's theory of hermeneutics, since his 'biting mockery' was directed towards fans of the games in general, and not towards Alypius in particular. This can be understood in the light of Augustine's theory in the *de Magistro*, that all instruction (*or* explanation *or* conveying of information; Latin *docere*) comes from the one true Teacher, namely Christ; it was effectively Christ rather than Augustine who was Alypius' teacher—and mocker. Alypius himself, when acting as clerk to the court, can 'laugh in his soul' at attempts at bribery (*Confessions* 6. 10. 16). Later, it is Continence personified who laughs at Augustine's inability to commit himself to sexual renunciation, as so many lesser men (and women) were doing (*tu non poteris quod isti, quod istae*).[69]

Three other positive evaluations of laughter also deserve attention. First, there is the imagined response of God's 'spiritual ones' (*spiritales tui*; probably mildly ironic) who might laugh at Augustine's account of his Manichee belief of good and evil as opposing physical entities; such laughter is permissible as long as it is 'kind and loving' (*blande et amanter*; *Confessions* 5. 10. 20). As this laughter is not edifying to Augustine himself, it must be at least harmless to those who are so amused. Secondly, there is the pleasure Augustine gets from conversation, laughter, and reading good literature (*colloqui... corridere... simul legere*) with his anonymous friend in

---

[69] The translation here emphasizes the pejorative force of the pronoun *iste*. Note that the repetition of *istae* (strictly redundant, on the principle that the masculine includes the feminine) stresses the importance of women as a model; *even* women can do this.

Thagaste. Thirdly, there is the spiritual profit to be gained from a kindly smile. In the depths of her despair over her son's condition, Monica is comforted by the dream-vision of a radiant young man, 'on a wooden rule', smiling cheerfully (*hilarem atque arridentem*) as he approached her. The smiling dream-figure seems to be something of a Christian topos; compare the response of Philosophy to Boethius' over-eager questions (*Consolation of Philosophy* 4. 6), or the smiling Saviour-figure of the Gnostic *Apocryphon of John* 22, 26, or Sulpicius Severus' dream-vision of the smiling Martin (*Epistle* 2), or (probably from a Jewish source) the smiling angel in *Joseph and Aseneth* 14–16. Similarly, Ponticianus gives Augustine a congratulatory smile (*arridens meque intuens gratulatorie*; compare Abraham's *exultatio gratulantis*) on finding him reading the Apostle Paul (*Confessions* 8. 6. 14). Any ascetic rejection of laughter is far from Augustine's mind.[70]

However, the distinction between joyful and malign laughter made in the *City of God* is already present in the *Confessions*.[71] If it is God who is the ultimate mocker, then this laughter itself inspires parodic imitation by the demons. The riotous student fraternity of 'Destroyers' at Carthage were them 'mocked... by the spirits that deceive in secret through the very fact that they loved to mock and deceive others' (*deridentibus... irridere*; *Confessions* 3. 3. 6).[72] Unbelievers are 'a source of delight and mockery' (*voluptati et derisui*) to the demons (*Confessions* 4. 2. 3). Spectators at the Games—typically demonic, for

---

[70] Of particular interest in this connection may be the intricate dialectic of laughter and smiles in the *Martyrium Pionii* 6–7. Pionius and his companion Sabina are variously mocked (καταγελάω, ἀναγελάω); Pionius responds with a pious aphorism, which evokes a smile (μειδιάω) from Sabina; asked if she is laughing (γελάω), she replies, 'If God wills... All who believe in Christ will doubtless laugh in eternal joy.' A very similar sequence from Acts of the Martyrs of Pergamum is noted *ad loc.* by Robert (1994: 68). It is tempting to suggest a wider pattern; in the world, Christians simply smile at the laughter of those around them, in the assurance that theirs will be the last laugh.

[71] And indeed elsewhere. Compare *Sermon* 198. 105. 464–8: 'Let [pagans] buy [Christian literature], read, and believe; or let them buy, read, and mock.'

[72] On the demonic love of mockery, compare Chapter 2. References to laughter are more frequent in biblical (and patristic) Latin than in Greek, as *irridere* and *deridere* translate not only Greek καταγελάω but also παίζω and ἐμπαίζω (though these are also rendered *deludere* and *illudere*).

Augustine—are mockers (*irrisores aut illusores*) of the gladiators, taking delight only in other people's suffering (*Confessions* 3. 8. 16). Augustine himself, as a Manichee, laughed at the Old Testament patriarchs and prophets, and was himself in turn mocked by God for his beliefs (*Confessions* 3. 10. 18). As Provine has noted, the similarities with language are close. Just as language brings people together in a social bond which has both pleasures and perils, so laughter can unite humans in an evil purpose. It was laughter, Augustine eventually concludes, which led him to embark on the notorious pear-stealing expedition in Book 2—'no one finds it easy to laugh alone', as he says (*nemo facile solus ridet*; *Confessions* 2. 9. 17). Such malicious laughter is very close to Halliwell's account of 'consequential laughter', but with an important distinction; whereas consequential laughter is by definition directed to some object outside itself, for Augustine this laughter may be an end in itself. That is not to say that he and his friends could not have identified some ulterior object for their laughter. One might imagine that the orchard owner was a notoriously mean and curmudgeonly fellow, and that the boys might have enjoyed the thought of his discomfiture through a kind of warped sense of justice; but even this is nowhere suggested. Their laughter has no *appropriate* object at all. Whereas classical theories of laughter from Plato onwards tend to assume it is a response to that which is laughable (τὸ γελοῖον, *ridiculum*), this particular instance of laughter is quite literally laughter at nothing.

An important consequence follows from this, even it is not fully developed at the time. Augustine does not reject the concept of the laughable altogether, in favour of a purely social theory of laughter. For laughter to occur, both elements—an object and a social context—seem to be necessary. Augustine is careful not to rule out altogether the possibility of solo laughter, 'if something overwhelmingly laughable (*nimie ridiculum*) comes to one's senses or one's mind'. Let us pursue for a moment the analogy with language. If, as Augustine suggests in the *de Magistro*, the function of language is to explain or teach (*docere*), and the ultimate Explainer is Jesus Christ, the other participant in all inner dialogue, then it may be that private laughter, at a truly laughable object, is really laughter shared with God, the ultimate Laugher. Such an explanation would help us make sense also of the fact that we can laugh apparently by ourselves when we recollect or read something amusing. On this analysis, however, we must allow also the possibility of solo laughter that is malicious or inappropriate—that is, effectively directed at nothing. If God is the sharer of all true laughter, then the social partner of such misdirected laughter is the demons.

7

Epilogue

A few years ago my elder son's nursery provided one of its regular reports on his progress in several key areas of development. The first was Communication and Language. The second was Manipulative Skills. Augustine would, I think, have enjoyed the juxtaposition, if (on his theory of hermeneutics) the meaning of a text lies in the *voluntas* or *intentio* of the hearer/reader as of the speaker/writer; the ability to manipulate others is, for him, a major element in his own acquisition of language:[1]

> *Confessions* 1. 6. 8: And then, little by little, I began to realize where I was, and formed the wish to display my wishes to those through whom they might be fulfilled; and I could not, since my wishes were inside, whereas the people were outside and could not by any perception of their own enter my soul. Therefore I began to hurl my arms and legs around—these being signs like my wishes, such and so few as I could; they were not really like them. And when I was not shown obedience, either because I was not understood or because it would have been bad for me, I grew angry that my elders were not my subjects, and that free men and women were not my slaves, and I got my own back on them by crying.

> *Et ecce paulatim sentiebam, ubi essem, et voluntates meas volebam ostendere eis, per quos implerentur, et non poteram, quia illae intus erant, foris autem illi nec ullo suo sensu valebant introire in animam meam. Itaque iactabam membra et voces, signa similia voluntatibus meis, pauca quae poteram, qualia poteram: non enim erant veresimilia. Et cum mihi non obtemperabatur vel non intellecto vel ne obesset, indignabar non subditis maioribus et liberis non servientibus et me de illis flendo vindicabam.*

---

[1] On the philosophical aspects of Augustine's discussion of language acquisition in the *Confessions*, see Burnyeat (1987).

Here we are still at the pre-linguistic stage, but we can see similarities with the observations we have made about language. Augustine's first attempts at communication are an attempt to impose his *voluntates*. It is impossible here to distinguish between the senses of 'wishing' and 'meaning', since what he means to convey as an infant are precisely his wishes, with a view to being obeyed.[2] God *is* his 'meaning' (*Confessions* 12. 28. 38), and—as we have suggested in Chapter 4—may even be invoked as such (*Confessions* 13. 15. 16). For humans, however, there is a constant gap between will and accomplishment. We seldom achieve a 'full *voluntas*', leaving the mind in the condition of commanding itself yet finding itself disobeyed (*Confessions* 8. 8. 19 to 8. 9. 21); as here, one *voluntas* is object of another, leaving open the possibility of an infinite regress of meanings. The use of the plural *voluntates* may reinforce the impression of the divided aims of humanity, as opposed to the simplicity of God; as we have seen in Chapter 5, these plurals are rather more frequent in the *Confessions* than in classical prose more generally.

The crying of babies is elsewhere described by Augustine as a 'shapeless' or 'ugly noise' (*informis vox*), albeit one with potential for being 'gathered up and shaped into words' (*quam possit postea colligere atque in verba formare*; *de Genesi ad Litteram* 1. 15. 21). In the context of the *Confessions*, it is impossible to miss the similarity with his exegesis in Book 12 of the opening verses of Genesis, *terra erat invisibilis et incomposita*, also glossed as *sine specie et informis*. Indeed, the creation process is described in near-identical terms as the imposition by God of *forma/species*, the key Neoplatonist concept of form and beauty, on a shapeless world. Again, then, we may see language as a form of human pro-creation.

This process marks a transitional stage in the child's life, from *in-fans* ('non-speaker') to boy.[3] This transition, however, is not without its perils:

---

[2] *Obtempero* covers a range of semantic possibilities, but it is notable how translators tend to play down its force: 'did not get my way' (Chadwick; Boulding); 'my wishes were not carried out/granted' (Pine-Coffin; Burton); 'did not get what I wanted' (Sheed).

[3] *Confessions* 1. 8. 13: *non enim eram infans, qui non farer, sed iam puer loquens eram*. A similar etymology is found in Greek also; compare the twelfth-century *Etymologicum Magnum* under μεῖραξ. Παρὰ τὸ εἴρω, τὸ λέγω, γίνεται εἶραξ. ὅθεν εἰράκιον καὶ μειράκιον. καὶ πλεονασμῷ τοῦ Μ, μεῖραξ, ὁ δυνάμενος ἤδη λέγειν.

Epilogue

Confessions 1. 18. 31: So it was I shared the signs for expressing my meanings with those I was among, and entered deeper into the squally society that is human life, dependent on the authority of my parents and the whim of my elders and fellow-humans.

Sic cum his, inter quos eram, voluntatum enuntiandarum signa communicavi et vitae humanae procellosam societatem altius ingressus sum pendens ex parentum auctoritate nutuque maiorum hominum.

In modern discussions, the development of human language is regularly correlated with evidence of changing patterns of human behaviour which, it is argued, could not have come about without it. It is an argument already anticipated in antiquity: Cicero had described how Reason had found humans 'making an inchoate and confused sound, their voices being not yet organized,' and how, having 'set words on things as though distinguishing tokens (*signa*)', she 'bound them to each other, dissociate as they had been, with language, the sweetest bond of all' (*hominesque anteae dissociatos iucundissimo inter se sermonis vinclo colligavit*; *de Re Publica* 3. 2. 3).[4] But *societas* is often a two-edged word for Augustine, representing anything from close personal involvement to a mere alliance of convenience; some fifteen years later, in *The City of God*, he would write variously of the *societas mortalium, societas angelorum, societas daemonum,* and *societas diabolica* (e.g. *City of God* 5. 17. 39; 10. 9. 43; 10. 11. 36).[5] In the *de Ordine* (2. 35) he had written positively about language as the product of reason and the precondition for stable society, in terms which recall Cicero's: 'The rational element in us, since there could be no alliance between one human and another unless they could speak to each other... perceived that names must be given to things' (*illud quod in nobis est rationabile... quia... nec homini homo firmissime sociari posset nisi colloqueremur... vidit esse imponenda rebus vocabula*).[6] Here in the *Confessions*, the abstractions have vanished; whatever the origins of language, in practical terms each new person is compelled to learn a language and so enrol in a particular social bond; that *societas* may be

---

[4] Discussion of this and other related passages in Gera (2003: 158–66).
[5] For a rich investigation of the relationship between community and language in Augustine, see Markus (1996: 105–20); on *societas* with demons through magic, pages 125–46.
[6] Discussion in Duchrow (1965: 94–5).

no more than a bond of mutual self-interest. This impression is strengthened by the adjective *procellosa*; Augustine makes frequent use in the *Confessions* of the Old Testament imagery of the sea as a primal force held in check by the power of Yahweh, often as a metaphor for the human condition (e.g. 13. 20. 28, with Clark 1996).

Furthermore, language involves a submission to authority—a key concept in Augustine, and again an ambiguous one. Within Latin linguistic theory the concept has a long pedigree. Varro had joined authority, custom (*consuetudo*), reason (*ratio*), and nature (*natura*) as the four organizing principles of Latin, though from Quintilian onward nature is usually omitted from the list (Law 1990). We have just seen how Augustine has already moved away from his earlier view of reason as the inventor of language. Here *auctoritas* is assigned a prominent role; but this term too is problematic. *Auctoritas* is traditionally the language of the *auctores*, the classic authors. It had long been pointed out that these *auctores* did no more than use the custom (*consuetudo*) of their day; in Quintilian's formula (*Institutio* 1. 6. 43), 'what is "old language" but the old custom of speech?' (*et sane quid est aliud vetus sermo quam vetus loquendi consuetudo?*). This is, as Law points out, not far removed from Augustine's own formulation at *de Doctrina Christiana* 2. 13. 19: 'what is well-constructed speech but the preservation of someone else's custom, reinforced by the authority of the speakers of old' (*quid est ergo integritas loquendi, nisi alienae consuetudinis conservatio loquentium veterum auctoritate firmatae?*). Augustine's definition, however, is notably more negative about *consuetudo* than is Quintilian; even in one's native tongue, it is always 'foreign' or 'someone else's'(*alienae*). We may note also that while Quintilian retrojects *consuetudo* into the past, Augustine projects *auctoritas* into the present. It is his parents—uneducated African provincials—who are his first *auctores*. This is further undercut by the gloss or expansion that follows his reference to parental authority: 'the whim of my elders and fellow-humans' (*nutu maiorum hominum*). Again, it is instructive to think what Augustine did *not* say. A phrase such as *auctoritate maiorum* would have conveyed a similar idea, if in more bland and conventional terms. Instead, *nutus* may indeed be no more than a synonym for *auctoritas*; but it may also suggest arbitrary judgement or even mere caprice, while the addition of *hominum* indicates a parity between Augustine and his notional 'elders and betters' (*maiores*). It would perhaps be an exaggeration to describe *maiorum hominum* as an oxymoron, but it is at least a paradox. Augustine's views on authority, then, are delicately balanced. Indeed, as O'Donnell (1992. ii: 60) points out, authority mostly 'appears in benevolent guise' in Augustine's early works, despite a 'lingering anxiety' he occasionally displays. In particular, the authority of the Christian Scriptures is one of his proofs of its validity, against the polemics of the Manichees. This is typically portrayed as an instance of the divine economy (οἰκονομία, *administratio, dispensatio*) of the world; God, the good estate-owner, intervenes both directly and through his 'bailiffs' (Moses and other Scriptural writers in the past; Christian bishops and preachers in the present) to see that it is kept in some kind of order.[7] The authority of Scripture, like that of the Church, is readily conceived in top-down terms; but the comparison with language may be instructive. The authority of language depends not only on the prestige of the *auctores*, but also on the practical realization of the value of language in human affairs; it is worth following previous patterns of speech not merely because of the prestige they enjoy, but because language has been found—at least to some extent—to work, and to offer pleasure. That it can do so is, for Augustine, ultimately through the *sermo* of God.

---

[7] The language of divine economy in the *Confessions* has not, to my knowledge, been fully explored. For some initial references to the key terms, see *Confessions* 11. 2. 2; 12. 23. 32; 12. 27. 37 (*dispensatio*); 12. 16. 23; 12. 26. 36; 12. 31. 42 (*administratio*).

APPENDIX

Greek Words in the *Confessions*

This list includes also Greek roots given Latin suffixes, but excludes the very small number of Latin words also found in biblical Greek.

Abyssus; Academicus; Aenigma; Aer; Agonisticus; Allegoria; Angelus; Antrum; Apostolicus; Apotheca; Aristotelicus; Aroma; Astrum; Aurora
Balanion; Baptismus; Barbarismus; Blasphemia; Blasphemare
Caliculus; Canistrum; Cataracta; Catechumenus; Categoria; Cathedra; Catholicus; Cedrus; Cetus; Chirographum; Chorda; Cinnamus; Collyrium; Comissatio; Cothurnus; Crapula; Criticus
Daemon; Daemonicola; Daemonium; Diabolicus; Diabolus; Drachma; Draco; Dyas
Ecclesia; Ecclesiasticus; Eleemosyna; Episcopaliter; Episcopus; Epistola; Eremus; Evangelium; Evangelizare
Genesis; Genethliacum; Gigas; Grammaticus; Gubernare; Gymnasium; Gyrus
Haereticus; Historia; Hymnus
Idolum
Laguncula
Machinamentum; Machinatio; Margarita; Martyr; Mathematicus; Melos; Monas; Monasterium; Musica; Mysterium; Mystice; Mysticus
Nauta
Oceanus; Opsonium; Orphanus
Paedagogus; Palaestra; Paracletus; Paradisus; Pausatio; Persona; Phantasia; Phantasma; Phantasticus; Philosophia; Philosophus; Plaga; Planus; Platea; Poena; Poeta; Poeticus; Presbyter; Propheta; Psalmus; Psalterium
Rhetor; Rhetorica
Scaenicus; Schola; Scholasticus; Soloecismus; Spongia; Stomachanter; Stomachus; Syllaba;
Tartareus; Thalamus; Theatricus; Theatrum; Thesaurizare; Thesaurus; Tornus; Tragicus; Typhus
Zelare; Zelus

Bibliography

Adams, J. N. (1984). 'Female Speech in Latin Comedy', in *Antichthon* 18: 43–77.
——— (2003). ' "*Romanitas*" and the Latin Language', in *Classical Quarterly* 53: 184–205.
Aitchison, J. (1996). *The Seeds of Speech*. Cambridge: Cambridge University Press.
Alexander, L. (1990). 'The "Living Voice": Scepticism towards the Written Word in Early Christian and in Graeco-Roman Texts,' in D. J. A. Clines *et al.* (eds), *The Bible in Three Dimensions*. Sheffield: University of Sheffield.
Allen, W. S. (1974). *Vox Graeca. A Guide to the Pronunciation of Classical Greek*. Second edition. Cambridge: Cambridge University Press.
Anderson, W. D. (1966). *Ethos and Education in Greek Music. The Evidence of Poetry and Philosophy*. Cambridge, Massachusetts: Harvard University Press.
Auerbach, E. (1965). *Literary Language and its Public in late Latin Antiquity and in the Middle Ages*. London: Routledge and Kegan Paul.
Auksi, P. (1995). *The Christian Plain Style. The Evolution of a Christian Ideal*. Montreal and Kingston, London and Buffalo: McGill-Queen's University Press.
Baldwin, B. (1983). *The Philogelos or Laughter-Lover*. Amsterdam: London Studies in Classical Philology.
Barker, A. D. (1996). 'Music', in S. Hornblower and A. Spawforth (eds), *Oxford Classical Dictionary*, third edition, 1003–12. Oxford: Oxford University Press.
Beinert, W. (1999). 'Regula fidei', in W. Kaspar *et al.* (eds), *Lexicon für Theologie und Kirche*, third edition, volume eight, 975–6. Freiburg *et alibi*: Herder.
Bennett, C. (1988). 'The Conversion of Vergil: The *Aeneid* in Augustine's *Confessions*', in *Revue des études augustiniennes* 34: 47–69.
Biville, F. (1994). 'Collisions synonymiques dans le lexique latin', in C. Moussy (ed.), *Les problèmes de la synonymie en latin*, 47–58. Paris: Presses de l'Université de Paris-Sorbonne.
Bonaria, M. (1956). *Mimorum Romanorum Fragmenta*. Genoa: Istituto di Filologica classica.
Braund, S. M., and Gill, C. (eds), (1997). *The Passions in Roman Thought and Literature*. Cambridge: Cambridge University Press.

Brown, P. R. L. (1991). *The Body and Society: Men, Women, and Sexual Renunciation in Early Christianity.* London : Faber and Faber.

Brunschwig, J., and Nussbaum, M. C. (1993). *Passions and Perceptions. Studies in Hellenistic Philosophy of Mind.* Proceedings of the Fifth Symposium Hellenisticum. Cambridge: Cambridge University Press.

Burn, A. E. (1905). *Niceta of Remesiana. His Life and Works.* Cambridge: Cambridge University Press.

Burnyeat, M. F. (1987). 'Wittgenstein and Augustine *de Magistro*', in *Proceedings of the Aristotelian Society* supplementary volume 61: 1–24; reprinted in G. B. Matthews (ed.) (1999). *The Augustinian Tradition,* 286–303. Berkeley: University of California Press.

Burton, P. (2000). *The Old Latin Gospels. A Study of their Texts and Language.* Oxford: Oxford University Press.

Caird, G. B. (1994). *New Testament Theology. Edited and completed by L. D. Hurst.* Oxford: Oxford University Press.

Chadwick, H. (1950). 'The Silence of Bishops in Ignatius', in *Harvard Theological Review* 43: 169–72.

—— (1991). *Saint Augustine. Confessions. Translated with an Introduction and Notes.* Oxford: Oxford University Press.

Chantraine, P. (1968–80). *Dictionnaire étymologique de la langue grecque. Histoire des mots.* Paris: Klincksieck.

Clark, E. G. (1996). 'Adam's Womb (Augustine, *Confessions* 13. 28) and the Salty Sea', in *Proceedings of the Cambridge Philological Society* 42: 89–105.

—— (1999). 'Translate into Greek. Porphyry of Tyre on the New Barbarians', in R. Miles (ed.) *Constructing Identities in Late Antiquity.* London and New York: Routledge, 112–32.

—— (2000). *Porphyry. On Abstinence from Killing Animals.* London: Duckworth.

—— (2005). *Augustine. The* Confessions. Second edition. Bristol: Bristol Phoenix Press.

Coleman, R. G. G. (1977). *Eclogues. Vergil.* Cambridge: Cambridge University Press.

—— (1989): 'The Formation of Specialized Vocabularies in Philosophy, Grammar, and Rhetoric; Winners and Losers', in M. Lavency and D. Longrée (eds) *Actes du Ve Colloque de Linguistique latine.* Louvain-la-Neuve: Peeters, 77–89.

Conte, G. B. (1986). *The Rhetoric of Imitation. Genre and Poetic Memory in Virgil and Other Latin Poets.* Ithaca and London: Cornell University Press.

Conybeare, C. (2002). 'The Ambiguous Laughter of Saint Laurence', *Journal of Early Christian Studies* 10. 2: 175–202.

—— (2006). *The Irrational Augustine.* Oxford: Oxford University Press.

Bibliography 181

Copenhaver, B. P. (1992). *Hermetica. The Greek Corpus Hermeticum and the Latin Asclepius in a new English translation, with notes and introduction.* Cambridge: Cambridge University Press.

Corbett, G. P. (2000). *Number.* Cambridge: Cambridge University Press.

Cox Miller, P. (1986). 'In Praise of Nonsense', in H. A. Armstrong (ed.), *Classical Mediterranean Spirituality*, 481–505. London: Routledge and Kegan Paul.

—— (1996). 'Jerome's Centaur. A Hyper-Icon of the Desert', in *Journal of Early Christian Studies* 4: 209–33.

Crystal, D. (1991). *A Dictionary of Linguistics and Phonetics* 3rd edition. Oxford: Oxford University Press.

Curtius, E. R. (1953). *European Literature and the Latin Middle Ages: translated from the German by Willard R. Trask.* London: Routledge and Kegan Paul.

Desclos, M.-L. (ed.) (2000). *Le rire des grecs. Anthropologies du rire en Grèce ancienne.* Grenoble: Jerôme Millon.

Dodd, C. H. (1935). *The Bible and the Greeks.* London: Hodder and Stoughton.

Douglas, A. E. (1990). *Cicero. Tusculan Disputations II & V, with a summary of III and IV.* Warminster: Aris and Phillips.

Duchet-Suchaux, M., and Lefèvre, Y. (1984), 'Les noms de la Bible', in P. Riché and G. Lobrichon (eds), *Le Moyen Age et la Bible*, 13–23. Paris: Beauchesne.

Duchrow, U. (1965). *Sprachverständisnis und biblisches Hören bei Augustin,* Tübingen: Mohr.

Dunbar, R. (1996). *Grooming, Gossip and the Evolution of Language.* London: Faber and Faber.

Ehrman, B. (2003). *Lost Christianities. The Battle for Scripture and the Faiths we Never Knew.* New York: Oxford University Press.

Elsner, J. (1998). *Imperial Rome and Christian Triumph.* Oxford: Oxford University Press.

Ernout, A, and Meillet, A. (1939). *Dictionnaire étymologique de la langue latine.* New edition. Paris: Klincksieck.

Erskine, A. (1997). 'Cicero and the expression of grief', in S. M. Braund and C. Gill (edd), *The Passions in Roman Thought and Literature*, 36–47. Cambridge: Cambridge University Press.

Evans, G. R. (1984). *The Language and Logic of the Bible. The Earlier Middle Ages.* Cambridge *et alibi*: Cambridge University Press.

Fantham, E. (1988). 'Mime. The Missing Link in Roman Literary History', in *Classical World* 82: 153–63.

Ferguson, E. *et al.* (eds) (1997). *Encyclopedia of Early Christianity*. Second edition. New York and London: Garland.
Fischer, B. (1951–4). *Vetus Latina. Die Reste der altlateinische Bibel*. 2. *Genesis*. Freiburg: Herder.
Fisher, P. (2002). *The Vehement Passions*. Princeton and Oxford: Princeton University Press.
Flores, R. (1975). 'Reading and Speech in St. Augustine's *Confessions*', in *Augustinian Studies* 6: 1–13.
Fögen, T. (2000). *Patrii sermonis egestas: Einstellungen lateinischer Autoren zu ihrer Muttersprache: ein Beitrag zum Sprachbewusstsein in der römischen Antike*. München: K. G. Saur.
Ford, L. S. (2003). 'Process Theology', in B. L. Marthaler *et al.* (eds), *The New Catholic Encyclopedia*, second edition, 730–2. Detroit *et alibi*: Thomson Gale.
Fruyt, M. 'Typologie des cas de synonymie', in C. Moussy (ed.), *Les problèmes de la synonymie en latin*, 25–46. Paris: Presses de l'Université de Paris-Sorbonne.
Fulton, R. (2006). ' "Taste and see that the Lord is sweet" (Ps. 33: 9). The Flavor of God in the Monastic West', in *Journal of Religion*, 86. 2, 169–204.
Gamble, H. Y. (1995). *Books and Readers in the Early Church. A History of Early Christian Texts*. Oxford: Oxford University Press.
García de la Fuente, O. (1994). *Latín bíblico y latín cristiano*. Madrid: Editorial CEES.
Geffcken, K. A. (1973). *Comedy in the* Pro Caelio, *with an appendix on the* In Clodium et Curionem. Lugduni Batavorum: Brill.
Gera, D. (2003). *Ancient Greek Ideas on Speech, Language, and Civilization*. Oxford: Oxford University Press.
Gibb, J., and Montgomery, W. (1908). *The Confessions of Augustine*. Cambridge: Cambridge University Press.
Goode, R. (2005). '*Looking for the Living among the Dead (Letters)'; Textual Transmission with First and Second Century Christianity*. PhD thesis: University of Birmingham.
Green, R. P. H. (1995): *Augustine: De Doctrina Christiana*. Oxford: Oxford University Press.
Green, W. M. (1959). 'A Fourth Century Manuscript of Saint Augustine?' in *Révue bénédictine* 69: 191–7.
Hadot, I. (1984). *Arts libéraux et philosophie dans la pensée antique*. Paris: Études augustiniennes.
Hagendahl, H. (1967). *Augustine and the Latin Classics*. Two volumes, numbered sequentially. Gothenburg: Acta Universitatis Gothoburgensis.

Bibliography

Halliwell, F. S. (1991). 'The Uses of Laughter in Greek Culture', *Classical Quarterly* 41: 279–96.
Jaffee, M. S. (2001). *Torah in the Mouth. Writing and Oral Tradition in Palestinian Judaism 200 BCE–400 CE.* Oxford: Oxford University Press.
Janda, L. (2000). 'Cognitive Linguistics', at <http://www.indiana.edu/~slavconf/SLING2K/ pospapers/janda/pdf>.
Janka, M. (1997). *Ovid 'Ars amatoria': Buch 2: Kommentar.* Heidelberg : C. Winter.
Janko, R. (1987). *Aristotle. Poetics I with the Tractatus Coislinianus, a Hypothetical Reconstruction of Poetics II, the Fragments of the On Poets.* Indianopolis and Cambridge: Hackett Publishing Company.
Jürgens, H. (1972). *Pompa Diaboli. Die lateinischen Kirchvätern und das antike Theater.* Stuttgart, Berlin, Köln, and Mainz: W. Kohlhammer.
Kaibel, G. (1899). *Comicorum Graecorum Fragmenta.* Berlin: Weidmann.
Kaimio, J. (1979). *The Romans and the Greek Language.* Helsinki. Societas Scientiarum Fennica.
Kannengiesser, C. (ed.) (2004). *Handbook of Patristic Exegesis: the Bible in Ancient Christianity.* Leiden and Boston: Brill.
Kaster, R. A. (1988). *Guardians of Language: the Grammarian and Society in Late Antiquity.* Berkeley, Los Angeles, and London: University of California Press.
—— (1995): *C. Suetonius Tranquillus: De grammaticis et rhetoribus.* Oxford and New York: Oxford University Press.
Kelber, W. (1958). *Die Logoslehre von Heraklit bis Origenes.* Stuttgart: Verlag Urachhaus.
Kennedy, G. (1978). *Encolpius and Agamemnon in Petronius,* in *American Journal of Philology* 99: 171–8.
Kirwan, C. (1994). 'Augustine on the Nature of Speech', in S. Everson (ed.), *Language (Companions to Ancient Thought 3).* Cambridge: Cambridge University Press.
—— (2001). 'Augustine's Philosophy of Language', in E. Stump and N. Kretzmann (eds), *The Cambridge Companion to Augustine,* 186–204. Cambridge: Cambridge University Press.
Klingshirn, W., and Safran, L. (2007). *The Early Christian Book.* Washington: Catholic University of America.
Kuschel, K.-J. (1994). *Laughter. A Theological Essay.* London: SCM.
Lampe, G. W. H. (ed.) (1961). *Patristic Greek Lexicon.* Oxford: Oxford University Press.
Langslow, D. R (2000). *Medical Latin in the Roman Empire.* Oxford and New York: Oxford University Press.

Lateiner, D. (1995). *Sardonic Smile. Nonverbal Behavior in Homeric Epic.* Ann Arbor: University of Michigan Press.
Law, V (1984). 'St Augustine's <De grammatica>: Lost or Found?' in *Recherches augustiniennes* 19: 155–83.
—— (1990). '*Auctoritas, Consuetudo* and *Ratio*', in G. L. Bursill-Hall, S. Ebbesen, and K. Koerner (edd), *de Ortu Grammaticae. Studies in Medieval Grammar and Linguistic Theory in Memory of Jan Pinborg,* 191–207. Amsterdam/Philadelphia: John Benjamins.
—— (2003). *The History of Linguistics in Europe. From Plato to 1600.* Cambridge: Cambridge University Press.
Lebek, W. D. (1970). *Verba Prisca: die Anfänge des Archaisierens in der lateinischen Beredsemkeit und Geschichtsschreibung.* Göttingen: Vandenhoeck & Ruprecht.
Lepelley, C. (1979–1981). *Les Cités de l'Afrique romaine au Bas-Empire* (two volumes). Paris: Études Augustiniennes.
Lieu, S. (1985). *Manichaeism in the Later Roman Empire and Medieval China. A Historical Survey.* Manchester: Manchester University Press.
Lilja, S. (1965). *Terms of Abuse in Roman Comedy.* Helsinki: Suomalaisen Tiedeakatemian Toimituksia/Annales Academiae Scientiarum Fennicae.
Lim, R. (1995). *Public Disputation, Power, and Social Order in Late Antiquity.* Berkeley and London: University of Chicago Press.
Long, A. A. (1999). 'Stoic psychology', in K. Algra, J. Barnes, J. Mansfeld, and M. Schofield (ed.), *The Cambridge History of Hellenistic Philosophy.* Cambridge: Cambridge University Press.
Lütcke, K.-H. (1990). '*Auctoritas*', in C. Mayer *et al.* (ed.), *Augustinus-Lexicon.* Basel: Schwabe and Co. AG.
Lyons, J. (1968). *Introduction to Theoretical Linguistics.* Cambridge: Cambridge University Press.
Maas, M., and Snyder, J. M. (1989). *Stringed Instruments of Ancient Greece.* New Haven and London: Yale University Press.
MacCormack, S. G. (1998). *The Shadows of Poetry. Vergil in the Mind of Augustine.* Berkeley and London: University of California Press.
McKinnon, J. (1987). *Music in Early Christian Literature.* Cambridge: Cambridge University Press.
Maier, H. O. (2004). 'The Politics of the Silent Bishop. Silence and Persuasion in Ignatius of Antioch', in *Journal of Theological Studies* 55: 503–19.
Marincola, J. (1997). *Authority and Tradition in Ancient Historiography.* Cambridge: Cambridge University Press.
Markus, R. A. (1990). *The End of Ancient Christianity.* Cambridge: Cambridge University Press.

Bibliography 185

—— (1996). *Signs and Meanings. World and Text in Ancient Christianity.* Liverpool: Liverpool University Press.
Marrou, H.-I. (1965). *Saint Augustin et la fin de la culture antique.* 4th edition. Paris: Editions E. de Boccard.
Mathieson, T. J. (1983). *Aristides Quintilianus On Music in Three Books.* New Haven and London: Yale University Press.
Mayer, C. P. (1969). *Die Zeichen in der geistigen Entwicklung und in der Theologie des jungen Augustinus.* Two volumes. Würzburg: Augustinus-Verlag.
Mikkola, E. (1964–5). *Die Abstraktionen in Lateinischen.* (two parts). Helsinki: Annales Academiae Scientiarum Fennicae, series B, 133: 1–231, and 137: 1–245.
Miles, M. R. (1979). *Augustine on the Body.* Missoula, Mont.: Scholars Press.
Mithen, S. (2005). *The Singing Neanderthals. The Origins of Music, Language, Mind and Body.* London: Weidenfeld and Nicolson.
Murphy, F. X. (2003). 'Hesychasm', in B. L. Marthaler *et al.* (eds), *The New Catholic Encyclopedia*, second edition, 811. Detroit *et alibi*: Thomson Gale.
Neu, J. (2000). *'A Tear is an Intellectual Thing.' The Meanings of Emotion.* New York and Oxford: Oxford University Press.
O'Donnell, J. J. (1992). *Confessions. Augustine.* Three volumes. Oxford: Oxford University Press.
O'Hara, J. J. (1996). *True Names. Vergil and the Alexandrian Tradition of Etymological Wordplay.* Ann Arbor: University of Michigan Press.
O'Meara, D. (2003). *Platonopolis. Platonic Political Philosophy in Late Antiquity.* Oxford: Oxford University Press.
Palmer, A. M. (1989). *Prudentius on the Martyrs.* Oxford: Oxford University Press.
Panayotakis, C. (1995). *Theatrum Arbitri. Theatrical Elements in the* Satyrica *of Petronius.* Leiden, New York, Köln: E. J. Brill.
Paschalis, M. (1996). *Virgil's Aeneid. Semantic Relations and Proper Names.* Oxford: Clarendon Press.
Pizzolato, L. F. (1972). *Le fondazioni dello stilo delle Confessioni di sant' Agostino.* Milan: Vita e Pensiero.
Plater, W. E., and White, H. J. (1926). *A Grammar of the Vulgate. An Introduction to the Study of the Latinity of the Vulgate Bible.* Oxford: Oxford University Press.
Provine, R. P. (2000). *Laughter. A Scientific Investigation.* London: Faber and Faber.
Quasten, J. (1983). *Music and Worship in Pagan and Christian Antiquity.* Washington, D. C.: National Association of Pastoral Musicians.
Reich, H. (1903). *Der Mimus. Ein litterar-entwickelungsgeschichtlicher Versuch.* Two volumes, numbered sequentially. Berlin: Weidmann.

Robert, L., *et al.* (1994). *Le martyre de Pionios prêtre de Smyrne*. Washington D. C.: Dumbarton Oaks.

Roberts, C. H., and Skeat, T. C. (1987). *The Birth of the Codex*. London: Oxford University Press, for The British Academy.

Roberts, M. (1989). *The Jeweled Style. Poetry and Poetics in Late Antiquity*. Ithaca and London: Cornell University Press.

Robinson, J. M. (ed.) (1990). *The Nag Hammadi library in English*. *Translated and introduced by members of the Coptic Gnostic Library Project of the Institute for Antiquity and Christianity, Claremont, California*. San Francisco: Harper and Row.

Ryan, J. K. (1960). *The Confessions of St Augustine*. Garden City, N. Y.: Doubleday.

Schoedel, W. R. (1985). *A Commentary on the Letters of Ignatius of Antioch*. Philadelphia: Fortress Press.

Shanzer, D. R. (2005). 'Augustine's Disciplines: *silent diutius Musae Varronis?*' in K. Pollmann and M. Vessey (eds), *Augustine and the Disciplines. From Cassiciacum to Confessions*, 69–112. Oxford: Oxford University Press.

Shumate, N. (1988). 'The Augustinian pursuit of false values as a conversion motif in Apuleius' *Metamorphoses*', in *Phoenix* 42: 35–60.

Sihvola, J., and Engberg-Pedersen, T. (1998). *The Emotions in Hellenistic Philosophy*. Dordrecht/Boston/London: Kluwer.

Solignac, A., *et al.* (1962). *Les Confessions. Texte de l'édition de M. Skutella; introduction et notes par A. Solignac; traduction de E. Tréhorel et G. Bouissou*. Bruges: Desclée de Brouwer (Bibliothèque augustinienne).

Sorabji, R. (1993). *Animal Minds and Human Morals: The Origins of the Western Debate*. London: Duckworth 194.c.99.110.

—— (2000). *Emotion and Peace of Mind. From Stoic Agitation to Christian Temptation*. Oxford: Oxford University Press.

Stanton, G. (2004). *Jesus and Gospel*. Cambridge: Cambridge University Press.

Stock, B. (1996). *Augustine the Reader. Meditation, Self-Knowledge, and the Ethics of Interpretation*. Cambridge, MA, and London, England: The Belnap Press of Harvard University Press.

Stroumsa, G. G. (2003). 'Early Christianity—a Religion of the Book?' in M. Finkelberg and G. G. Stroumsa (eds), *Homer, the Bible, and Beyond*, 153–74. Leiden: Brill.

—— (2004). 'Christ's Laughter. Docetic Origins Reconsidered', in *Journal of Early Christian Studies* 12: 3: 267–88.

Tolkien, J. R. R. (1975). *Tree and Leaf. Smith of Wootton Major. The Homecoming of Beorhtnoth Beorhthelm's Son*. London: Unwin.

Trask, R. L. (1999). *Language. The Basics*. London: Routledge.
Trevett, C. (1983). 'Did Ignatius Combat a Third Error?' in *Journal of Ecclesiastical History* 34: 1–18.
van der Meer, F. (1983). *Augustine the Bishop. The Life and Work of a Father of the Church*. Translated B. Battershaw and G. R. Lamb. First edition 1961. London: Sheed and Ward.
van Deusen, N. (1989). *The Harp and the Soul. Essays in Medieval Music*. Lewiston, New York, and Lampeter: Edwin Mellen.
Vecchio, S. (1994). *Le parole come segni. Introduzione alla linguistica agostiniana*. Palermo: Novecento.
Verheijen, M. (1949). *Eloquentia pedisequa. Observations sur le style des Confessions de saint Augustin*. Nijemegen: Dekker & van de Vegt.
Walsh, P. G. (1988). 'The rights and wrongs of curiosity (Plutarch to Augustine)', in *Greece and Rome* 35: 73–85.
Wilkinson, L. P. (1963). *Golden Latin Artistry*. Cambridge: Cambridge University Press.
Wisnieski, R. (2000). '*Bestiae Christum loquuntur* ou des habitants du désert et de la ville dans la *Vita Pauli* de saint Jérôme', in *Augustinianum* 40: 105–44.
Wölfflin, E. (1888). 'Atellanen- und Mimentitel', in *Rheinisches Museum* 43: 308–9.
Young, F. M. (1979). 'The God of the Greeks and the Nature of Religious Language', in W. R. Schoedel and R. L. Wilken (eds), *Early Christian Literature and the Classical Intellectual Tradition in honorem R. M. Grant. Théologie historique* 53: 45–74. Paris: Beauchesne.
―― (1999). 'The *Confessions* of Saint Augustine. What is the Genre of this Work?' in *Augustinian Studies* 30: 1: 1–16.

Index locorum

Biblical citations
Genesis 1. 1 29; 1. 8 29; 1: 21 128; 3. 16 161; 3: 21 111; 6: 5 123 n. 15; 11: 1–9 8; 17–18 166; 40: 17–18 127
Exodus 24: 3–8 93; 32: 1–20 93; 34 93
Deuteronomy 17: 18 91; 28: 58 91; 28: 61 91; 29: 20 91; 29: 27 91
Judges 12: 1–6 8
1 Regnorum (= 1 Samuel) 3: 1 27
3 Regnorum (= 2 Samuel) 11: 14–17 93; 21: 17
4 Regnorum (= 2 Kings) 22–3 91
Esther 6: 1 92
Psalm 1: 1 128; 2: 4 166; 4: 3 24; 14: 3 25 n. 48; 18: 2 17 n. 27; 18: 4 30; 28: 5 65; 32: 9 3; 33: 9 84; 44: 2 103; 51: 8 166; 68: 34: 21–5 40; 35 18; 39: 16 40; 47: 2 114; 50: 10 113; 50: 19 113; 69: 4 40; 73: 13 15 n. 24; 79: 8 143; 85: 16 58; 100 145–6; 103: 2 111; 103: 3 29 n. 58; 115: 10 20; 115: 11 124; 115: 16 58; 118: 16–17 28 n. 55; 118: 154 102; 136: 3 150 n. 36; 144: 3 114; 147: 5 79; 148: 5 3; 148: 9 65; 148: 12 145
Proverbs 2: 1 28 n. 55; 3: 32 28; 3: 34 113, 114; 4: 20 28 n. 55; 6: 2 29 n. 58; 7: 4 28 n. 55; 7: 21 29 n. 58; 19: 21 123; 19: 27 28 n. 55
Ecclesiastes 7: 4 166; 7: 30 121; 12: 12 93; Isaiah 1: 18 77, 83; 29: 18 91; 33: 15 25 n. 48; 34: 4 111; 45: 23 4 n. 8; 53: 12 79; 66: 18 4 n. 8
Jeremiah 9: 5 25 n. 48; 9: 23–4 44 n. 16; 31: 15 153; 32: 12–16 91; 36: 4–32 91
Ezekiel 3: 1–2 91; 11: 19 93; 36: 26 93
Daniel 1: 4, 17; 1: 17 92
Hosea 1: 1 28 n. 55; 4: 14 52 n. 31
Micah 1: 1 28 n. 55
Joel 1: 1 28 n. 55
Ezra 4–6 92
Zechariah 8: 16 25 n. 48
Wisdom 11. 21 79, 106

Ecclesiasticus 21: 23 166
Tobias 10: 4 160
1 Maccabees 1: 59–60 92
Matthew 1: 23 100; 2: 18 100, 153; 3: 3 100; 4: 1–11 93; 6: 6 163; 10: 20 79; 13: 45–6 128; 13: 57 13 n. 19; 14: 26 131; 19: 21 99; 23: 8 3, 17 n. 27; 26: 30 142
Mark 1. 34 21; 5: 38 154; 6: 4 13 n. 19; 6: 21–5 153; 6: 49 131; 13: 9 52 n. 31; 14: 26 142; 14: 72 153; 15: 28 79
Luke 1: 20–2 21; 1: 38 58; 4: 17–21 109, 111 n. 30; 7: 13 153; 7: 22 21; 8: 14 122, 123; 8: 52 153; 12: 47–8 52 n. 31; 18: 3–5 126

John
Chapter One 1: 1–18 8; 1: 10 15 n. 24; 1: 18 20 n. 36; 1: 20–1 18 n. 30
Chapter Two 2: 11 12
Chapter Three 3: 21 11; 3: 36 12 n. 19
Chapter Four 4: 26 16; 4: 34 12; 4: 44 13 n. 19
Chapter Five 5: 24–6 12 n. 19; 5: 47 94
Chapter Six 6: 38 12; 6: 61 28; 6: 63 16
Chapter Seven 7: 17 12; 7: 19 13
Chapter Eight 8: 25 104; 8: 35 15, 16; 8: 38 16; 8: 40 25; 8: 44 30
Chapter Nine 9: 21–3 12 n. 19; 9: 31 12; 10: 10 12 n. 19
Chapter Ten 10: 25 16; 10: 35 28 n. 55
Chapter Eleven 11: 15 154
Chapter Twelve 12: 38 28
Chapter Fourteen 14: 6 28; 14: 10 16
Chapter Fifteen 15: 25 28
Chapter Seventeen 17: 17 28
Chapter Eighteen 18: 17 18 n. 30; 18: 20 16; 18: 25 18 n. 30
Chapter Nineteen 19: 22 94
Acts 2: 1–13 8
Romans 1: 21 17 n. 27, 123, 125; 2: 14 94; 8: 22–6 157; 8: 28 163; 12: 12–13 96

190 Index locorum

1 Corinthians 1: 24 81: 1: 30 81; 2: 13 112; 4: 16 99 n. 15; 4: 20 112; 12–14 8; 11: 1 99 n. 15; 14: 15 143; 15: 52 101; 15: 54 29
2 Corinthians 3: 6 72, 94; 4: 10 115; 4: 13 20; 5: 2–4 157; 9–12 44 n. 16
Galatians 2: 14 4
Colossians 2: 8 80; 3: 8 30 n. 59; 3: 15 141 n. 20
Ephesians 4: 25 25 n. 48; 4: 29 30; 5: 19 141 n. 20
Philippians 2: 11 4 n. 8
1 Timothy 1: 6 24 n. 45; 5: 14 999 n. 15
Titus 1: 10 24; 3: 3 122; 3: 9 121
James 1: 17 38; 4: 1–3 122; 5: 12 141 n. 20
1 Peter 5: 8 99 n. 15
Revelation 3: 18 127

Non-biblical citations

Acta III Concilii Carthaginiensis 11 41

Ambrose of Milan
Hymn 2. 1 32

Apocryphon of John 22 170; 26 170

Apuleius
The Golden Ass (*Metamorphoses*) 3 45; 3. 11 167 n. 65

Aristides Quintilianus
de Musica 1. 19 149; 2. 6 139 n. 16; 2. 16 151

Aristotle
Ethica Nicomachea 1105b19–1106a13 156 47
de Partibus Animalium 3. 10. 673A. 8 165

Auctor ad Herennium 4. 11 113; 4. 14. 20 45 n. 20; 4. 52. 65

Augustine
City of God 2. 7 46 n. 22; 2. 12 46 n. 22; 5. 17. 39 175; 6. 5 82; 10. 9. 43 175; 10. 11. 36 175; 14. 9 154–5; 16. 26 166; 18. 18 60; 18. 52 73 n. 20; 22. 5 76; 21. 14. 18 168 n. 66
Confessions Book One 1. 1. 1 20, 79, 113, 114–115; 1. 4. 4 116, 135; 1. 5. 5 21; 1. 6. 7 21, 168 n. 67; 1. 6. 8 168, 173; 1. 8. 13 174; 1. 7. 11 169; 1. 1. 10 11; 1. 5. 6 20; 1. 6. 7 158, 168; 1. 7. 11 158; 1. 8. 13 70; 1. 9. 14–15 168; 1. 9. 14 59; 1. 12. 19 79; 1. 13. 20 36; 1. 13. 21 40; 1. 13. 22 36, 71, 85; 1. 13. 23 71; 1. 14. 23 122, 168; 1. 17. 27 36; 1. 18. 28–9 64, 71; 1. 18. 29 94; 1. 18. 31 174–5
Book Two 2. 1. 1 37, 125; 2. 2. 3 122; 2. 3. 5 73; 2. 3. 7 58; 2. 4. 9 84; 2. 5. 10 124; 2. 9. 17 171
Book Three 3. 1. 1 33; 3. 2. 2–3 41; 3. 3. 6 60 n. 46, 64, 170; 3. 4. 7–8 79–80; 3. 4. 7 74, 95, 102; 3. 4. 8 80; 3. 5. 9 112; 3. 6. 10 38, 84, 130; 3. 8. 16 141, 171; 3. 10. 18 171; 3. 11. 19 106, 162; 3. 12. 21 162; 3. 15. 25 38
Book Four 4. 1. 1 82 n. 35; 4. 2. 2 24, 74, 82; 4. 2. 3 170; 4. 3. 4 64, 113; 4. 3. 5 64, 113; 4. 4. 9 85, 159, 160; 4. 5. 10 159; 4. 6. 9 113; 4. 6. 11 159; 4. 7. 12 159; 4. 8. 13 22, 23 n. 41, 102; 4. 10. 15 33; 4. 11. 16 33; 4. 14. 21 75, 80; 4. 15. 26 24; 4. 15. 27 113; 4. 16. 30 74–5, 77; 4. 19. 30 77
Book Five 5. 1. 1 103; 5. 2. 2 162; 5. 3. 3 23 n. 41, 96; 5. 3. 5 79, 81, 123; 5. 4. 7 79, 106, 123; 5. 6. 10 24 n. 44, 83–4; 5. 6. 11 71 n. 15, 83; 5. 7. 12 23 n. 41; 5. 8. 14 84; 5. 8. 15 36, 48–52, 160; 5. 9. 17 82; 5. 10. 18 58; 5. 10. 19 23 n. 41; 5. 10. 20 130, 167 n. 65, 169; 5. 12. 22 57, 74 n. 21; 5. 9. 17 78; 5. 15. 24 131; 5. 23. 13 75
Book Six 6. 1. 1. 36; 6. 2. 2 20 n. 36, 127, 147; 6. 3. 3 91 n. 5, 162; 6. 4. 5 24 n. 44; 6. 4. 6 72, 108; 6. 5. 7 23 n. 41, 86; 6. 5. 8 113, 128 n. 22; 6. 6. 3 85; 6. 6. 9 84, 85, 169; 6. 7. 12 106; 6. 8. 13 150; 6. 9. 14 43–8; 6. 9. 15 128; 6. 9. 17 113; 6. 10. 16 169; 6. 10. 17 121; 6. 11. 20 162; 6. 12. 21 150; 6. 13. 23 84; 6. 13. 24 123
Book Seven 7. 1. 2 131; 7. 2. 2 32; 7. 5. 7 131; 7. 8. 12 127; 7. 9. 13 96; 7. 9. 14

Index locorum

65, 123; 7. 13. 19 65; 7. 19. 25 32, 154; 7. 20. 26 102 n. 20; 7. 21. 27–8; 7. 21. 27 96, 145; 7. 21. 27 38
Book Eight 8. 2. 4 65, 128; 8. 3. 7 124; 8. 4. 9 103; 8. 5. 10 73; 8. 6. 14 170; 8. 6. 15 97–8, 127 n. 21, 145; 8. 8. 19 174; 8. 9. 21 174; 8. 10. 22 24; 8. 10. 24 124, 145; 8. 12. 28–9 163; 8. 12. 28 127 n. 21; 8. 12. 29–30 107; 8. 12. 29 96; 8. 12. 30 107, 163
Book Nine 9. 1. 1 24 n. 44, 58, 122; 9. 2. 2 82; 9. 4. 7 82; 9. 4. 9–10 24; 9. 4. 11 29, 101; 9. 4. 12 21; 9. 7. 15 144; 9. 8. 17–18 52–6; 9. 12. 29–31 144; 9. 12. 32 146–7; 9. 9. 19 26, 84; 9. 9. 20 56; 9. 10. 23–4 22; 9. 10. 23 84; 9. 12. 33 105, 164
Book Ten 10. 3. 3 13 n. 21; 10. 4. 5 24; 10. 6. 8 18; 10. 6. 9–10 18; 10. 9. 16 73, 77; 10. 12. 19 77, 86; 10. 16. 24 77; 10. 21. 30 74; 10. 23 34 20 n. 36; 10. 30. 41 127 n. 21; 10. 31. 46 127 n. 21; 10. 33. 50 148–9; 10. 38. 62 30; 10. 43. 70 127 n. 21
Book Eleven 11. 2. 2 177 n. 7; 11. 8. 10 13, 17; 11. 9. 11 78; 11. 12. 14 85; 11. 22. 28 20, 124; 11. 25. 34 24; 11. 27. 36 33; 11. 25. 38 24; 11. 29. 39 12411. 30. 40 24
Book Twelve 12. 4. 6 85; 12. 10. 10 78; 12. 13. 16 29; 12. 16. 23 163; 12. 23. 32 177 n. 7; 12. 26. 26–7 30; 12. 26. 36 74; 12. 27. 37 177 n. 7; 12. 28. 38 174; 12. 28. 39 16; 12. 28. 38 24 n. 44; 12. 31. 42 72, 105
Book Thirteen 13. 11. 12 107; 13. 15. 16–18 111; 13. 15. 16 174; 13. 19. 24 77; 13. 20. 26 30; 13. 15. 18 29; 13. 18. 23 81; 13. 19. 24 83; 13. 20. 28 176
contra Academicos 3. 18. 37 76
contra Cresconium 1. 14. 17 76; 1. 19. 23 78
contra Iulianum 3. 2. 7 76
de Doctrina Christiana praefatio 72 n. 16; 1. 1 74 n. 21; 2. 13. 19 176; 2. 117–31 76 n. 25; 2. 133 74 n. 21; 2. 136–7 79 n. 30; 2. 144–5 80 n. 32; 3. 2 108; 3. 87–9 71 n. 14; 4. 10. 24 117 n. 6; 4. 60 74 n. 21; 4. 25. 67 67 n. 6
de Genesi ad Litteram 1. 15. 21 174

de Magistro 11: 38 17 n. 27
de Ordine 1. 8. 22 143; 2. 12. 35 72 n. 17; 2. 35 20
Enarrationes in Psalmos 50: 19 117; 94. 1 142; 95. 2 142
Epistle 1A 110–111; 55. 20. 37 111 n. 29; 91. 4 46 n. 22; 138. 16 58 n. 45
Retractationes 1. 4 66; 1. 11 17 n. 27
Sermon 198. 105 464–8 170 n. 71; 288 12 n. 24; 288. 3 161
Soliloquies 1 115; 14 82 n. 36
Tractatus in Iohannem 49. 21 154

Aulus Gellius
Noctes Atticae 11. 7 42

Basil the Great
Address to Young Men 6 138
Homilies 2. 30B 156; 4. 5 156
Vita Macrinae 33 145 n. 30

Boethius
Consolation of Philosophy 4. 6 170
de Musica 138–9

Caelius Aurelianus
de Morbis Acutis 2. 8. 35 127 n. 20

Catullus 64. 1–2 1 n. 1

Censorinus
de Die Natali 10. 3 75 n. 23

Charisius
de Grammatica 1. 9 120

Cicero
ad Atticum 6. 3. 1 152; 14. 12. 3 68
Academica 1. 7. 25 68
Brutus 75 139
de Finibus 3. 2. 5 68; 5. 29. 87 79 n. 31
de Fato 28 67 n. 6
de Inventione 1. 5 74 n. 22; 1. 6–7 72 n. 17
de Natura Deorum 2. 1. 3 86
de Officiis 1. 37. 134–5 77 n. 28
de Oratore 1. 167 74 n. 22; 1. 235 72 n. 18; 1. 55. 236 44, 45 n. 20; 2. 216ff 61; 2. 235 165; 2. 236 61; 2. 251 44 n. 16

Index locorum

de Senectute 49. 6 78 n. 29
Laelius 1. 24. 38 77 n. 28
Orator 77
Philippic 2. 65 55
Pro Caelio 27. 65 45
Republic 1. 10. 16 79 n. 31;
  3. 2. 4 175
Topica 30 120
Tusculan Disputations 1. 5 78 n. 29; 2. 55
  152

Clement of Alexandria
Stromateis 2. 5 167; 5. 9. 57. 2–3
  5 n. 11

Codex Theodosianus 15. 7. 12 41

Corpus Hermeticum 1 161

Diogenes Laertius
adversus Professores 5. 31 151 n. 38

Dionysius of Halicarnassus *see* Pseudo-Dionysius of Halicarnassus
Eustatius 19–20

Egeria
Peregrinatio 28. 4 54 n. 27

Etymologicum Magnum 174 n. 3

Evanthius
de Comoedia 4 61–2

Gospel of Truth, The 19–20 94 n. 10;
  22–3 94 n. 10

Heraclitus
Fragment 2 30 n. 60

Homer
Iliad 6. 166–70 93 n. 8; 16:
  458–61 135
Odyssey 8: 499–534 40 n. 8

Horace
Odes 1. 28. 1–2 78 n. 29; 3. 21. 9–10
  77 n. 28
Satires 1. 5. 30 127

Iamblichus
de Vita Pythagorica 68. 72 7 n. 13;
  110–11 138

Ignatius of Antioch
ad Ephesios 4. 1–2 3–4; 15. 2, 19. 1 5 n.
  11, 7 n. 13
ad Magnesios 8. 2 5 n. 11; 10. 3 4
ad Philadelphios 1. 1 5 n. 11 6. 1 5
ad Romanos 2. 1, 8. 2 5 n. 11
ad Smyrnaeos 10. 1 5 n. 11
ad Trallenses 9: 1 5 n. 11

Jerome
Epistle 7. 2 101 n. 18; 22. 35 6; 106. 82
  103 n. 23; 107. 8 140; 107: 9 143
Vita Pauli 8

John Cassian
Instituta 2. 10 157–8

Joseph and Aseneth 14–16 170

Juvenal 6. 579 127

Lactantius
Fragmentum de Motibus Animi 155

Longus
Daphnis and Chloe proem 40 n. 8

Lucian
Timon 5 5 n. 11
Vitarum Auctio 3 7

Macrobius
Saturnalia 2. 7 5 n. 11; 3. 14. 7 139; 5. 17.
  5 50

Martianus Capella
de Nuptiis Mercurii et Philologiae 3. 229
  72 n. 17; 9. 955 149 n. 34

Martyrium Pionii 6–7 170 n. 70; 6 44 n. 15
Menander
fragment 740 151

Nicetas of Remesiana
de Bono Psalmodiae 2 141

Index locorum 193

Origen
contra Celsum 2. 12, 3. 51 5 n. 11

Ovid
Fasti 4. 516 97 n. 13
Metamorphoses 8. 633–99 97 n. 13
Tristia 2. 273 75

Palladius
Historia Lausiaca 49 7

Peregratio Egeriae see Egeria

Petronius
Satyricon 88 74, 81 n. 34

?Plutarch
Consolation to Apollonius 130. c 151

Philo of Alexander
Abraham 36. 201

Philogelos 87 47

Plato (includes pseudo-Plato)
Phaedrus 274ff 89
Protagoras 347D-348A 137–8
Republic 394D 60 n. 47; 397A-400E 138; 440A 60 n. 47; 467B 60 n. 47; 514 37; 606C 60 n. 47
Seventh Letter 344ff 89
Plautus
Curculio 77 52

Pliny (the Younger)
Epistle 3. 5. 2 94–5; 4. 19. 4 140

Pliny (the Elder) see also Pliny (the Younger)
Historia Naturalis 35. 76 68

Plotinus
Enneads 1. 2. 2–3 155–6

Porphyry
de Abstinentia 2. 6. 34 143; 3. 3 23 n. 42

Prudentius
peri Stephanon 9 40 n. 8

Pseudo-Dionysius of Halicarnassus
Ars Rhetorica 10. 7–10 42

Quintilian
Institutio Oratoria 1. 4. 4–5 81 n. 34; 1. 6. 26 120; 1. 6. 43 176; 1. 33. 8 139 n. 15; 1. 39 42 n. 13; 2. 14. 14 72 n. 18; 2. 16. 2 74 n. 22; 6. 3. 25 165; 9. 2. 31 77 n. 27

Rhetorica ad Herennium see Auctor ad Herennium

Rufinus of Aquileia
Historia Monachorum 1 7 n. 14; 4 6; 15 7 n. 14; 22 7 n. 14

Sallust
Catilinarian Conspiracy 25 57, 139–40
Jugurthinum War (Jugurtha) 35 58; 30. 4 75

Seneca (the Younger)
Epistle 88. 20 72 n. 17

Servius
Commentarius in Aeneida Book Four preface 50; 9. 499 152

Suetonius
Nero 49. 1 140
Tiberius 42 53

Sulpicius Severus
Dialogus 1. 9 47
Epistula 2 170; 3 156–7
Vita Martini 27. 1 167

Terence
Adelphoe 867 39, 59
Andria 229 53 n. 35
Eunuchus 583–91 40, 46 n. 22

Tertullian
de Carne Christi 9. 7 154

Theocritus
Idyll 1. 96 152 n. 39

Tibullus
1. 10. 40 97 n. 13; 2. 5. 26 97 n. 13

Vegetius
Mulomedina 2. 11. 3 127 n. 20

Virgil
Aeneid 1. 209 152; 1. 453–93 40 n. 8; 4. 237 50; 4. 308 50; 4. 370 50; 4. 547 50; 4. 595 50; 4. 667 50; 4. 677 50; 4. 685 50; 6. 20–33 40 n. 8; 6. 465 50; 8: 608–731 40 n. 8; 9. 492 36; 10: 464–72 135
Eclogue 6. 42–5: 1–2

Index Rerum

'abstract' nouns 118–119
Adeodatus 144
adverbial accusative 25–6
alphabet 94 n. 9
Alypius 43–8
Ambrose 9, 54, 75, 143–7
archaism 42–3, 86
authority 54, 176–7
biblical Latin Chapter 5 *passim*
clausula 54, 163
codex 109–110
Codex Vercellensis 108–9
cognitive linguistics 119
contrastive linguistics 119
'Courtier Literature' 92
curriculum 39
dative/ablative plural 117–126, 163
Dido 50–1, 52
dialectic 22, 31–2, 76–8
Donatists 92, 110
economy 86, 129 n. 22, 177
ecphrasis 40
emotion 135
endiathetic logos 129–30
etymology 132 n. 25, 146
eucatastrophe 62 n. 52
Evodius 144–5
exegesis 31
genitive of quality 52, 162
genre 35–7
groaning 157
historic present 100 n. 16
imparisyllabic nouns 131
incarnation 135
inconcinnitas 57
language, acquisition of 173; Augustine's philosophy of, 10 n. 17; in the

Bible 8–9; origin of 1–2, 19–20, 175; unique to humans, 19–20;
laughter 133, 164–72
Licentius 143
loan-words 126–32, 140–1; Chapter 3 *passim*
Manichaeans 17, 96, 108, 109,130–1, 177
markedness 69
memory 96, 147
metaphor 19 n. 33, 65 n. 3, 100
mime 41–52
Monica 22, 26, 48–52, 52–56, 143, 160–2
novelistic 56–60
number (as grammatical category) 116–126
Philodemus 138
pleasure 21–2, 33
plural forms 29 n. 58; *see also* number
Ponticianus 96, 97–99
Pythagoras 138–9
Quedlingburg Itala 109
reading Chapter 4 *passim*
Scipio Aemilianus 139
scroll 109–110
silence 2–7
singing 133, 137–151
smiling 170
society 175–7
Socrates 137
substitutability 69
synonymy 69–70
token of identity 44
Tychonius 108
Varro 146
weeping 152–8, 158–164
Wisdom literature 28
writing Chapter 4 *passim*

Index Verborum Graecorum

ἀγοραῖος 44 n. 15
ἀληθής 27
ἀληθινός 27
ἀπάθεια 155
γράφω 89
δέρω 52
δημιουργέω 12 n. 18
διαλέγομαι 77
διαλεκτή 27
διαλεκτική 77
διάλογος 27, 77, 145
ἐγκράτεια 164
εὐαγγέλιον 116
ἔχω 12 n. 19
ἰουδαΐζω 4

κτίζω 12 n. 18
λαλέω 16, 100
λέγω 100
λόγος 23, 28, 30 n. 60, 34 n. 63
μετριοπάθεια 151, 155, 159–60, 163–4
μυθικός 82
ὁμιλία 28–9, 78
πάθος 136, 151
πάσχω 136
ποιέω 12 n. 18, 13 n. 20
πράσσω 13 n. 20
ῥητορική 82
φιλοσοφία 80
φημί 27

Index Verborum Latinorum

aer 130
adversor 99 n. 13
aeditumus 45
aedituus 45
affectus 136
agonisticus 63
aio 100
amor 38 n. 3
ancilla 53
antrum 130
anus 53
apporto 46
arithmetica 68
astronomia 68
barbarismus 63, 64
canistrum 126
cantio 150
cathedra 129
cedrus 64–5, 65
cetos 129
circumfero 115
carmen 150
cogitatio 123
collyrium 127
consuetudo 113–114, 176
cothurnus 64–5
clanculo/clanculum 46, 53
colloquor 22, 83–4, 98
conversio 61–2
criticus 63
decrepitus 53
defectus 38
delectatio 124
desertum 128
dialectica 76–8
dico 113
dimensio 78
dispensator 128–9, 130
disputo 77, 81, 83, 145
dissero 77
dominus 58

dyas 131
eiulo 51, 152, 161
eloquentia 74, 82
eloquium 102–3
episcopus 128–9, 130
eremus 128
et 114–115
euge 40
fabulosus 82
facies 119–120
facio 12–13
facundia 75
fallacia 51
for 100
garrio 23–4
genethliaca 64
geometria 68, 79
gloriosus 44
grammatica 68, 71
grandiusculus 53
gymnasium 63–4, 65
harmonia 68
humilis 112–113, 120
in 15
incantare 150
informis 161, 174
ingurgito 55
inquam 100
interrogatio 67, 85
irrisio 60
lautitia 122
libri 102
litterae 71–2, 102
litteratio 72–3
litteratura 72–3
loquacitas 82
loquax 23–4
loquor 16–26, 75, 82, 100, 113
ludificatio 59
ludus 59
luxuries 120

Index Verborum Latinorum

machinamentum 63
machinatio 63
materies 120
mathematicus 64, 79
margarita 129
melos 148–9
meribibula 52–3
monas 131
monitum 120
monitus 120
motus 136
munditia 122
musica 68
mutus 23
natura 176
numerus 79
omnipotens 116
oratio 125
palaestra 64
pedisequus 45
persona 38
perturbatio 136
phantasma 131
philosophia 68, 80
philosophor 80
planus 64
praedico 20 n. 36
progenies 120
psallere 139
quaestio 121–2
ratio 176
regula 107–8

rhetor 64
rhetorica 68, 74
sanguis/sanguen 117
sapientia 76, 80–1
sapor 84–5
schola 64, 78
scholasticus 46–7
scriptura 102
sermo 26–33, 98, 101–2
sermocinor 78
sermocinatio 28–9, 77–8
solitudo 128
soloecismus 64
sonitus 120
sonus 120
species 119–120
spectaculum 38
spes 120
spongia 131
suavitas 122
sub- (as preverb) 45
syllaba 64
temulentus 53 n. 35
trinitas 131
typhus 64
umbra 37–8
vapulo 51–2
verax 26–7
verbum 28
verus 26–7
volo 104–5, 107
voluntas 123, 124; see also volo

Printed in Great Britain
by Amazon